Deviant Acts
Essays on Queer Performance

Deviant Acts
Essays on Queer Performance

edited by

David Cregan

Carysfort Press

A Carysfort Press Book

Deviant Acts: Essays on Queer Performance
edited by David Cregan

First published as a paperback in Ireland in 2009 by
Carysfort Press Ltd
58 Woodfield
Scholarstown Road
Dublin 16
Ireland

ISBN 978-1-904505-42-6

Typeset by Carysfort Press Ltd

Printed and bound by eprint limited
Unit 35
Coolmine Industrial Estate
Dublin 15
Ireland

Cover design by eprint

This book is published with the financial assistance of
The Arts Council (An Chomhairle Ealaíon) Dublin, Ireland

Contents

Acknowledgements

As the editor of *Deviant Acts: Essays on Queer Performance* I would like to thank Carysfort Press, in particular Eamonn Jordan, for their encouragement and support during this project. I am most grateful to all of the contributors to this volume for their hard work and dedication. Finally I would like to thank Anna McMullan and Brian Singleton for their encouragement and guidance through my years of research and writing.

Illustrations

1 | Introduction

David Cregan

In his book *The Politics of Irish Drama* Nicholas Grene describes the erotic energy of *The Playboy of the Western World* which served to offend those who did not like what was being implied about Irish character in its representations of Irishness:

> As the repressed physicality of the sexual was allowed to appear from under the normal decencies of its covering, so sex was proximate to violence and both made manifest the actuality of a specific location. Again and again distinctions, differences and the ideological labelling that went with them were jumbled in unsorted contiguity. Such contamination of confused categories was a deeply disturbing affront to the middle-class nationalist community whose self-image depended on such moral classification.[1]

These social protestations against the idea of Irishness as represented on the National Stage indicate an important shift in Irish cultural politics, one that would impact the possibility of the emergence of gay and lesbian identities for decades to come. While early nationalism based its identity project on reconfiguring the negative British imagery of Ireland, post-liberation Ireland began to devolve into its own essentialization of the nature of the 'true' Irish citizen, forcing the suppression of alternative life choices and marginalized identities through a civic conversation based on a catholic morality rather than the broad based human rights of an emerging democracy.

These events of moral prudery and aversion to sexuality being theatrically represented, even in its most banal forms, are the historical antecedents which limited and prohibited Irish playwrights for decades. It is not until 1968 that the Dublin Theatre Festival produces a drama with an openly gay character. Thomas Kilroy's play *The Death and Resurrection of Mr. Roche* opened at the Olympia Theatre during the festival and was set in present day 1960s Dublin. At the centre of the play is the character of Kelly. Kelly is a country bachelor renting a basement apartment in Dublin. The action takes place between Saturday evening and Sunday morning, and portrays the weekly routine of a small group of friends who ritually drink the weekend away. Into these late night revelries comes the openly gay character of Mr. Roche, accompanied by a young man. Kilroy uses Roche's sexuality to articulate the latent sexual anxieties of Kelly. Kelly lashes out at Mr. Roche:

> **KELLY.** Get him away, away to hell. Dirty, filthy pervert. If you don't do anything about it I am telling you I will. I'm telling you that now. [*He exits to bedroom where at first he stands indecisive and nervous. Later he bends to look through and listen at the keyhole or walks about the room.*][2]

As events unfold Kelly, predictably, admits to a previous homosexual encounter and his own sexual denial. But what is most interesting about this groundbreaking play for gay and lesbian issues in Ireland is its portrayal of the open homosexual character as object. Kilroy certainly represents the social anxieties surrounding homosexual identity in 1960s Ireland, but he does so as object rather than subject. The gay character is the antagonist, the problem, the source of the necessary dramatic conflict; an object of curiosity but nonetheless an object who is defined by the ideas and opinions of others around him rather than through his own articulation of self or experience.

In 1971 Brian Friel introduces a gay character into his own writing in his play *The Gentle Island*. The play is set on the small island of Inishkeen off the coast of County Donegal in the north-west of Ireland. The inhabitants of the island are emigrating due to fading resources with the exception of Manus Sweeney and his family. When two travelling strangers come to visit this remote island they become entangled in the fear and neurosis of this failing Irish family. Manus's son Philly becomes involved in a sexual relationship with one of the strangers, Shane, and is caught by his wife Sarah. The sexuality of this family is as dysfunctional as their interpersonal relationships, and Friel uses homosexuality to bring these frailties to a dramatic head. In the end of the play Sarah shoots and kills Shane. Homosexuality is again a point of conflict, an accusation, and an object of scrutiny in what Nicholas Grene calls 'the social policing of sexual relationships'[3] in Friel's writing.

It is important to note that although entertainment in the United States was a huge influence on Irish culture during this period of the 1960s and 1970s, the sexual revolution in the US was perhaps only stimulating the imagination of the general Irish population. While the civil rights movement in the US was certainly inspiring the Irish Republican Army (IRA) in Northern Ireland, it was impossible even to acquire contraception in the Republic of Ireland. After the events of Stonewall in New York in 1969 the organization the Gay Liberation Front (GLF) was formed and did, in fact, extend its influence into Ireland through Ireland's close proximity to the influential branch of the GLF working out of London. The manifesto of the GLF created a language through which gay and lesbian men and women could reconfigure their objectified identities:

> The emphasis was on pride and affirmation; these gay people were blatant, outrageous and flamboyant. Discarding an identity conditioned by notions of sickness and sin, they represented homosexuality as a revolutionary path towards freedom. They engaged in public displays of affection and violated gender conventions. Sexual expression was seen as a form of personal, political action that was subversive, liberating and a way of building solidarity. 'Coming Out', the public affirmation of gay identity, became a key political act.[4] This important shift in queer language would ultimately influence Frank McGuinness, the first Irish dramatist to rescue the Irish homosexual from the assigned status of object to the self-defining position of subject.

While representations of Irish identity have broadened in recent decades, the academic discourse on this diversity is still in need of development. This book is aimed at opening conversations about identity and citizenship in Ireland through the concept of performance. The essays included in this volume address a range of alternative performances that range from theatre to film, from parades to drag artists.

In chapter one Eibhear Walshe examines representations of Oscar Wilde in plays by the beloved Micheál MacLiammóir, Terry Eagleton, and Tom Kilroy. He explores the intersection of Wilde's high-profile homosexual life and questions of Irish queer identity in the twentieth century. This chapter highlights the groundwork of the earliest queer performances that can be constituted as Irish, performances that lay the foundation for every chapter that follows. In a similar attempt to queer history, Michael Patrick Lapointe reveals latent homoeroticism in the writing of one of the founding fathers of the Irish Literary Theatre, Edward Martyn. What is wonderful about both of these essays is their illumination of a past that refuses the desired homogeneity of burgeoning Irish identities, detailing the not-so-conservative past that many scholars of Irish subjects have turned into a cliché.

All too often in Irish Studies, Northern Ireland goes under-examined. This book contains two remarkable essays on the North. In Kathryn Conrad's piece she contextualizes queer performance in the North through the important practice of parades in Northern Irish identity politics. In this highly theoretical piece Conrad employs the fun of camp to reveal the power of queer politics in Belfast through the city's Pride Parade. Her photographs are not to be missed! Niall Rea approaches queer performance in the North through a detailed exposition of an unperformed 1988 production of *Ecce Homo* by the Belfast Community Theatre. Niall's piece examines the construction process of a gay performance that aspires to function as a drama of liberation. This type of research articulates otherwise under-documented attempts of queer artists to introduce alternative identities into mainstream culture.

One of the qualities that make this project extraordinary is the way in which the contributors press the boundaries of conventional drama studies in order to reveal remarkable theatricality in untraditional spaces. Fintan Walsh's analysis of the Dublin based drag artist Panti, and the multifarious ways in which she shapes queer identity through public performance, disrupts the traditional idea of performance itself and introduces contemporary theories of identity to analyse Panti's position in cosmopolitan Dublin. Not only is this essay fabulously fun as it chronicles the career of one of the best drag queens ever, it presses Irish academic discourse to modernize and move beyond the constrictions that have virtually ignored the imperatives of performance studies.

Brian Merriman's contribution details his career as a social activist and an artist. Brian outlines the development of the International Dublin Gay Theatre Festival which he founded and still heads. While the history of the rapid growth and popularity of the festival is fascinating, the strength of this piece is Brian's insight into the place of gay and lesbian theatre practice in Irish culture. What is most compelling about this piece is Brian's assertions as to why he has met continual and persistent roadblocks in his attempts to acquire funding from the Irish government. His candour is raw throughout, and is imbued with the passion and commitment of an artist and a citizen.

Mária Kurdi, Todd Barry, and Kathleen Heininge write about contemporary Irish authors. Mária's work with Emma Donohue deals with lesbianism and the biography play. By examining Donohue's use of history, Mária describes how the often-silent historical experience of lesbians can find voice through contemporary writing. She does so by focusing on character construction and relationality. Todd Barry employs a similar type of historical revision, but examines queer identity and its relationship to space in the writing of Frank McGuinness, Brian Friel, and Brendan Behan. Heininge is not as concerned about history as she is about the contradictions inherent in private and public experience in queer Irish performance. She reads Gerry Stembridge's play *The Gay Detective* in order to expose the complexity of postmodern Irish identities.

Drama studies are never quite complete without an examination of the transition from the page to the stage, from text to performance. In my own contribution to this book I look at the Conall Morrison production of Oscar Wilde's *The Importance of Being Earnest* in order to criticize how unsubstantial queer ideas are without understanding theory as performance paradigm. Samuele Grassi highlights gender as aesthetic paradigm in his study of the artistry of Dublin based Glasshouse Productions.

This book represents a variety of perspectives as well as methodologies. I have included in this collection an essay by Charlotte McIvor on two of the films of Neil Jordan that deal with transvestism. While film is not a traditional category of theatricality or performance, Charlotte's essay has at its heart the 'Irish question'. Her research carries this project beyond the localness of Ireland to the global dimension of Irishness as it is consumed by mass media. The inclusion of this essay is for its content as well as for its invitation to broaden categories of analysis and performance in an era of technology and global identities.

Overall, the aim of this book is to chronicle a variety of queer performances, and to open the debate amongst theorists of Irish culture about an inherent conservatism in scholarship. In order to do so I have crossed methodological and geographical boundaries. The contributors to the volume are from Italy, the United States,

Hungary, Ireland, and Canada. They are scholars, social activists, directors, and artists, and represent the diverse conflation of practices which enrich the exciting and ever changing world of drama and performance studies.

---

[1] Nicholas Grene, *The Politics of Irish Drama: Plays in Context from Boucicault to Friel* (London: Cambridge University Press, 1999), p. 86.

[2] Thomas Kilroy, *The Death and Resurrection of Mr. Roche* (London: Faber and Faber, 1969), p. 28.

[3] Grene, p. 211.

[4] Kieran Rose, *Diverse Communities: The Evolution of Lesbian and Gay Politics in Ireland* (Cork: Cork University Press, 1994), pp. 5-6.

2 | Queering Oscar:
Versions of Wilde on the Irish Stage and Screen

Eibhear Walshe

In this essay, I propose a reading of three plays, three dramatized versions of the life and of the sexuality of Oscar Wilde. All three texts have been performed in Ireland. I will consider the ways in which Wilde's homosexuality is figured, either as an absence or as a disruptive presence within Irish cultural discourse. There have been a number of plays written in Ireland where Wilde features as a character[1] but I choose three influential texts to discuss here and compare them with a film, *A Man of No Importance*, where Wilde's presence within the Ireland of the 1960s is represented. Firstly, I consider the work of Micheál MacLiammóir (1899-1978). Micheál MacLiammóir, born Alfred Willmore in London in 1899, gaelicized his name, reinvented himself as an Irishman and moved to Dublin, setting up his Gate Theatre with his life partner, the director Hilton Edwards. With his widely performed one-man stage show, first played in 1960, *The Importance of Being Oscar,* MacLiammóir created an acceptable version of Wilde, his life and his writings for a wide audience in Ireland and elsewhere. The many and popular performances of this show were crucial for the process of cultural acceptance for Wilde, yet I argue that this play heterosexualized Wilde, ignored the sexual nature of his downfall, and found tragedy and pathos in his fate. The focus of the second half of the essay will be dramatizations of Wilde's life by contemporary playwrights such as Terry Eagleton's 1989 *Saint Oscar* and Tom Kilroy's 1997 *The Secret Fall of Constance Wilde* and films like Barry Devlin's screenplay for the 1994 film *A Man of No Importance*. In these latter texts, the writers attempt to make direct links between Wilde's Irishness and his sexuality as Irish cultural perceptions of queerness changed, each with differing dramatic results. As Micheál MacLiammóir wrote, 'Wilde was the invisible but by no means inaudible bond who made the road I was facing less chilly ... That magician whose name was my secret for ever more.'[2]

In the late 1920s, Micheál MacLiammóir set up the Gate Theatre with his life partner, the director Hilton Edwards, and quickly established himself as a central figure in Irish theatrical life. His widely performed play *The Importance of Being Oscar* (1960) presented an acceptable version of Wilde, his life and his writings for a wide audience in Ireland and abroad. The many performances of this popular show were crucial for the process of cultural acceptance and rehabilitation of Wilde's name in Ireland, but the openly gay MacLiammóir and Edwards achieved this trans-formation, this revolution, by heterosexualizing Wilde. Taking their cue from *De Profundis*, they reconstructed Wilde as helpless victim, sidestepping any details of his sexual downfall and finding tragedy and pathos in his fate. MacLiammóir performed his 'safe' version of Wilde's life in theatres, schools and on television all over Ireland from 1960 to 1970 and thus facilitated a sea-change in Irish attitudes towards Wilde. In his 1968 memoir of the show, published under the title *An Oscar of No Importance,* MacLiammóir per-mitted himself some frank speculation on Wilde's sexuality: 'How fortunate he was. Not merely because without the catastrophe he would be remembered as the author of a handful of underrated and little read books and plays, but, by the very nature of the scandal that ripped the last rags of decency from him, posthumous writers can discuss him and his work with complete frankness, as no other homosexual artist, leading a discreet and reasonable private life, can even in our time be discussed.'[3] As a result of this one-man Wilde show, new versions of his sexuality could be accommodated and presented in mainstream social discourse in Ireland, permitting a contemporary reclaiming of Wilde the Gay Irishman.

For nearly fifty years the invented figure Micheál MacLiammóir actor, dramatist, painter, designer, Gaelic scholar, theatre manager (and 'Corkman'), dominated Irish theatre with his programme of experimental, poetic and continental dramas. In his own Gate Theatre, founded in 1928 with Hilton Edwards, Micheál MacLiammóir provided a less insular, more cosmopolitan, alter-native to the state-subsidized Abbey Theatre and maintained a counterbalance to the peasant dramas and rustic comedies of establishment theatre with a programme of Wilde and Coward, Ibsen, Pirandello, Eugene O'Neill, Anouilh and others. Terence Brown considers their contribution to Irish cultural life thus: 'Only the work of a few individual poets, novelists and artists of the nineteen-twenties gave any hint that the dismal obscurity that Shaw feared might not envelop the country, as with Micheál Mac-Liammóir presenting European drama at his Gate Theatre and his Irish language theatre in Galway.'[4]

Just as significantly, Micheál MacLiammóir was also that most unique of figures within post-independence Ireland: the openly homosexual public figure. In a state where homosexual acts were criminalized until 1993, and the homoerotic was censored and expunged from all official literary and cultural discourse MacLiammóir and Edwards survived, and even flourished, as Ireland's only visible gay couple. A strikingly handsome man in his youth, Micheál MacLiammóir maintained his looks into old age with the aid of paint and powder, a familiar and popular figure on the streets of Dublin. This was no mean achievement within a culture where in 1941 Kate O'Brien, Micheál MacLiammóir's friend and contemporary, had an entire novel banned for one homoerotic sentence. When MacLiammóir died in 1978, the President of Ireland attended his funeral, as did the Taoiseach and several government ministers, and Hilton Edwards was openly deferred to and sympathized with as chief mourner. Yet Micheál MacLiammóir, supposedly Cork-born Irish actor and writer, never actually existed. As I have stated, it was a name and a personal history conjured up by London-born actor Alfred Willmore when he left England for Ireland in 1917. Born in Kensal Green in London in 1899, he had no Irish connections whatsoever. He had been a success as a child actor, working with Sir Herbert Beerbohm Tree amongst others, and had then attended the Slade School of Fine Art. However, just before graduating from the Slade, Willmore abandoned his studies and went travelling. In the short term, he was fleeing Britain because of conscription during World War I, and possibly because of the attentions of an older, wealthy lover; as his biographer Christopher Fitz-Simon argues, 'There is no reason to doubt that as Alfred's seventeenth birthday approached he would have been dreading the arrival of his call-up papers.'[5] More acutely, he was also seeking, in the aftermath of the Wilde trials, an acceptable persona within which to be both homosexual and, at the same time, visible. Alan

Sinfield, in his study *The Wilde Century*, contends that a particular and threatening concept of 'the Homosexual' came from Wilde's public persona and was implicated in his disgrace:

> The dominant twentieth-century queer identity, I argue, has been constructed in this kind of process, mainly out of elements that came together at the Wilde trials, effeminacy, leisure, idleness, immorality, luxury, decadence and aestheticism.[6]

H. Montgomery Hyde comments that when the Woldfenden Report on Homosexual Offences and Prostitution was published in England in 1957 'it received a very largely favourable press and was welcomed by practically every organization which had submitted evidence to it, as well as by leading spokesmen of most of the Christian denominations'.[7] In 1954, the centenary of Wilde's birth, Micheál MacLiammóir wrote to some of the Irish newspapers suggesting that members of the public might subscribe to the placing of a suitable tablet on the facade of the house in which Wilde had been born at 21 Westland Row, Dublin. The interest in Wilde culminated in the one-man show, *The Importance of Being Oscar*. It was created by Micheál MacLiammóir and Edwards and then directed by Edwards. It was first performed on 15 September 1960 at the Curragh Barracks in County Kildare, for Irish Army officers and their families. Later transferring to the Gaiety Theatre in Dublin on 3 October, *The Importance of Being Oscar* came as a much-needed boost, providing them with widespread commercial and critical success. Christopher Fitz-Simon records that: '*The Importance of Being Oscar* opened to a very warm response. All the reviews next day were more than favourable ... '.[8] This success led to a series of American and European tours and, eventually, a television dramatization. Another biographer calls this time in their career, the 'Reingreencarnation'.[9] This, in turn, led to a world-wide tour of the play and great financial success.

Given that the name of Wilde had been employed throughout the twentieth century as a shorthand code for homosexual identity, Micheál MacLiammóir's reading of Wilde in *The Importance of Being Oscar* (1963) was very partial, shaped by a need to present an acceptable version of Wilde and of his fate. Contemporary lesbian and gay theorists have reclaimed Wilde as a powerfully disruptive figure, a sexual rebel and a social transgressor. However, in this version MacLiammóir fixes on Wilde the tragic hero, not Wilde the rebel, Irish or otherwise. Hilton Edwards introduced the published text of the performance in the following terms: 'It shows him to have been aware, from the first, of the inevitability of his tragedy.'[10]

In his narrating within *The Importance of Being Oscar*, MacLiammóir chose to distance himself from Wilde, recounting his life and his writings rather than impersonating Wilde directly. This allowed him to construct a Wilde of his own making. Edwards and MacLiammóir took Wilde's fall from grace as their theme and saw that fall as consequent on his fatal glorification of the erotic: 'I did but touch the honey of romance/And must I lose a soul's inheritance?'[11] However, the honey of Wilde's romance in this version is predominantly heterosexual. Wilde's key act of transgression, his infatuation with Bosie, is referred to in one telling phrase: 'That Tiger Life'.[12] Setting a tone of world-weary despair and ennui, Micheál MacLiammóir keeps all his sexual referents strictly heterosexual. In the first half of the presentation, Wilde's passion for Lily Langtry and his love for Constance, his wife, are recounted. Indeed the readings from *Salome* and *The Picture of Dorian Gray* concentrate on Herod's lust for Salome rather than on her eroticization of Iokanaan's body, and on Dorian's murderous instincts, rather than on Lord Henry's and Basil's love for Dorian's beauty. After these straight moments from Wilde's writings, MacLiammóir inserts a short interval. During the interval, Wilde's affair with Bosie, his 'Tiger Life' with London rent boys and the three trials are presumed to have taken place.

In the second act, the play deals solely with Wilde's prison writings and the consequences of Wilde's sexual deviancy are concentrated on, rendered with pathos and melodrama. Wilde's dignity in prison and in exile, his composed yet passionate reproach to Bosie in *De Profundis*, the stark anguished compassion of *The Ballad of Reading Gaol* all serve to increase a sympathy with the erring outcast. His final fable, *The Doer of Good*, although dealing with lust and the despair of the erotic, is firmly heterosexual. However, playing Wilde, or at least interpreting Wilde as predominantly straight, led to questions that Micheál MacLiammóir was not quite ready to answer. Joan Dean has researched the two North American tours of *The Importance of being Oscar*, and her account of various reviews reveals that there was a greater cultural difficulty with Wilde and with the hidden theme of his homosexuality in the United States than in Ireland. The first American performance of the show began in the Lyceum Theatre on Broadway on 14 March 1961 and led to a four-week season.

American reviews, positive in many ways, were, at the same time, as blunt as they could be about the gay implications of the subject and of the production. *The New Yorker* commented that: 'Despite Mr. MacLiammóir's innumerable skills, his performance will of necessity appeal only to a fairly specialized audience.'[13] *The World Telegraph and Sun* believed that: 'the show can only have a specialized appeal.'[14] As Joan Dean has written, 'encoded was a bristling over of any, let alone, a sympathetic treatment of homosexuality. If it wasn't just a disease, it certainly was still a crime.'[15] Despite some hostility, *The Importance of being Oscar* returned to the United States in October 1961 for an extended tour, where the First Lady, Jackie Kennedy, attended a performance of the play in Washington, D.C. In *An Oscar of No Importance*, MacLiammóir recounts an incident during his later South African tour of the show when a woman journalist challenged him directly on the subject of Wilde's sexuality and, by implication, his own:

> 'You', began a small, plump, very firm-looking lady, gazing at me through her spectacles as though she would burrow into the depths of my soul, 'are going to act as Oscar Wilde?' 'Not act as him: I try to interpret him.' 'Well then, I would be interested to know, as you have chosen him rather than another writer, what is your own attitude to the question of male homosexuality?' I gazed back at her in a prolonged moment of silence, as of deep cool waters whose apparent tranquillity might be haunted by many sharks ... Did she mean among cattle or human beings? But I never received an answer.[16]

The 1960s were an important decade for the republishing of Wilde's texts and his rehabilitation as an artist. Although emboldened by the success of the one-man show, there is evidence that they were still hesitant about highlighting the homoerotic in their theatrical work. Indeed, it was not until Micheál MacLiammóir was in the final decade of his life that he wrote his most directly 'gay' play. Changes in British law and in censorship in the theatre and the experience of working on Wilde all had a cumulative effect on MacLiammóir's writings on the homoerotic. Alan Sinfield writes that:

> It is no accident, then, that the English legislation governing both theatre and homosexuality was reformed when the Labour Party was elected with a big majority on a modernizing platform in 1966 ... The Woldfenden proposals were enacted in 1967 and theatre censorship was abolished in 1968 ... It enabled many gay men and lesbians to refuse the discreet spirit

of the law and, with varying degrees of flamboyance, to come out.[17]

Thus Micheál MacLiammóir's memoir, *An Oscar of No Importance*, is a revealing account of the way in which the one-man show on Wilde brought him face to face with the nature of Wilde's sexuality and with the implications for his own creativity.

In many ways, *An Oscar of No Importance* (1968) is, as the title suggests, a mirror text for *The Importance of Being Oscar*. All the evasions of the stage play are dealt with directly in the memoir. In considering the relation of the play to the memoir, it seems as if MacLiammóir found the public arena of theatre an unsafe place in which to speculate on Wilde's sexual nature. Where the play concentrates on the normative aspects of Wilde's life and writings, the memoir displays no such reticence. It opens with surprising directness, relating a childhood incident where he quizzed his embarrassed father as to the exact nature of Wilde's unspeakable crime, eventually provoking this outburst: 'What was wrong with Oscar Wilde? He turned young men into women.'[18] In the course of the memoir Micheál MacLiammóir explores his professional and personal bonds with Wilde: 'that magician whose name was my secret for evermore'.[19] He even allows himself to theorize on Wilde's sexual identity. He claims a more direct kinship with Wilde than in his previous writings: 'Wilde was the invisible but by no means inaudible bond who made the road I was facing less chilly.'[20]

In relating the process by which he devised the one-man show with Edwards, he incorporates a candid account of Wilde's sexuality into the memoir, but adopts a tone of objectivity through-out. His attitude to Wilde is one of worldly understanding: 'All right, so he was "So" (the twenties slang-word for the contemporary word 'queer').'[21] His account of Wilde's sexual history is forthright and clear-sighted:

> He had been initiated into homosexual practices, as the legend has asserted, by Robert Ross himself, and difficult as it may be for the mind of today wholeheartedly to believe that this was in truth his very first experiment, there is a great deal of evidence to show that he had been in fact passionately in love with his own wife, and had been strongly attracted throughout his earlier manhood by many other women. It was likely too that it was the experience with Ross that decided him to accept himself for the future completely as a pederast and to lose all his previous interest in the opposite sex. Robert Ross stated that the affair began in 1886, the same year that English law

adopted the statute that nine years later was to cause Wilde's arrest and imprisonment: one could be forgiven for wondering could it have been the very same day that Queen Victoria signed the statute? At the very same moment, it may be, when Wilde decided to respond to the enamoured Ross, so closely the web seems woven about him.[22]

Micheál MacLiammóir finds Wilde's blatant disregard for potential notoriety disturbing and seeks to explain the almost suicidal disregard that Wilde had for public opinion and for the legal consequences of his sexual transgressions. Side by side with this unease at Wilde's supreme confidence is a need to find such open-ness commendable.

Dramatizations of Wilde's life in Ireland like Terry Eagleton's 1989 *Saint Oscar* and Tom Kilroy's 1997 *The Secret Fall of Constance Wilde* and films like Barry Devlin's screenplay for the 1994 film *A Man of No Importance* continue to make direct links between Wilde's Irishness, his sexuality and his subversiveness. These two stage versions of Wilde's life re-introduce Wilde's dangerous 'Tiger Life' with a vengeance and are in stark contrast to his careful, distanced and de-sexualized presentation. But in other ways, these later plays seek to explain Wilde's same-sex desire by viewing it as an attraction towards androgyny, a need to fuse male and female and, especially in Kilroy's play, Wilde's sexuality is thus presented as the source of suffering and degradation.

In 1989, Field Day, a company with a clear political sense of connection to Irish Cultural nationalism, produced Terry Eagle-ton's play *Saint Oscar*. Eagleton brings Wilde back to 'life', making him the central character, and the link between dissident sexuality and colonial subversion is explored as the drama unfolds. The English-born Eagleton writes of Wilde as an English writer but from a position of identification with and allegiance to Ireland and his play was produced within an Irish context. Dispensing with linear progression, and indeed with dramatic tension, Eagleton creates a play in which Wilde calls up his life and arbitrarily discourses with those central to his life – Speranza, Bosie, Edward Carson. Unlike *The Importance of Being Oscar*, *Saint Oscar* represents Wilde's homosexuality in a much more direct way, reflecting societal changes in Ireland in the intervening twenty-five years. In an *Irish Times* article on the play, it is explained that: 'While he (Eagleton) didn't set out to write an allegory of the present-day Anglo-Irish situation, he found it impossible to write about past conflicts between England and Ireland, without reflecting them, if only indirectly, to what is happening today ... Words he put in Oscar's mouth have a pert and ironic ring in the post-Guilford haze (The Guilford Four).'[23] Sexual frankness is central to the play, despite Eagleton's comment in his introduction that

> Much previous work on Wilde has centred on his homosexuality ... but if I have tried to avoid writing a gay play about him, this is not only because as a heterosexual I am inevitably something of an outsider in such matters but because it seems to me vital to put that particular ambiguity or doubleness back in the context of a much wider span of ambivalence.[24]

However, the play is direct and even celebratory of Wilde's iconic 'queer' sexuality, although Eagleton does make Wilde's status as colonial jester in London – 'a parodist and parasite'[25] – and Wilde's undermining of British cultural imperialism his main focus. This bawdy, often witty, sexually explicit directness is demonstrated by the opening ballad: 'The moral of our tale is plan for to tell:/Unnatural practices land you in hell/If you're Quare and you're Irish and wear a daft hat/Don't go screwing the son of an aristocrat.'[26]

In an effort to come to terms with Wilde's sexuality, Eagleton relies on an androgynous notion of sexuality, as does Kilroy. In *Saint Oscar* Wilde describes his birth as 'A monstrous birth. When they pulled me out they screamed and tried to kill me on the spot. A cock and a cunt together, the one tucked neatly within the other.'[27] In the play, it is the mother, Speranza, who is blamed for this hermaphroditic birth, as Wilde accuses her, 'who was it unmanned me?' and he goes on to explain: 'Don't you see, mother, something went awry with me within the furry walls of your womb. Your little boy is flawed, botched, unfinished. I had my own body but I was too greedy for flesh. I wanted yours, too. The two don't mix well.'[28] Eagleton is unequivocal in his portrayal of Bosie as a pernicious influence on Wilde – 'I love him ... as Saint Sebastian loved the arrows'[29] – but is even-handed in demonstrating Wilde's own deliberate courting of his trials and his fall from grace. As Eagleton constructs Wilde, disgrace was the only place for him to go, the only logical end to his stance of transgression and subversion. Eagleton finds a kind of gallows humour in all this and celebrates Wilde's sabotaging of British imperialism. In the review by David Nowlan in *The Irish Times:*

Mr Eagleton has tried to personify Wilde the person outcast from family, nation and sex, the nation-victim of another establishment. But the parable does not work dramatically.[30]

The novelist and playwright, Tom Kilroy produced two dramas on the life of Oscar Wilde in the late 1990s. In an *Irish Times* interview called 'Kilroy Is Here' in October 1997, he explains:

It is now more than two years since playwright Tom Kilroy, speaking at the annual Synge Summer School at Rathdrum, County Wicklow, read extracts from a new play, then only at the work-in-progress stage. At that time it was called Wife for Mr. Wilde. The Oscar Wilde emerging from Kilroy's text was a cold creature, somewhat at variance with the more popularly held image of Wilde the tragic, gifted, victim figure, so hopelessly out of place even in the Age of Decadence.

While focusing on Wilde's cool, anarchic intelligence, Kilroy appeared to be balancing Wilde's intolerant self-delusion and quest for perfection against the realism of his unfortunate wife, Constance. 'For Wilde', argued Kilroy,

style was a mode of freedom in the widest possible sense of the word ... for Wilde; life was a contradiction, a condition of being human which can only be met by an enlarged performance of mockery and camp, a bid to outdo the ordinary, the mundane.

As ever, Wilde was the central figure, his wife a passive onlooker, the good wife who said nothing. But during the writing process, something in Kilroy's imagination shifted ... In *The Secret Fall of Constance Wilde,* Constance Holland Lloyd, betrayed wife and disillusioned romantic, asserts herself and confronts her husband, forcing him to acknowledge the squalor behind the epigrams. 'You never face the situation as it really is,' she says, 'Never! Nothing exists for you unless it can be turned into a phrase.' Throughout the play Constance struggles with her own self-disgust for being complicit in the charade of their public life as well as the rage directed at Oscar's folly and duplicity. For Kilroy this is not, despite its historical context, an historical play. It is more concerned with two individuals and their contrasting views of the truth as well as

trying to present two very different views of normality. There is conflict between them in their understanding of what the world is about. I set out to place the Wildean wit in a context where laughter would be very difficult. It is important for me that I don't take sides. I don't think you can take sides.

Above all, it is about a man and a woman faced with their differences and the resulting collision. Images of entrapment dominate the work, reinforced by the use of marionette puppets, and the respective trauma suffered by Wilde, Constance, and Lord Alfred Douglas at the hands of their fathers is a powerful theme. It is also quite Japanese in staging. Interested in classical Japanese theatre, particularly Bunraku puppet theatre, Kilroy, who has visited Japan a few times, spent several months there some years ago. 'We are using these huge figures; they're about 15 feet high,' he enthuses, explaining that the idea is to juxtapose the human figures of the actors with the inhuman shapes of these menacing giant puppets. Kilroy sees Constance as 'a radical young woman – she was disappointed but she was not prepared to go along with the lies. She even changed her sons' names. That was a pretty dramatic thing to do in the 19th century.' She was determined to protect her sons from the influence of Douglas, 'Bosie,' whom she viewed as a greater threat than Oscar. [31]

The Secret Fall of Constance Wilde is, dramatically, an intense and often traumatic representation of Wilde's life from the perspective of his wife, Constance. In the play, Wilde's fall into sexual sin and the inevitability of his public disgrace is connected to a secret darkness that haunts Constance. Kilroy brings into the familiar historical narrative of Wilde's life a new element, sexual abuse. In Kilroy's version, Constance Lloyd is drawn toward Wilde and marries him, partly as a consequence of sexual abuse in childhood. As the play unfolds, the ugly reality of Wilde's other life, his homosexual affair, becomes entangled with Constance's dark secret and the tainted legacy of her past, her secret fall:

> You – I. All connected. Everything connected. You know I was unable to face that – thing without you being by my side? I used to think: nothing can touch me, married to this brilliant, outrageous man! I am safe beneath this glittering surface! Whereas the truth was you were drawing me into horror, step by step, like a dangerous guide, the horror of myself.[32]

As with Eagleton's play, Wilde's homosexuality is interpreted as an impulse towards androgyny, a supposed yearning for the fusion of male and female together. Kilroy has Wilde declaim:

> I must have it! I will have it! Neither man nor woman but both ... The great wound in Nature, the wound of gender, was healed ... Woman, this is our secret history, the history of the Androgyne.[33]

In Wilde's own writings, this interest in the Androgyne is not particularly evident, Wilde's particular imaginative preoccupations being with absolute beauty and, latterly, with the Christ figure as aesthetic forefather. In Kilroy's version of the central relationships, Bosie is hateful, Wilde is weak, Constance is strong, angry, no longer the passive victimized wife but a woman who has informed herself as to Wilde's real sexual nature and so not afraid to name it. She tells Bosie: 'You and Oscar are Urnings. That is the term used by the German expert on sexual behaviour, Karl Heinrich Ulrich.'[34]

Kilroy returned to the figure of Wilde in 2004 with his unperformed play, *My Scandalous Life*, a dramatic monologue with Alfred Douglas as the central figure, set in England in 1944, the year before his death. In this play, Douglas meditates on his own life after the trials, his various court cases, his marriage, the tragic mental illness of his only son and the poisonous legacy of his turbulent association with Wilde – 'Oscar Wilde, did you say? That's all you lot ever ask about.'[35] Douglas, in this account, is devious, self-deceiving and filled with hatred and rancour especially against Robert Ross; but, Kilroy imagines a kind of wisdom achieved by Douglas in spite of his paranoia and anger, an understanding of the bond between himself and Wilde. This crucial moment of insight into the bond between Wilde and Douglas is rare in depictions of their fatal association and worth noting. At one point in the play, Douglas is questioned by one of his young friends about *De Profundis* and Wilde's motivation in writing such a cruel and relentless indictment of the man he loved. 'Why, he asked eventually, why had Oscar Wilde written that terrible letter about me when he was in prison when he and I clearly loved one another to the end? Oh innocence! Innocence! I found the look on the boy's face unbearable. He wanted some answer but was terrified that the answer would destroy some belief which he held dear.'[36] Kilroy imagines Douglas replying in terms that suggest plausibility and a dignity to the enduring connection between the two men.

> I told him that prison was about failure ... that at the very heart of existence is this well of failure and that to look into this black pool was to cleanse oneself, forever, of all illusion, about others, about oneself. How could I explain that Oscar, too, had looked into this pit and then wrote that terrible letter about me? How could I explain that that was the reason, too, why I could forgive him? You see, we had both become truth-tellers, able to cut through deception, especially our own self-deception.[37]

Wilde also features as a symbol of sexual disturbance in the 1994 film, *A Man of No Importance,* written by Barry Devlin and set in Dublin in 1963, the same period for the Gate's production of *The Importance of Being Oscar.* The central character is called Alfie Byrne and the reference is Joycean for some reason, Alfie Byrne being a famous Lord Mayor of Dublin, but perhaps Devlin is using the name to connote an essential Dublinness. Alfie, a Dublin bus conductor and lover of Wilde's poetry and plays, is a virginal middle-aged gay man who lives with his sister and directs productions of Wilde's plays in the local parish hall using his regular customers on the bus. Alfie is encoded as gay with his love of reading, his interest in cooking (even venturing to make Spaghetti Bolognese for his bewildered sister) and a strong lisp added to his flat Dublin working-class accent. As the play opens to the sound of Eartha Kitt singing Cole Porter's 'Let's Fall in Love', Alfie is walking alone by the river Liffey reading *The Ballad of Reading Gaol* in a strongly exaggerated Dublin accent and throwing his green carnation into the water. The object of his affections is the handsome young bus driver that he works with, Robbie, who he calls Bosie, or Dear Boy and whom he is asking to take part in his production of *Salome.* This is to be Alfie's masterpiece, and a new arrival on his bus, the beautiful young Adele Rice, a country girl newly arrived in Dublin, is immediately claimed as his perfect princess, his Salome.

As the production of *Salome* progresses, the forces of Catholic moral repression in the figures of the local parish priest and the butcher become perturbed about the possibility of 'indecent dancing', and Alfie's production in the parish hall is threatened by clerical intervention and possible closure. Wilde's name is constantly evoked within the film, with Alfie quoting Wilde's poems to his early morning passengers, much to the distrust of his Northern Irish supervisor, the crudely drawn villain of the piece. Indeed most of the characters are crudely drawn, either loveable simpletons quoting Wilde in comic Irish accents or dim-witted moralists without imagination or intelligence seeking to oppose the saintly. The threat of homosexuality, Alfie's, is the impending revelation of the play, with Wilde as his mentor and warning. At one point, Alfie visits a gay pub in Dublin alone and gazes furtively across the room at a handsome blond man, terrified when his gaze is mockingly returned with a theatrical kiss. In another scene, the stupidity of the Irish Catholic moralist is illustrated when discussing the current political scandal of 1963, the Profumo case, where a government minister, John Profumo, was discovered to be sharing a lover with a Russian diplomat. His mistress was introduced to him by a society doctor and homoeopath, Stephen Ward, and the right-wing butcher announces to Alfie and his sister that Stephen Ward was guilty of the most serious crime known to humanity, the sin of homoeopathy.

As Alfie begins to come out to his young friend, his Salome, those around him increase the pressure to marry him off and put a stop to the play. The point of crisis comes when he sees his work-mate and love object Robbie, his Bosie, in a passionate kiss with a girlfriend. Determined now to assert his own sexual needs, Alfie dresses up as Wilde, with a wide brimmed hat, a draped scarf and less than discreet eye make-up and goes back to the gay bar. 'A queer looking tulip' as one barman remarks, Alfie has made his homosexuality visible by dressing as Wilde, perhaps also in imitation of MacLiammóir, and the young gay men in the pub dressed in contemporary 1960s fashion react badly. The cruel blond young man, 'called Kitty', responds to Alfie's advances by bringing him outside into the alleyway where Alfie is beaten and robbed by the other gay men. As he lies bleeding, Alfie's gaze lingers on the stars above, a visual pun on one of Wilde's most famous lines and then he is rescued by a kindly young policeman who complains 'He's not going to press charges. They never do. The usual thing.'

'As he has learned, by assuming the mantle of gayness in his performance as Wilde, Alfie's desires have become public property', writes Maria Pramaggiore.[38] Outed as much by the homophobic attack by other gay men as by dressing like Wilde, Alfie explains and defends his loneliness and his unrequited passion for the heterosexual Robbie to his sister:

> The very idea that I might want or love him or ever feel special towards him would be so repulsive to him that he wouldn't be able to get far enough away from me ... Me hands are innocent of affection.

The cruel bus inspector, now named as Carson, taunts Alfie, telling him that he should be locked up for what he is. 'I am in prison, I've been in prison all my life and the one bird that sang to me there through me prison bars has upped and flown away'. 'Oscar Wilde?' Inquires the homophobic Carson. 'Alfred Byrne, I fear', Alfie replies and as Carson retreats, Alfie defends himself by quoting verbatim from Wilde's speech from the dock defining the Love that Dare not Speak its Name, to the applause of his bus passengers.

The film ends as it began, with a reading from *The Ballad of Reading Gaol*. But significantly, it is read by Robbie, Alfie's 'Bosie', who has learnt of Alfie's outing and compassionately tells him 'I don't care what you get up to. I'm your pal and I know who Bosie was', and the two men rehearse the poem to the strains of Eartha Kitt singing, 'Let's Fall In Love', Cole Porter's hymn to the diversity of sexual attraction and desire ... Referring to the inherent meaning in *A Man Of No Importance*, the critic Maria Pramaggiore writes that

> Questions of Ireland's internal diversity are central to the film ... Alfie's fondness for Oscar Wilde situates sexual pluralism at the centre of discussions about Irishness in historical and contemporary contexts. Because Wilde was Anglo-Irish and thus Protestant, and Alfie and his passengers are Catholic, Alfie's infectious admiration for the playwright asserts that Irish artists and national heroes, often one and the same, need not be Catholic or heterosexual. Here the reference to the Irish theatrical tradition asserts the fact that non-normative subjectivities – here, sexual outlaws – have been a part of the modern Irish nation and the post-modern Irish Diaspora.[39]

It is true that the availability of Wilde to a Dublin Catholic working–class man as a symbol of his own sexual identity does mean a kind of cultural inclusiveness, but the film does project a kind of retrospective liberalism around Alfie's gayness, with most of the heterosexual characters being both sympathetic and tolerant. All clerical homophobia is comical and easily deflated. The only real menace and violence comes, perhaps ironically, from other gay men when Alfie impersonates Wilde. Reviews of the film were not positive. *The Irish Independent* called it a 'seriously inept movie'.[40] *The Irish Times* carried a review called' 'Wild About Oscar' where Michael O'Dwyer wrote:

> But this was a time when 'the love that dare not speak its name' was still considered unspeakable, and while the movie displays an affectionate and jovially nostalgic feel for the period, it eschews any predictable 'Rare old Times' trappings and firmly sets about exposing the bigotry and hypocrisy that lurked beneath the superficial bonhomie.[41]

Overall, in these dramas and texts, Wilde's own life served as a useful trope from which to dramatize homosexuality, coloured by the prevalent cultural assumptions around same-sex desire in Ireland and the need to 'other' any dissident sexuality. The unambiguous nature of Wilde's life and his conviction for gross indecency provided a useful metaphor for those Irish cultural commentators and writers wishing to track prevalent views and perceptions around male homosexuality. Each of these plays is a hallmark for evolving perceptions of Wilde and, by extension, of sexual otherness. Micheál MacLiammóir was careful to negotiate the difficult and troubling sexuality for which Wilde was condemned and to translate it into an acceptable and discreetly tragic melodrama. On the other hand, Eagleton and Kilroy are more direct in their presentation of his sexuality and they both reinstate dissident sexuality and sexual sin as a central part of the drama of Wilde's life. Only Eagleton allows that sexual sin to be seen as something subversive and radical, whereas Kilroy situates his version of Wilde within a familiar discourse of trauma and self-disgust.

To conclude, I would argue that each of these texts demonstrates that Wilde, as an emblematic figure of dissidence, disgrace and desire, continues to draw Irish dramatic imaginations towards the complex yet stimulating challenge of representing same-sex desire and these performances of his life on the Irish stage themselves perform Irish social and cultural attitudes towards sexual difference. In a sense, Wilde is constantly being made and remade, invented and re-invented as Ireland remakes its own modernity in the light of the radical cultural reinventions of the last fifty years.

---

[1] In particular, I refer to John Boyd's *Speranza's Son*, produced in the Lyric Theatre in 1982 and Ulick O'Connor's *A Trinity of Two*, produced in the Peacock Theatre, Dublin, in 1988. I draw some of the materials for this essay from my previous essays, *Wild (e) Irish. Ireland in Proximity,* Ed Alderson et al. (London: Routledge, 1999) and *Game To The Last: Inventing MacLiammóir. Sex, Nation and Dissent* (Cork: Cork University Press, 1997). This forms part of my forthcoming book on Wilde and Modern Ireland.

[2] Micheál MacLiammóir, *An Oscar of No Importance* (Dublin: Dolmen Press, 1963), p. 25.

[3] Ibid, p. 37.

[4] Terence Brown, *Ireland: A Social and Cultural History* (London: Harper Perennial, 2004), p. 137.

[5] Christopher Fitz -Simon, *The Boys* (Dublin: Gill & Macmillan, 1994), p. 41.

[6] Alan Sinfield, *The Wilde Century* (London: Cassells, 1994), p. 11.

[7] H. Montgomery Hyde, *The Other Love* (London: Heinemann, 1970), p. 233.

[8] *The Boys,* p. 231.

[9] Michael Ō'hAodha, *The Importance of being Micheál* (Kerry: Brandon Press, 1990), p. 159.

[10] Hilton Edwards, Introduction, *The Importance of Being Oscar*, p. 5.

[11] IBO, p. 15.

[12] Ibid., p. 37.

[13] *The New Yorker* 25 March 1961.

[14] *The World Telegraph and Sun* 15 March 1961.

[15] Joan Dean, 'MacLiammóir's Oscar and the American reclamation of Wilde', pp. 6-7. Unpublished essay, I am grateful to her for all her help.

[16] IBO, p. 138.

[17] Alan Sinfield, *Out On Stage* (New Haven: Yale University Press, 1999), p. 265.

[18] ONI, p. 1.

[19] Ibid., p. 4.

[20] Ibid., p. 24.

[21] Ibid., p. 29.

[22] Ibid., p. 62.

[23] *The Irish Times* 1 November 1989, p 12.

[24] Terry Eagleton, *St Oscar* (Derry: Field Day, 1989), pp. x-xi.

[25] Eagleton, p. viii.

[26] Ibid, p. 6.

[27] Ibid.

[28] Ibid, pp. 13-17.

[29] Ibid, p. 23.

[30] *The Irish Times* 26 September 1997, p .1.

[31] *The Irish Times* 2 October 1997, p. 12.

[32] Tom Kilroy, *The Secret Fall of Constance Wilde* (Dublin: Gallery Press, 1997), p. 66.

[33] Ibid, p. 20.

[34] Ibid, p. 30.

[35] Tom Kilroy, *My Scandalous Life* (Meath: The Gallery Press, 2004), p. 9.

[36] Ibid, pp. 25-26.

37 Ibid, p. 26.

38 Maria Pramaggiore, *The Irish In US*, ed. Diana Negre (Durham: Duke University Press, 2006), pp. 124-25.

39 Ibid.

40 *Irish Independent* 21 April 1995, p. 26.

41 *The Irish Times* 21 April 1995, p. 15.

3 | The Politics of Camp:

Queering Parades, Performance, and the Public in Belfast

Kathryn Conrad

Despite the recent resumption of the Northern Ireland Assembly and a recommitment of major political parties to working together on Northern Irish governance, and despite the public perception of increasing tolerance,[1] Northern Irish society would seem to be as divided as ever before. For instance, the number of 'peace lines'[2] dividing Protestant and Catholic housing areas doubled between 1995 and 2005, with most of the walls located in Belfast.[3] As of 2006, 80% of people lived in 'single identity' communities.[4] The Good Friday Agreement (1998) effectively reified the 'two-community' model of politics,[5] and neither the subsequent St. Andrews Agreement nor the quotidian workings of politics has done much to unsettle this model.

Perhaps one of the most obvious and contentious displays of identity, particularly in post-ceasefire Northern Ireland, has been through parades. Parading peaks during the Orange marching season, which takes place every summer and is concentrated around the 12th of July in commemoration of William of Orange's 1690 victory at the Battle of the Boyne. After the violent confrontations and protests surrounding the Drumcree parade in Portadown, the Parades Commission was established in 1998 to monitor and regulate controversial parades.[6] Parading, like self-imposed religious housing segregation, does not appear to have diminished; in 2005, for instance, the Parades Commission lists 391 Orange parades; in 2008, it lists 1334.

Parading is not limited, however, to loyalist and nationalist groups. 1991 saw the first Gay Pride parade in Belfast, and Belfast Pride has increased in the number of participants and observers ever since. Pride's popularity has certainly accompanied an increase in visibility of gays and lesbians and an increased recognition of the claims to rights by those identifying thus. Although Pride seems to offer yet another identity to add to the parade of identities in Northern Ireland, I would suggest a different reading of the yearly event, which takes place near the end of the summer 'marching season'. In the context of Northern Ireland, Belfast Pride proffers an alternative to the performance of 'identity' and 'tradition' represented by the loyalist and nationalist parades. Specifically, the Belfast Pride parade has camp elements, and camp in this public context provides an alternative to the entrenchment of identity and identity politics as well as to the public forms such politics take in Northern Ireland.

Making a New Camp

Richard Kirkland is the first critic to have, provocatively, brought the notion of camp to bear on Northern Irish cultural productions. He writes that

> camp ... fulfils a number of important roles within bourgeois society. In exposing the shallowness of identitarian constructions of the self through a determined focus on the surfaces of their manifestation, it is a celebration of those identities while at the same time containing a more dangerous awareness of their ultimate interchangeability. Its intimacy with those codes, the profound knowledge of the society it demands, similarly allows for a demarcation of a culture while, as [Richard] Dyer reminds us, providing a mode of cultural survival in the face of real or imagined violence.[7]

He suggests that 'camp is ... transgressive of the limits by which identity normally offers itself' (130). And indeed, these descriptions echo the way camp functions in Belfast Pride. Those who practice camp within the parade are double-voiced, echoing the structures of the majority culture(s) while at the same time providing a comic commentary on them through parody.

Kirkland's analysis draws heavily on Susan Sontag's 'Notes on Camp', which he describes as 'one of the most vivid engagements with the concept' (Kirkland, 128) and to which I will return as well. He accepts Sontag's suggestion both that camp is an aesthetic position and that what it responds to is 'instant character'.[8] As such, 'camp ... seems to invite an actual commitment to identity's formal structures. In this way camp becomes an unlikely ally, if not of identity itself, then at least to the symmetries and oppositions on which it is dependent' (Kirkland, 130). Kirkland's notion of camp is also heavily indebted to Judith Butler's theory of gender per-formativity.[9] For Kirkland, 'camp becomes indicative of an over-determined identity formation'(127). By the time he engages in close reading of 'camp' formations (which he characterizes as belonging to one of three 'forms': dissenting camp, unionist camp, and nationalist camp), camp has become a 'spectacular critique (a critique *through* spectacle) of the earnest values it wishes to promote' (135). For Kirkland, camp is unintentional parody, parody through excess, parody through failed repetition *à la* Butler. Although he acknowledges that camp is often seen as 'highly conscious', his examples – of, for instance, Ian Paisley performing the role of Protestant martyr in the Crumlin Road jail, or the contradictions between didacticism and sentimental self-regard in Bernadette Devlin's autobiography – suggest a notion of camp that, following Sontag, is 'pure Camp': a 'seriousness that fails' (Sontag, 59) that is then identified (and in Sontag's vision, but not Kirkland's, 'redeemed') by its audience as camp.

The idea that nationalist and loyalist, as well as 'dissenting' (expressly non-aligned, liberal humanist), discourses and forms are worthy objects of camp appropriation is, it seems to me, an important contribution to thinking about Northern Irish political discourse. However, Kirkland's identification of what constitutes camp in the Northern Irish context and how it works, I might suggest, would be unrecognizable to most practitioners of camp. It is important to explain his failures of understanding of camp in order to reclaim what I find more valuable about Kirkland's contribution.

The first and most obvious critique of Kirkland is that he erases homosexuality almost entirely from his discussion of camp even as he relies on gay critics such as Dyer for his elaboration of the concept. In a footnote, Kirkland writes that 'it is necessary to place Dyer's cheerful analysis in the context of other more militant reclamations of camp by queer theory', citing as an example Moe Meyer's claim that camp 'embodies a specifically queer cultural discourse' and that the un-queer have no access to camp except through appropriation (Kirkland, 181). Indeed, Sontag's famed essay has itself been critiqued as being appropriative of homosexual discourse, taking a homosexual cultural practice and suggesting it as a more general aesthetic response; in contrast, Esther Newton's study *Mother Camp* can be seen, as Fabio Cleto points out, as a text that gives camp 'a stable referent': 'the sensibility/taste described by Newton is no longer the Sontagian sign and expression of an era, but rather an exercise in homosexual taste and a mode of existence'.[10] I will stake my tent and suggest that camp, at least for the majority of the twentieth and twenty-first centuries, is a queer phenomenon.

Why queer? Certainly camp, as many critics have suggested, has been closely tied to male homosexual culture in particular, whether or not the concept actually originated there (Cleto, 21). But more to the point, as Cleto suggests in his analysis of the instability of the origins and meaning of both 'camp' and 'queer', queer, like camp, is a destabilizing discourse, and indeed, as he suggests, both are 'cognate terms: camp is queer as a mode of being, as posturing a body, as a modality of distribution within social spaces and within the economy of the social contract, and as a mode of com-munication ...' (30).

This list is evocative, but it still does not explain why Kirkland's use of camp as an analytical category fails. Camp is, to be sure, notoriously difficult to write about. I would offer that critics – and by no means is Kirkland alone, given that scholars of camp seem to have as many definitions of camp as a drag queen has sequins – have trouble defining camp because they cannot decide where the camp actually lies: in the object, in the reception, in the 'sensibility' or aesthetics, in the worldview, or in the performance. I will add my sequins to the dress with the following attempts at clarification.

First, camp always involves a performance. It can be a performance of reception of an object or person. This is how the Queen Mother can be a camp icon (an example used by Richard Dyer[11] and cited by Kirkland [134]): she is not innately camp, and indeed no *object or person* is, but one can perform a response to her that claims her as camp. Of course, other performances are both more obviously camp and more obviously performances, like drag. Camp, in short, is not 'performa*tive*' in the Butlerian sense of a discourse that forms a subject through reiteration; it is, rather, *performance* by a knowing agent. It is an active choice. Sontag cites Wilde in *An Ideal Husband*: 'To be natural is such a difficult pose to keep up' (Sontag, 58). The camp performer recognizes the performance, the pose, *as* performance. Esther Newton, and several critics after her refer to this aspect of camp as its theatricality,[12] and it is important, I think, to distinguish deliberate theatricality from agentless performativity.

Second, the performance of camp, whether that performance is a response to an object as 'fabulous' or a Celine Dion song sung in drag or the hosting of a Pee-Wee Herman pyjama party, is necessarily part of an exchange. It is dialogic; camp does not happen in isolation. Sedgwick evokes this sense of camp in her discussion of camp-recognition, as opposed to kitsch-attribution:

> Camp [as distinguished from kitsch] seems to involve a gayer and more spacious angle of view ... Unlike kitsch-attribution, then, camp-recognition doesn't ask, 'What kind of debased creature could possibly be the right audience for this spectacle?' Instead, it says *what if*: What if the right audience for this were exactly *me*? What if, for instance, the resistant, oblique, tangential investments of attention and attraction that I am able to bring to this spectacle are actually uncannily a response to the resistant, oblique, tangential investments of the person, or of some of the people, who created it? And what if, furthermore, others whom I don't know or recognize can see it from the same 'perverse' angle? Unlike kitsch-*attribution*, the sensibility of camp-*recognition* always sees that it is dealing in reader relations and in projective fantasy (projective though not infrequently true) about the spaces and practices of cultural production.[13]

I do not believe that Sedgwick is suggesting that the 'recognition' of camp is a 'recognition' of anything innate, but rather a re-cognition, a re-thinking, from a 'perverse' (or *queer*) angle of view. To recognize camp, one must be part of a discourse, an exchange; one must be hailed by camp. This dynamic can also be understood in the context of public sphere theory, to which I will return. It is also the very reason both Sontag and Kirkland may partially fail in their analysis in different ways: Kirkland sympathetically cites Sontag's claim that 'to name a sensibility, to draw its contours and to recount its history, requires a deep sympathy modified by revulsion' (Sontag, 53, cited in Kirkland, 135). The 'revulsion' experience implies that neither Sontag nor Kirkland really identifies with the 'resistant, oblique, tangential investments of the person, or of some of the people, who [create] camp' (Sedgwick, 156).

Third, camp involves a seeming paradox in that it is simultaneously exclusive and potentially inclusive. It is exclusive insofar as it is a response of the marginalized to their marginal status that preserves, reclaims, and refigures that status, but only by those who are sympathetic. Further, if one is not hailed by camp, if one does not recognize a fellow-feeling in camp as Sedgwick suggests, then one is appropriating the discourse. The parallel might be in the use of 'dyke' or 'nigger': if one is not hailed by those terms in their reclaimed context, one cannot safely use the terms without condescension. In this sense, camp performs as a counter-public discourse, as Michael Warner defines the concept. It

> maintains at some level, conscious or not, an awareness of its subordinate status. The cultural horizon against which it marks itself off is not just a general or wider public but a dominant one ... The discourse that constitutes it is not merely a different or alternative idiom but one that in other contexts would be regarded with hostility.[14]

In this sense, I might also suggest that camp occupies a discursive space both inside and outside the dominant culture: with one foot inside the culture enough to know it and care about, and another foot outside, able to see with the critical (and parodic) view of the marginalized.

Perhaps most importantly, however – and this is where Kirkland's analysis misses the sense of camp in practice utterly – camp is funny. Whether the laughter is with *or* at the camp performance, camp is meant to engender laughter. And in that, it has the potential to be inclusive and even, as Sontag implies, generous. The use of humour in response to the conflict in Northern Ireland is by no means a new approach; one can name many artists, such as Stewart Parker, Robert McLiam Wilson, and Paul Muldoon who, in different ways, have incorporated humour, albeit often of a dark sort, in their work. But the playful and good-humoured public parody that Pride's camp performances enact of the actual signs and structures of the conflict – from identity to parading to flags – is both a novel approach *and* a political one, despite Sontag's (in)famous assertion that 'comedy is an experience of under-involvement, of detachment', and that the 'camp sensibility' is, 'it goes without saying', 'disengaged, depoliticized – or at least apolitical' (Sontag, 54). As Caryl Flinn notes, most critics would not agree with Sontag's sentiments here, instead 'adher[ing] to the basic belief in camp's ability to unmoor dominant ideological structures and values – not an apolitical act, to be sure'.[15] Camp's ability to unmoor is located in its exploitation of excess for comic effect – excessive seriousness, excessive feathers, excessive sentiment.

Excess reveals the form for what it is: form, not nature, not inevitability. In the context of a Northern Irish political environment in which 'two community' rhetoric has become ever more entrenched, such destabilization of supposed inevitabilities is essential for the political health of the region.

Camping in Belfast

Belfast's gay pride parade has been taking place since 1991, growing from a small parade (or 'dander', as early organizer and long-time officer of the Northern Ireland Gay Rights Association, PA MagLochlainn, has always preferred to call it), attended by gay rights supporters from Belfast as well as London/Derry, Dublin, Cork, and elsewhere, to a large multi-event celebration known as Belfast Pride. Pride culminates with a parade comprising hundreds of participants, from individuals to organized groups and Belfast gay-friendly businesses. Even from the beginning, some Belfast Pride participants, like Pride parade-goers in many parts of the world, engaged in camp performance and fancy dress costuming. In recent years, elements of the parade have run the gamut from the high seriousness of human rights activism to the camp performances of drag queens, parade floats, dancers, and costumes, quite often accompanied by amplified disco music.

One might argue that the camp performances are at odds with serious activism, but I would argue that the effect is otherwise: the camp performances help the diverse audience of Pride accept with equanimity the other messages the parade offers. Camp delivers politics with a smile and a wink – an approach that, as I have suggested elsewhere, has been part of an effective strategy of address both to the queer counter public and to the wider public to which the parade is addressed.[16]

Pride has more obviously had a political impact as part of a larger lesbian and gay rights discourse, but its various strategies of address – including camp – impact more with lesbians and gays or the larger queer counter public that the parade addresses.[17] I have argued that one of the ways Pride challenges Northern Irish politics is through a reversal of the surveillance gaze to which all Northern Irish people are subject:

> This returned gaze is not a mere recapitulation of the politics of surveillance, but rather an exposure, literal and figurative, of the economy of surveillance: to turn a camera on a protester is

to say that queers are subjects with a gaze as much as they are objects of it. Mostly, the parade says 'watch us', changing the very nature of that watching through the strategic assumption that the parade audience is a mostly sympathetic, open-minded public.[18]

But Pride not only turns the gaze back on the viewers, as I have argued elsewhere; the returned gaze creates a dialogue. In concert with the camp performances in particular, the Pride parade invites participation from its audience and is apparently so effective in this invitation that 'the borders of the parade are remarkably fluid; many members of the audience become marchers'.[19] It is perhaps this dialogism – and humour – that allows the parade participants so effectively to 'camp up' some of the sacred cows of Northern Irish political life such as political flags, parading, and parade counter-protests (see figs. 1 and 2). Although these elements are not the focus of the parade, their presence both signals that Pride is part of the political culture and is performing a critique of it, seeing mainstream culture from the particular 'perverse' angle of view that Sedgwick celebrates.

One of the more contentious elements of Northern Irish visible political culture, for instance, is the display of flags; such displays have been the focus of much political discussion, negotiation, anger, and resistance in Northern Ireland.[20] It has also been the subject of camp performance in Belfast Pride: not simply satire, not protest, but the particular combination of affection, knowledge, humour, excess and critique that camp can produce. The camp humour of gay boys and girls in white jeans and white shirts and brightly coloured cowboy hats holding a Union Jack where the blue has been replaced by pink both deflates the high seriousness of Northern Irish obsession with flags and exhibits, presumably, some level of affection for that obsession (see fig. 3). Who knew that the Union Jack could be fabulous if it were just a bit pinker? The same can be said of the giant rainbow flag that runs the length of a city block (see fig. 4), used in other Pride celebrations but taking on a particular resonance in a Northern Irish context. 'You call that [tricolour or Union Jack] a flag? THIS is a flag,' it seems to say. It, like the empinkened Union Jack, celebrates the form while perverting the content.

Conclusion

Camp is no mere repetition of form to the point of unconscious parody, as Kirkland suggests. Nor is it, on the other extreme, merely postmodern ironic positioning; it is not nihilistic. It is, I might suggest, a politics of affection, even when the satiric knife may cut a bit deeply. And camp humour in the context of a public parade, I would suggest, offers 'different ways of imagining stranger sociability and its reflexivity', as Warner describes the queer counter public (Warner, 122); it 'challenges the limits of public space and the place of the body in that space' (Conrad, 'Queering', 601). It does this through performing the same forms to which people are accustomed, but in a different way, one that draws the audience into dialogue and which has the potential to reposition those who are in dialogue with it, to allow them to see things they take for granted from a different perspective. And in so doing, it betrays what Sontag gestures toward when she says that 'camp taste is a kind of love, love for human nature' (Sontag, 65).

By turning an exclusive form of address outward to a larger public, the camp elements of Belfast Pride seem to suggest, in the paradox that is peculiar to camp, that we can all partake of this exclusive form. It gestures to shared forms that ossify identities, cultures, practices, communities, traditions, and politics, empties them of their high seriousness, and provides a different perspective and an opportunity for a different path. I remain hopeful that more and more people will find themselves hailed by camp and in so doing seek a more generous and 'perverse' angle of view on Northern Irish politics.

My thanks to Darryl Wadsworth and Robert Lachance for their insight and contributions to my thinking about camp.

---

1 *Northern Ireland Life & Times Survey: Community Relations*, 2007. See http://www.ark.ac.uk/nilt/2007/Community Relations/index.html (accessed 24 November 2008).

2 high dividing walls, also called 'interfaces'.

3 John O' Farrell, 'Apartheid', *New Statesman* 28 November 2005. See http://www.newstatesman.com/200511280006 (accessed 20 November 2008).

4, John Kampfner, 'Divided in Peace', *New Statesman* 20 November 2006. See http://www.newstatesman.com/200611200028 (accessed 20 November 2008).

5 For analysis of the implications of the language of the Good Friday Agreement, see especially Dominic Bryan, 'The politics of community', *Critical Review of International Social and Political Philosophy* 9.4 (December 2006), pp. 603-17; Kathryn Conrad, *Locked in the Family Cell: Gender, Sexuality, and Political Agency in Irish National Discourse* (Madison: University of Wisconsin Press, 2004), chapter 3; Alan Finlayson, 'Culture, politics and cultural politics in Northern Ireland', *New Formations* 43 (2001), pp. 87-102; and Kathryn Conrad, 'Queering Community', *Critical Review of International Social and Political Philosophy* 9.4 (December 2006), pp. 589-602.

6 See Northern Ireland Parades Commission website, http://www.paradescommission.org (accessed 24 November 2008). For more analysis of Orange parades and the nationalist and loyalist parading traditions of Northern Ireland more generally, see Dominic Bryan, *Orange Parades: The Politics of Ritual, Tradition, and Control* (Ann Arbor: University of Michigan Press, 2000); Neil Jarman, *Material Conflicts: Parades and Visual Displays in Northern Ireland* (Oxford: Berg, 1997); Jarman and Dominic Bryan, *Parade and Protest: A Discussion of Parading Disputes in Northern Ireland* (Coleraine: Centre for the Study of Conflict, University of Ulster, Coleraine, 1996); and the Conflict Archive on the Internet (CAIN), http://cain.ulst.ac.uk/index.html (accessed 20 November 2008).

7 Richard Kirkland, *Identity Parades: Northern Irish Culture and Dissident Subjects* (Liverpool: Liverpool University Press, 2002), p. 130. Subsequent references will be cited in the text.

8 Susan Sontag, 'Notes on Camp', *Camp: Queer Aesthetics and the Performing Subject: A Reader*, ed. Fabio Cleto (Edinburgh: Edinburgh University Press, 1999), p. 60. Subsequent references will be cited in the text. Cited in Kirkland, 129.

9 See Judith Butler, *Gender Trouble: Feminism and the Subversion of Identity* (New York and Routledge: Routledge, 1999).

10 Fabio Cleto, Introduction, Cleto, *Camp*, p. 89. Subsequent references will be cited in the text.

11 Richard Dyer, 'It's Being So Camp As Keeps Us Going', Cleto, *Camp*, p. 113.

12 Esther Newton, 'Role Models', Cleto, *Camp*, p. 103.

13 Eve Kosofsky Sedgwick, *Epistemology of the Closet* (Berkeley and Los Angeles: University of California Press, 1990), p. 156; emphasis in the original. Subsequent references will be cited in the text.

14 Michael Warner, *Publics and Counterpublics* (New York: Zone Books, 2002), p. 119. Subsequent references will be cited in the text. For a fuller discussion of Belfast Pride, read both in the context of public sphere theory and Northern Irish politics, see Conrad, 2006.

15 Caryl Flinn, 'The Deaths of Camp', Cleto, *Camp*, p. 439.

16 Conrad, 'Queering Community', p. 601. Subsequent references will be cited in the text.

17 Ibid.

18 Ibid.

19 Ibid.

20 For a fuller discussion of the significance of flags, see Dominic Bryan and Gillian McIntosh, 'Sites of Creation and Conflict in Northern Ireland', *SAIS Review* 25.3 (2005), pp. 127-37. See also CAIN.

4 | Lesbian Versions of the Female Biography Play: Emma Donoghue's I *Know My Own Heart* and *Ladies and Gentlemen*

Mária Kurdi

The Irish-born writer, Emma Donoghue, author of widely acclaimed, award-winning novels and anthologized short stories, is also a leading feminist historian who explores changing notions about and linguistic representations of sex between women in her works of non-fiction. Her 1993 study of British lesbian culture during the late seventeenth and eighteenth centuries (1668-1801), *Passions Between Women*, contains invaluable data and source material regarding the subject, offering a detailed discussion of the related discursive practices and their operation in the given socio-cultural context. Besides producing fiction and scholarly work, Donoghue has also written works for the stage, stating, in an interview that

> Drama for me has provided the biggest excitements of my career. There's nothing like working with a group of actors in rehearsal, seeing them add at least 100 percent to the material, seeing them act it out on stage and make it real and live and exciting in a way that I'm not sure a novel can be. And theatre is unspeakably live ... if it works well it can hold people gripped.[1]

Two of her plays are available in print: *I Know My Own Heart* (first performed in 1993) and *Ladies and Gentlemen* (first performed in 1996). They fit into the Donoghue canon as dramatized interpretations of the lesbian experience by giving voice to historical characters, who lived in early nineteenth-century Britain and late nineteenth-century America respectively. The protagonist of *I Know My Own Heart* is Anne Lister (1791-1849), a woman belonging to the landed class who, as testified by her journals, had love affairs with women. Primarily, the play focuses on her feelings for a farmer's daughter, Marianne, and the dilemmas inherent in the relationship for both under the pressures of the patriarchal society. Annie Hindle (ca. 1847-19??), the English-born protagonist of *Ladies and Gentlemen* is presented at the time of her return to the stage as male impersonator after a few years' absence during which she lived in seclusion married to a woman, her former dresser called Ryanny. The play is constructed of a series of recollections, which portray the history of the two women's relationship. To a degree, Donoghue's works for the stage continue the explorations of *Passions Between Women* in a different performative genre noted for its evocative immediacy by the writer herself, and look at the century following the one studied in the book revealing how varied and decisive a period it was as far as both the individual expression and the communal treatment of same-sex attachment between women were concerned.

In the introduction to their 1997 volume *Gender and Sexuality in Modern Ireland*, Anthony Bradley and Maryann Gialanella Valiulis argue that the recent 'progressive social changes or disturbing revelations' in the Republic of Ireland 'have given an urgency to the issues of gender and sexuality, and have been accompanied by a growing intellectual awareness of the extent to which social experience, past and present, is gendered'.[2] An obvious sign of the thorough revisioning of Ireland's gender politics at the time was the decriminalization of homosexuality in 1993. Notably, the first two lesbian-feminist plays for the Irish stage had been written a few years before 1993, to 'challenge the sexual imbalance prominent in Irish theatre and society at large' by Joni Core, in the wake of which came Louise Callaghan's attempt to dramatize the life of Kate O'Brien.[3] Having left Ireland for Canada in 1990, Donoghue, however, set neither of the plays examined here in Ireland of the 1990s, where the lesbian experience had just started to become more visible as part of the above cited increasing concern with the implications of gender and sexual practices for the society. She places the subject in a broader, international perspective by introducing English, American, and Irish protagonists who are based on real persons, having lived at the two ends of the nineteenth century and in markedly different social circumstances. *I Know My Own Heart* and *Ladies and Gentlemen* treat historical material similarly to several pieces of Donoghue's fiction. Her historical retrospect is explained in the above cited interview as follows: 'It's not like I have one of those wonderfully varied biographies to draw on, of being a rodeo woman and nun. I don't have great decades of experience of life ... so I have to rely on my research skills quite a lot.'[4]

The two dramatic works qualify as versions of the biography play, presenting a kind of gender-sensitive as well as interrogative life-writing for the stage which defines its own strategies against the male-dominated traditions of the genre. Neither do they share a conceptual basis with contemporary, postmodern examples of the biography play which stage a variety of cultural constructions and media-represented versions of the main character, revealing but a void at the centre. As a feminist writer Donoghue is not interested in the concept of the disappearance of the subject, yet her approach undermines its stability when couteracting the lesbian subject's exclusion from theatrical representation. Theorizing biography plays by women Ryan Claycomb in *Modern Drama* claims that

> Instead of focusing on recovering the identities of the women themselves ... they focus on the real-life acts and transgressive gender performances of feminist and protofeminist women. These plays avoid merely holding up historical women as museum pieces removed by time from their audiences; they choose, instead ... [to] turn their critical eye to the historical gender performances being recovered, as well as to the process of that recovery, the performance of doing biography itself, and the paths by which we, as postmodern readers and audience members, have access to these historical acts.[5]

Donoghue's biography play constructs disjointed narratives alongside the employment of 'scenic presentation ... to create a realistic atmosphere',[6] by which she reflects on the protagonists' subjective landscape and strife for agency at the expense of attempting to offer as complete a picture of the chosen lives as possible. Moreover, the writer's enterprise is unique in that she cuts across the boundaries of genre and gender, integrating specific features of lesbian feminist dramaturgy. This chapter intends to analyse how these dimensions and choices underpin both plays, as well as to investigate the historical and cultural embedding of the lesbian protagonists' subjectivity and self-professed otherness. At the same time, the essay will be concerned with the potential of the multiple effects that such an experimental combination evokes to refresh the understanding of alternative generic and gender formations.

Through several examples of the contemporary female biography play from the English-speaking world, including *Blood and Ice* by Liz Lochhead about the person of Mary Shelley, Claycomb points out that they are imbued with acts and tropes of performance to 'foreground the representations of subjectivity'.[7] Donoghue's protagonists are shown performing what had made their figures known. Anne Lister, whose journal written in secret codes about her relationships with women was found and decoded only long after her death, and Annie Hindle, 'the first woman ... to specialize in male impersonation in the music hall'[8] often appear involved in writing and performing on stage respectively. Along with its contradictions, the progress in the history of women's developing opportunities for creative expression throughout the nineteenth century becomes foregrounded by the performance of these activities.

Anne and her long-time friend Tib read from Jane Austen's new novel in *I Know My Own Heart*; the intertextual insertion calls attention to writing by women as the main form of how they could assert their subjectivity with comparative freedom for much of the nineteen hundreds. The quotation which describes Emma's 'admiring those soft blue eyes'[9] of Harriet seems to illustrate that within the female-authored novel may be found a coded text which implies its author's unconventional desires, functioning not unlike the journal Miss Lister was keeping. Austen's novels and this play by Donoghue are set in the same period and feature a similar country lifestyle. They also share the writing of letters as a strategy to suggest that middle-class women's communication with each other often took such forms due to the scarcity of occasions or places, save the church, where they could have met and talked unchaperoned outside the carefully guarded confines of the family home. Evaluating Jane Austen's letters, Deborah Kaplan claims that Austen and the women (relatives and friends) who were the addressees of the majority of her letters 'experienced the doubleness of participation in both a woman's culture and the general, gentry culture'. In contrast with her novels, which represent 'a public and ideological form' and, thus, 'resist expression of cultural contra-dictions', Austen's letters, representing an uncensored, private genre, 'express multiple, indeed even opposing, cultural values'.[10] It is with a similar effect that, beside the frequently performed act of

Anne writing her journal, the female characters' penning of letters to each other is staged in *I Know My Own Heart*. Marianne's decision to leave her husband and stay with Anne is rejected by the latter: 'My aunt would never permit it, what with my uncle bedridden and your husband likely to ride up at any moment with a brace of pistols' (137). The letter Marianne writes to Anne upon her arrival back home words the ambiguity of having to do the consensually right thing while personal feelings revolt against it: 'My dearest, truest husband, here I am back in Lawton Hall. I shrink from sharing a house with Charles ... '(139).

The English-born Annie Hindle, the protagonist of *Ladies and Gentlemen*, came on the scene in the United States 'when the female emancipation movement was growing more vociferous and demanding. On stage, unruly women disguised as men were less threatening ... '.[11] Thus the socio-cultural changes permeating the contemporary discourse of gender facilitated Annie's debut as a dedicated cross-dressing performer, starting to pursue an inevitably public form of creative art. Part of the entertainment provided by the vaudeville and variety shows that emerged in post-bellum American society included the performance of both female and male impersonators: 'female assumptions of male identity appeared in the theatre as a novelty, a salacious turn, a secular Johnny-come-lately' as Laurence Senelick observes.[12] On the one hand, female members of Annie Hindle's audiences may well have cherished a secret longing to dress and behave as freely as men, thus for them to watch Annie's acting male in an unrestrained manner was perhaps a kind of wish-fulfilment. Male spectators, on the other hand, were gratified to see that the transgressive inclinations of woman, the never fully reliable 'other', could be contained in a public institution, the theatre; a place known for creating illusion while leaving reality intact as nineteenth-century popular drama trained the audience. In this Donoghue play, a life centred on performance is portrayed, doubling the characteristic that theatre 'proceeds through a process of impersonation and role-play', with which *Ladies and Gentlemen* enhances its dramatic potential to 'function as a critical site for exploring the constitution of identity through performativity'.[13] Donoghue's title, *Ladies and Gentlemen*, in this respect may be seen as invested with dual meaning. While it evokes a crucial theme of the play, gender, it exposes its constructed status through its coincidence with a well-known staple of the theatre and the world of performance, namely the phrase used to address an audience. The two meanings interact in an intriguing way: the binary formulation of the subject of gender carried by the title is undermined as the reference to theatre suggests that the gender divide is created through acts of illusion, which makes it slippery and opens it up to interrogation. Concurrently, '*in the dressing-room of a New York vaudeville theatre*'[14] as setting the items of costume, make-up and other requisites like the wig, false moustache or beard emphasize that theatre is a privileged site of performative acts to reinforce or unfix gender through self-conscious role-playing and playing with roles.

Drag performance, however, is not necessarily recognized as parody. Implicated as it inevitably is in hegemonic power relations, it may signify many different, even contradictory things to its viewers.[15] Annie's inspired exploration of masculine identity manages to persuade women attending her shows that she could be taken for a real, desirable man. The drama includes a letter from one of her young female admirers, who makes the confession: 'Darling Mr Hindle, please oh please oh please leave off this pretence that you are a woman only dressed as a man ... I told my mother I know you are a real true man and I intend for to marry you' (38). The possibility of equating the performing female body with authentic masculinity highlights that the latter is itself an act, contrary to beliefs about its allegedly stable nature. For Annie, male impersonation does not mean a mere imitation of men's behaviour, a speciality of her performance being that she appeared not in the stereotypical roles that lovers of the music-hall had been accustomed to, but acted as an individual. Not just mimicking clichés of masculinity but creating something new, she surpasses the citational nature of the performative act, and achieves what Judith Butler posits as the possibility of 'a different sort of repeating, in the breaking or subversive repetition of that style'.[16] Believing in the transformational power of role-playing Annie re-negotiates gender by unfixing the norms that define masculinity as a stable category and constructs herself to look 'the model of modern man' on stage, a protean being as her favourite song, 'A Real Man', puts it into words (103):

> I've been to the east and I've been to the west
> From Philly right through to San Fran
> Of the fellers I've met I'm the out-and-out best
> I'm the model of modern man.

Further associations are propelled as a reference in the drama reminding us that this was the time when Oscar Wilde, whose principles notoriously contested the limitations of Victorian identity formation on virtually all fronts, gender and sexuality included, visited the United States to give lectures on aesthetics.

Biography plays by women, to refer to Claycomb again, explore as well as critique the past[17] by portraying the lives they focus on in context. The mores of the respective societies, with their coercive influence on the protagonists themselves as represented in Donoghue's works, form a significant part of this critique, from the particular angle of how psychologically and discursively trans-gressive gender behaviour managed to assert itself, and how these assertions were received. As an heiress to landed property, Miss Lister's life in *I Know My Own Heart* is conspicuously enmeshed in problems related to class differences, the private interest compromised by communal expectations. In her comments on the play, Anna McMullan observes: 'the central character is not romanticized – we are aware of her class position operating in relation to her socially marginalized sexuality, producing a complex profile of privilege and constraint, confidence and vulnerability'.[18] Social prejudice seems to overwhelm individual needs: when Anne Lister notices her sexual attraction to the daughter of a farmer, Marianne Brown, it is not so much sexual inhibitions but class-conscious reservations that she has to overcome in herself. Paradoxically, women of similar social standing did not arouse suspicion even if they maintained a very close friendship, since 'The generality of people don't suspect that such a thing [female homosexuality] exists' as Marianne remarks (117). It is in this context that Anne's encouraging Marianne, already her secret lover, to marry her older suitor, a man of means and with a good name can be understood. However, the grammatical nuances of her discourse betray how ambivalent she is concerning the subject:

> **ANNE.** Lawton Hall is a prosperous estate; I seem to recall visiting it as a child. I should rejoice at such a marriage for you.
> **MARIANNE.** Would you?
> **ANNE.** I said should, not would. I ought to rejoice at it, and I would certainly seem to (112).

'Should', however, is not the same as 'would', she quickly adds, because she is also aware of the emotional cost to both of them of her partner having, as a married woman, all the usual legal and bodily duties. However, there is no way for the two women to live together; only complete financial independence could make it possible for women to abandon their social bindings and start a new life like the Irish Ladies of Llangollen who, according to historical record, had inherited family money to sponsor their unconventional set-up far away from their original home.

In *Ladies and Gentlemen* Annie Hindle does have the financial background to marry her lover, the Irish-born dresser Ryanny, but they cannot continue as an accepted 'normal' couple in their own environment, even though it is the bohemian world of vaudeville shows. The troupe's boss, Tony Pastor, appears in Donoghue's play in a way that complicates if not subverts the idealized image theatre history seems to have of him as an ambitious manager bent on serving audience needs to guard his reputation and remain financially successful in a highly competitive cultural milieu. Therefore he tends to measure even the private behaviour of members of the troupe against the moral views of the public, conservative and unflinchingly heteronormative though they may well be. True, his worried harangues such as: 'I don't want any whiff of scandal attached to my Grand Speciality Troupe, you hear? ... It makes me nervous as hell having Ella hang round with that Mansfield moll' (33) provoke laughter. Yet they underscore that the performers are not at all free from the cultural and economic constraints of Victorian America. Tony has a 'show-book', which prescribes what the impersonator is to do on stage to provide the audience with the amount of fun they expect for their money. A woman impersonating the opposite gender on stage, even to great audience acclaim, was one thing, but appropriating the male prerogative and living with a wife in public was quite another. Consequently, the newly-wed Annie and Ryanny have to leave for Annie's New Jersey cottage where Annie soon finds herself missing the challenges of the theatre as her career. The couple live in comparative isolation during the five years of their marriage: the ladies in the neighbourhood, who habitually talk about them as 'those Hindle sisters' (71), would be shocked if they knew the truth and probably react in a way that Annie and Ryanny, with clichéd citations and excess, perform as a little scene to amuse themselves:

> **RYANNY.** *(Being Mrs Bagnall)* Ye-es, Miss Hindle? Do you
> wish to pur-*chase* a cherry pie?
> **ANNIE.** *(In an Irish accent)* Mrs Big-nose, I'll have you know
> that I have not, for some years now, been a Miss.
> **RYANNY.** And the lucky gentleman is ...

ANNIE. A lady. *(Ryanny shrieks)* I mean, me sister here is actually me wife.
RYANNY. Incest! Abomination! *(pretending to faint)* Fetch me my smelling salts! (71)

As this little play-within-the play through its comic effects demonstrates, late nineteenth-century society is far from being ready to accept same-sex partnership, let alone marriage, as a viable option for either women or men.

Both Donoghue plays foreground costume and female corporeality, utilizing the dualism that the body is both a sign of social positionality and cultural experience, whereas it also reflects individual desire to gain liberation from rules and prescriptions of gender normalization to evoke subjectivity as a process rather than a fixture. Body and dress encode the lesbian characters' relation to what Susan Bordo identifies as 'the inscription of phallocentric, dualistic culture on gendered bodies',[19] their obligatory acceptance of or voluntary resistance to it or the choice of contestatory variants between these two poles. In *I Know My Own Heart* Anne Lister likes to wear a large, loose black cloak to cover her sex and does not ornament herself like the 'weaker women in captivity', to borrow the precise and insightful wording of Elizabeth Barrett Browning from her poem written to George Sand.[20] Anne 'rides a horse called Lord Byron' (104), the often mentioned animal being a fetish-like indicator of her owner's desire to fly free from all kinds of socio-cultural bonds. Due to the strict binaries of the era she can have only 'fancies about dressing entirely in men's clothes', yet she manages to cultivate a distinguished look of difference and her manners are, in Marianne's description, 'softly gentlemanlike' (105). However, the attempted gender-neutrality of her costume tends to deceive people who, like most of society, have no understanding of ambiguity as a creative force, but are instead threatened by it: Anne reports indecent assaults on her from both men and women. To look different also entails isolation; Annie realizes that she could enjoy more female company if, paradoxically, she abandoned the expression of her individuality through a particular choice of clothes and changed them for the 'frills and bonnets' (134) that belong to the conventional gear of female masquerade and making use of them would establish a place for her in the community of females. The 'natural' is, thus, pinpointed as part of a complex system of practices that function to reinforce constructed divisions as well as to exclude and even abject the liminal.

Costume physically and metaphorically operates in *Ladies and Gentlemen* as a characteristic marker of the actual overlapping of what is conventionally held as everyday reality on the one hand and the world of performance with its supposed secrets and mysteries on the other. Arguing with her dresser about 'men's clothes', her professional wear, Annie asserts:

> **RYANNY.** But do you like wearing men's clothes?
> **ANNIE.** They're only called that because men got a hold of them first. You bet your sweet life I like 'em; they've got pockets for everything (22).

With the stress on practicality and usefulness, another widespread social ideal of the era, Annie thoroughly unsettles the notional basis of the practice that these clothes are destined to be worn by one gender and not by the other. The issue of what kind of clothes to use or what kind of performance to engage in is, at the same time, associated with the subject's sense of identity and social situation. Back on stage, after she has lost her wife, Ryanny, to breast cancer, Annie experiences profound existential anxiety: 'I don't know what to wear. I don't know what to say. I don't know who to be' (67). The inability to play any role signals confusion and diagnoses depression, for which the cure is shown in donning a gendered garment and restarting her career as a performer. In a man's jacket again, Annie's realization, 'This is all I've got' (100) confirms that performance is a metaphor for life, which renews itself after the damage death has incurred and carries potential freedom for the player through expanding the ontological borders of the self. *Ladies and Gentlemen* dramatizes imagined situations from a lesbian performer's biography allowing us to see how the marginal experience is able to reflect on crucial human issues of identity.

A significant piece of stage property in *Ladies and Gentlemen* is the dummy called Miss Dimity. Miss Dimity is originally part of the troupe's dressing room, eventually making its way as a present from their former colleagues into the private home of Annie and Ryanny. Annie welcomes its arrival with the ambiguous phrase: 'Another woman. How unsuitable!' (78), referring to its displacement and nakedness by the same stroke. Bringing a bare, imitation female body into focus, which is to be given character by the kind of clothing imagined and selected for it, the haunting presence of Dimity suggests that woman as a sexed sign is open to a scale of potential meanings. In both Donoghue plays lesbian sexuality is represented in its own right, emphasizing that it can be a site of pleasurable experimentation with the body, an assertion which parallels the writer's perception as articulated in another interview:

> I'm biased here (*laughs*) but in terms of the details of technique, lesbians are often very imaginative because there's no one thing they've been traditionally told to do ... We listen to each other's bodies more, I suppose, because we haven't been brought up to believe that sex is one particular act.[21]

The bodily sensations and acts expressing same-sex love between women are performed or mentioned in the plays as similar but also different from those characteristic of heterosexual attraction and sexual practice, challenging the cultural inclination to restrict them by walls of artificially constructed stereotypes. When the issue of jealousy arises between the lovers, Donoghue has her lesbian protagonist in *I Know My Own Heart* state a view that sounds vital for all humans of all times:

> **MARIANNE.** It's different with a man.
> **ANNE.** It is not.
> **MARIANNE.** How would you know? You've never been with a man, you don't know how ... how nothing it is. A damp fumble in the dark, an insignificant spasm.
> **ANNE.** Insignificant?
> **MARIANNE.** It never really touched me. You know that, and yet you've let a woman inside you, the place I thought belonged to me.
> **ANNE.** It's my body, it belongs to none of you (154-55).

Although a site of the sexual exchange, the body remains a constituent of subjectivity, 'a point of overlapping between the physical, the symbolic, and the sociological' as Rosi Braidotti cogently summarizes.[22] The title of *I Know My Own Heart* resonates with a sentence from the beginning of the first chapter of Jean Jacques Rousseau's *Confessions*, which, brought into inter-textual play with the Donoghue narrative, evokes the meaning that self-knowledge is gained through listening to the body as much as to the intellect.

Another way of reflecting on the complex operations of the body is provided by including instances of illness, which assume metaphorical meaning in the action of the two plays. The female characters in *I Know My Own Heart* are infected by venereal disease, a phenomenon widely present but rendered invisible because they are barred from discourse in the society; an exclusion which, in fact, hindered proper and effective treatment. Anne complains:

> The doctor's examination was so humiliating; he averted his gaze and poked his hand up my skirt as if opening a drain. Then he asked if I was married, and I said, 'No, thank God,' without thinking. So I told him that I must have caught the infection from a married friend whose husband was dissipated, because I remembered visiting the water closet just after her (142).

The disease here is an indicator of the unhealthy nature of the cultural requirement that sex in marriage was compulsory for woman, her body being no longer her own, while men were permitted to enjoy unlimited promiscuity. In a recollected scene of *Ladies and Gentlemen*, featuring Annie's first comeback on stage, the bruises and blue marks on her face and body tell of a largely hidden but not infrequent aspect of heterosexual marriage: domestic violence. These blows are usually suffered by a wife from a dissatisfied or frustrated husband. Ryanny's death in the same play is evidently based on historical fact, yet the stress on its premature occurrence seems to corroborate with the idea, brought home through their isolation, that there is no future in terms of social integration for same-sex married partners under nineteenth-century circumstances.

Admittedly, the cultural construction, involving continual deconstruction and re-construction of gendered and sexual identities, can take place only within existing power relations. Lesbian subjectivity is theorized in terms of how far women's same-sex relations replicate or, rather, complicate, or even contest the normative gender categories set up by the discourse of heterosexuality. To investigate the ways in which the identity of women involved in lesbian relationships is represented necessitates the consideration of the butch/fem categories as a framing discourse. The butch/fem binary has generated debates about lesbian roles in recent decades, while also serving as a vehicle of juxtaposition with heterosexual complementarity. Having charted the nature and the implications of these debates among feminists, Mary F. Brewer concludes that

> Within the discourse of butch/fem, context is everything, and feminists must be careful not to conflate the power relations of heterosexuality with those of the sex act itself. Power is experienced in many different ways in butch/fem relationships

as opposed to straight men and women. Therefore, alternative meanings should be possible.[23]

In *Ladies and Gentlemen* Annie Hindle, the protagonist, as it happened in history, marries her dresser, the Irish-born Annie Ryan, rechristened Ryanny. Anne Lister, in *I Know My Own Heart*, cannot marry her lover Marianne Brown, but gives her a ring to wear. They often refer to each other as wife and husband, thinking of theirs as a married relationship based on desire but necessarily involving problems like separation and jealousy. Both couples, it seems, define themselves according to the norms of mainstream culture, yet the way they feel and act as lesbians subverts rather than duplicates the masculine-feminine divide because it happens in contexts undetermined or only partly determined by the dominant ideology. Context has a dual importance and weight; while interrogating the self-defining features of the construction of lesbian subjectivity the plays work also as biographical narratives authenticated by their detailed social and cultural embedding. In addition, as a critic comments, the two plays' 'historical context and basis in real life events succeeded in opening new areas of lesbian experience that had not been accessible to Irish theatre audiences before'. [24]

The 'gentlemanlike', androgynous-looking Anne in *I Know My Own Heart* plays a multiplicity of roles, depending, besides the changes in her subjective emotional landscape, on how far the outer world interferes with the cultivation of her female relationships. Donoghue, in *Passions Between Women*, citing Lillian Federman's relevant study, refers to 'romantic friendship' that 'in the English upper and middle classes until the late nineteenth century ... was seen as harmless or silly at worst and at best as the most edifying of social bonds'.[25] Like many contemporary ladies Anne Lister has had a long-term friendship of this kind with Tib, a woman her social and intellectual equal. Sex enters the relationship when Anne· feels increasingly neglected because Marianne, her wife-in-secret now legally married to a man, lives elsewhere, has new interests and 'also loves her house, her fine dresses, her social standing ... ' (134). It is Tib, characteristically the emotionally stronger of the two friends, who makes the first step by calling Anne 'irresistible' like a woman. She then surprises her '*with a long kiss*' (134), and proves to be an excellent lover in bed. In their altered relationship Anne turns out to be more fem, and she also switches from the initial acting of butch to this role when, after a long interval, Marianne comes to visit her again, putting an end to months of waiting: '*(Having a multiple orgasm as quietly as possible) ... (To herself)* No one else *ever* gave me a kiss like that' (153). Wavering and transitions between 'butch desire and fem receptivity' in the play underscore that lesbian sexuality has more faces than 'the masculine/feminine, active/passive binaries'.[26] The roles of desiring and desired are blurred in Donogue's alternative dramatic world.

In the portrayal of lesbian subjectivity *Ladies and Gentlemen* seems to offer less flexible formations at first sight. Annie, under a male name, and Ryanny get married in church by a minister with all the customary paraphernalia, which includes having a '*husband-and-wife photograph*' (65) taken of them. However, their courage to have their same-sex marriage sanctified is itself a highly subversive historical act, especially from twenty-first century hindsight when gay marriage is still not legal and fiercely protested against in many countries of the world. Annie and Ryanny's domestic life together, as a recollected scene demonstrates, is based on the complementarity of housewife and husband, mutually teasing each other as in heterosexual marriage. Yet, their bantering exchange is playful, suggestive, and disruptive of rules rather than citational:

> **RYANNY.** Every time I have the fruit bowl nicely arranged, you pinch something and topple my bananas.
> **ANNIE.** How have you managed to put up with me for four years, Mrs. Hindle? (70)

What reminds one of heterosexual patterns in the Annie-/Ryanny relationship is further undermined by Donoghue's choice to foreground an object of 'everyday use'. At the beginning of the drama Annie enters the scene carrying '*a quilt, carpet bag and letter box*' (7). The quilt is a piece of genuine patchwork, Annie's much cherished item of heritage from the already dead Ryanny, who possessed it as a specific treasure made by her mother back in Ireland. Wrapped around each other's shoulders at some crucial points in the drama, the quilt provides not only warmth but the feeling of continuity with other female bodies, emphasizing that across racial and sexual divides women can build their own distinctive culture which has both enduring and sustaining values.

Donoghue's works, thus, illustrate Claycomb's observation that biography plays 'show their subjects in communities and not as discrete entities',[27] and do even more: they recover not only their chosen heroines' complex subjectivity through acts of performance but, not unlike what happens in Gertrude Stein's *The Auto-*

biography of Alice B. Toklas, also lift their closest companions out of oblivion. Marianne, Anne Lister's lover in *I Know My Own Heart*, appears not just as a farmer's aspiring daughter who became attracted to same-sex love by chance, but a woman who, undergoing contradictory sexual experiences, also learns to know her own heart. In the later play, *Ladies and Gentlemen* Ryanny has run away from a convent in Ireland, a near synecdoche for the country itself as it was then, to settle down in America. Her progress to forge an independent gender identity for herself while being an emigrant with a highly conservative upbringing in her background allows the audience to see her achievement in a special light. Mary Trotter notes that through Ryanny Donoghue 'challenges representations of nineteenth-century Irish women in Irish theatre and culture as either iconic figures who symbolize the oppressed nation ... or passive supporters of a patriarchal status quo'.[28] Under a creatively transformed androgynous name, Ryanny becomes a figure emblematic of the potential that Irish women, drawing strength from their mini-communities, can recast and reinvent themselves.

Widening their own biography-focussed borders by appropriating techniques of lesbian feminist drama, Donoghue's works, to borrow Deirdre Heddon's words, utilize 'personal material as a resource' with the result that 'its assumed relationship to the "real" affords it particular power', because the awareness that 'something really happened invests it with a political urgency'.[29] By this they support an agenda, albeit indirectly: the stories of Anne Lister, Annie Hindle and their companions model the discovery of alternative, fluid gender identities against the hegemony of gender and its restrictive corollary. In so doing, they are exploring the past to open new ways towards a more flexible sexual politics in the present and the future. At the same time, the plays confirm Lis Whitelaw's contention that lesbian-feminist authors of lesbian biographies endeavour 'to ensure that lesbian lives are understood for what they are, and not viewed through the distorting glass of heterosexual preconceptions and prejudice'.[30]

It is noteworthy that Donoghue's lesbian dramatic characters are travellers like herself: Annie Hindle and Ryanny have left England and Ireland respectively, while Anne Lister is ready to leave England for Paris at the end of *I Know My Own Heart*. However, they can be identified as nomadic subjects not only on account of their geographical displacement, but because, to rely on Braidotti's theory of nomadism, they learn to refuse containment and the conventional mode of 'settling into socially coded modes of thought and behaviour'.[31] Ultimately, *I Know My Own Heart* and *Ladies and Gentlemen* are concerned with the issue of how to achieve greater human freedom in socio-cultural as well as sexual terms through a revised sense of the links between performance and subjectivity, bodily inscriptions and their alterability. They evoke and reinforce these links as both roots and routes, reminding us that a critical consciousness of creative resistance to the various forms of ideological pressure is a potential to work for and work with.

[1] Stacia Bensyl, 'Swings and Roundabouts: An Interview with Emma Donoghue', *Irish Studies Review* 8.1 (April 2000), p. 80.

[2] Anthony Bradley and Maryann Gialanella Valiulis, eds, Introduction, *Gender and Sexuality in Modern Ireland* (Amherst: University of Massachusetts Press, 1997), p. 1.

[3] Louise O'Shea, 'Sapphic Stages: Irish Lesbian Theatre', *Irish Journal of Feminist Studies* 5. 1-2 (2003), p. 105.

[4] Bensyl, p. 76.

[5] Ryan Claycomb, 'Playing at Lives: Biography and Contemporary Feminist Drama' *Modern Drama* 47.3 (2004), pp. 527, 535.

[6] Stephanie Kramer, 'Imaging/Imagining Women's Lives: Biography in Contemporary Women's Drama', *Contemporary Drama in English*: *Anthropological Perspectives*, ed. Bernhard Reitz (Trier: Wissenschaftlicher, 1998), p 77.

[7] Claycomb, p. 238.

[8] Laurence Senelick, *The Changing Room*: *Sex, Drag and Theatre* (London and New York: Routledge, 2000), p. 329.

[9] Emma Donoghue, *I Know My Own Heart, Seen and Heard: Six New Plays by Irish Women*, ed. Cathy Leeney (Dublin: Carysfort Press, 2001): 133. Subsequent references are cited in the text.

[10] Deborah Kaplan, 'Representing Two Cultures: Jane Austen's Letters', *The Private Self: Theory and Practice of Women's Autobiographical Writings*, ed. Shari Benstock (Chapel Hill and London: The University of North Carolina Press, 1988), p. 212.

[11] Senelick, p. 340.

[12] Senelick, p. 326.

[13] Lib Taylor, 'Shape-shifting and Role-splitting: Theatre, Body and Identity', *Indeterminate Bodies*, eds Naomi Segal, Lib Taylor, and Roger Cook (London: Palgrave Macmillan, 2003), p. 168.

[14] Emma Donoghue, *Ladies and Gentlemen* (Dublin: New Island, 1998), p. 7. Subsequent references are cited in the text.

15 Nikki Sullivan, *A Critical Introduction to Queer Theory* (Edinburgh: Edinburgh University Press, 2003), p. 91.

16 Judith Butler, 'Performative Acts and Gender Constitution', *Literary Theory: An Anthology*, eds, Julie Rivkin and Michael Ryan, 2nd edn (London: Blackwell, 2004), p. 901.

17 Claycomb, p. 542.

18 Anna McMullan, 'Gender, Authorship and Performance in Selected Plays by Contemporary Irish Women Playwrights: Mary Elizabeth Burke-Kennedy, Marie Jones, Marina Carr, Emma Donoghue', *Theatre Stuff: Critical Essays on Contemporary Irish Theatre*, ed. Eamonn Jordan (Dublin: Carysfort Press, 2000), p. 43.

19 Susan Bordo, 'The Body and the Reproduction of Femininity', *Writing on the Body*, eds, Katie Konboy, Nadia Medina, and Sarah Stanbury (New York: Columbia University Press, 1997), p. 104.

20 'To George Sand', *The Norton Anthology of English Literature*, gen. ed. Stephen Greenblatt, vol. 2, 8th edn (New York and London: W.W. Norton & Company, 2006), p. 1083.

21 Emma Donoghue, From 'Causing a Stir: An Interview by Liam Fay', *The Field Day Anthology of Irish Writing, Vol. IV: Irish Women's Writing and Traditions*, eds, Angela Bourke, et al. (Cork: Cork University Press in association with Field Day, 2002), p. 1067.

22 Rosi Braidotti, *Embodiment and Sexual Difference in Contemporary Feminist Theory* (New York: Columbia University Press, 1994), p. 4.

23 Mary F. Brewer, *Race, Sex and Gender in Contemporary Women's Theatre* (Brighton, Portland: Sussex Academic Press, 1999): p. 140.

24 O'Shea, p. 107.

25 Donoghue, *Passions,* p. 18.

26 Brewer, p. 143.

27 Claycomb, p. 326.

28 Mary Trotter, 'Re-Imagining the Emigrant/Exile in Contemporary Irish Drama', Modern Drama 46.1 (2003): p. 44.

29 Deirdre Heddon, 'Performing Lesbians: Constructing the Self, Constructing the Community', *Auto/Biography and Identity: Women, theatre and performance*, eds, Maggie B. Gale and Viv Gardner (Manchester and New York: Manchester Univerity Press, 2004): p. 228.

30 Lis Whitelaw, 'Make Of Our Lives A Study: Reading and Writing Lesbian Biography', *Volcanoes and Pearl Divers: Essays in Lesbian Feminist Studies*, ed. Suzanne Raitt (London: Onlywomen Press, 1995): p. 121.

31 Braidotti, p. 5.

5 | Touching, Feeling, Cross-Dressing:
On the Affectivity of Queer Performance.
Or, What Makes Panti Fabulous.

Fintan Walsh

'...on some level, our pleasure is our resistance.'[1]

This chapter approaches queer performance as a distinct sub
cultural tradition in Ireland. While a wide range of plays, theatre
productions, and festivals have carried issues concerning gender
and sexual diversity from the periphery to the mainstream,
including work of significance to feminist, gay, and lesbian politics;
this essay seeks to uncover, in part, the development of a specific
queer performance tradition that does not engage directly with the
dominant social order by way of normative modes of communication or cultural critique. In particular, the study considers
how a range of performance practices, sites, and modes of
relationality have been harnessed by queers to create liveable spaces
for undesirable lives: the coming together of bodies in gay bars,
fetish clubs, hill walks, political protests, choirs, alternative
pageants, and drag shows.[2]

It might be useful at this point to clarify my use of the term
'queer'. From a certain perspective all live performance might be
aligned with this adjective, as so often the contingency of the event,
not to mention the indeterminacy of desire and identification
among those present, speaks to the slipperiness of all identity. But
further to this, the term queer – as distinct from gay, lesbian or
what might be considered as mainstream theatre and performance –
signifies a much wider range of difference that the former categories
do not. Jill Dolan stresses the value of using the words gay and

lesbian alongside queer in relation to theatre 'to remind us of history, to remind us of differential power, to remind us that however fluidly we might practice and perform our identities, regulatory systems tend to fix them and to legislate against them, through juridical, medical and educational discourses in which the theatre we make and write about must intervene'.[3] While this is a valuable reminder of the importance of historicizing both theatre and theory, like most discursive classifications, it is also somewhat exclusive, for not all those who identify as queer do so with gay and lesbian movements, the identity categories themselves, or even, for that matter, something called 'theatre'. In fact, the term 'gay theatre' is usually conferred retrospectively, as in Alan Sinfield's' work. And, as Tim Miller and David Román remind us, 'queer theatre audiences, like all theatre audiences, defy simplistic categorizations and resist overly determined preconceptions concerning why we are even at the theatre'.[4] Queer, then, seems to be the most useful term to index the multiplicity of open, contradictory, and contentious forms, practices, and identities such as those I am interested in addressing here. Noreen Giffney suggests that we might speak of 'quare' 'to articulate the specificities, nuances, and methodological tensions between expressions of queer theory in an Irish context and theoretical formulations of queer theory originating in an Anglo-North American context', and in order to signal the relationship between queer studies and discourses of feminism, lesbianism, and post colonialism that already inflect Irish studies.[5] Without borrowing the term, this paper echoes the value of doing queer in context.

Those who live through or alongside the queer culture about which I write (Irish, Dublin-centred) will know of the many braided performative gestures that constitute it and us. Similarly, they will know of the centrality of cross-dressing, guerilla drag, and gender-fuck to many forms of queer sociality. Although this is not specific to Irish culture, it is true to say that these specific modes of expression and interaction are especially prevalent and well-developed languages. We might understand this pattern in light of Ireland's rich history of popular theatre, its rigid construction of gender types, or its skill in subversive mimicry, finely honed within the folds of a wider system of postcolonial resistance. Regardless of its original impulse, when taken up by Dublin based artists such as Shirley Temple Bar, Heidi Konnt, the Shamcocks, and Miss Panti, cross-dressing enters the realm of queer performance art, and as such, demands recognition within Irish theatre and performance scholarship.

Outside of Irish studies, much has already been written about the practice of cross-dressing. Peggy Phelan, speaking within the tradition of outspoken critics Marilyn Frye and Janice Raymond, has noted how gay male drag in particular runs the risk of misogyny by fetishizing the category 'woman'. In *Unmarked: the Politics of Performance* (1993) she contends: 'Gay male cross-dressers resist the body of woman even while they make its constructedness visible.'[6] Countering this, other critics have asserted the strategy's value in disrupting the illusion of gender and sexual coherence. On this, Judith Butler's discussion of the documentary *Paris is Burning* (1990) has been particularly influential: 'In imitating gender, drag implicitly reveals the imitative structure of gender itself – as well as its contingency. Indeed, part of the pleasure, the giddiness of the performance is in the recognition of a radical contingency in the relation between sex and gender in the face of cultural configurations of causal unities that are regularly assumed to be natural and necessary.'[7] In the case of Irish drag performance, we can hold both theories in useful regard. While cross-dressing might well be understood to upset gender categories, there are many examples from the Irish queer performance repertoire where the personae invoked are the derisive legacies of colonialism and cultural nationalism such as the comely maiden, the dancing schoolgirl, the virgin, the whore, the mother, the religious authoritarian, the patriarch, and the stage Irishman. While some performers might build their particular personae on one such category, other acts might embody them occasionally or for an isolated outing. Collectively, these acts trouble restrictive and oppressive identity formations by disidentifying with the divisive logic of heteronormativity, while simultaneously creating queer space within the Irish cultural imaginary.

The following pages focus on this generative dimension to queer culture. What interests me is not only what queer performance might undo rhetorically or epistemologically, but what kind of world it opens up affectively. Following this line, the essay will focus on self-styled 'gender illusionist' Miss Pandora 'Panti' Bliss as an embodied archive of queer feeling, by examining the performer's contribution to queer culture on relational terms. In drawing queers together through her warm, familial persona – Aunty Panti – while exploring all registers of touch, the chapter argues that Panti resignifies the principle of contagion that is so central to homophobic discourse by letting queer feeling freely flow, while simultaneously effecting an uncanny imaginary dwelling space that is no place like home.[8]

Crossing Clothes, Crossing Culture

Following a number of years in Tokyo, where she performed as part of the drag duo CandiPanti, Panti launched her career in Dublin in 1996 as host of the *Alternative Miss Ireland* (AMI) queer beauty pageant. Conceived in the mind of art graduate Rory O'Neill as a mid-Atlantic aunt returned home, Panti entered the scene as an oddly recognizable figure that – like anyone's favourite single, zany, and possibly lesbian aunt come to visit – inspired intrigue and attraction in equal measure; while retaining for herself the outsider's facility to comment upon the culture in which she found herself. However, while Aunt Panti may have been an imaginary construction, the social and political dynamics she referenced were real. For instance, Panti was not the only person returning home at this time. Following mass immigration during the 1980s many aunts, uncles, sons, and daughters were similarly returning to enjoy the benefits occasioned by the country's financial boom. Three years after the decriminalization of homosexuality, Ireland was not only on the brink of economic regeneration but cultural cross-fertilization. Finding herself in a country on the cusp of change, and boasting trans-credentials like no other, Panti was in a unique position to participate in this reimagining process.

The AMI is perhaps the most significant event through which Panti has perfected her persona and negotiated a specific performance style. Since its first production in 1987, the pageant, modelled on Andrew Logan's *Alternative Miss World* and organized around regional heats, has staged an irreverent take on the sanitized depictions of gender and sexuality typical of normative beauty pageants world-wide, while also engaging with a specifically Irish tradition of gender appropriation, and contests such as *The Rose of Tralee* and *Miss Ireland*. In this, the performance exists as an important community-driven political forum dedicated to both cultural interrogation and transformation.[9] Drawing on Panto-mime's tradition of playing highly current politics in humourous but no less committed terms, the event also known as Gay Christmas quickly became an important arena through which Panti began to deploy drag as a vehicle for activism while encouraging similar modes of intervention among others.

This particular approach to queer politics found further progression in collaborative partnerships to emerge from AMI. Working with producers, promoters, and artists that included individuals such as Trish Brennan, Niall Sweeney, and Tonie Walsh, Panti proceeded to appear at a number of performance-based pub and club nights throughout the 1990s such as Gag, Powderbubble, HAM, Gristle, while also running the long-standing Casting Couch Karaoke night. In addition, Panti regularly appeared at Pride parades throughout the country, frequently speaking passionately about issues affecting LGBTQ people. The leading lady at these events, Panti typically performed a range of tasks such as hosting, singing, lip-synching, dancing, lecturing or, notoriously, pulling all manner of objects, including rosary beads, from her 'rosy rump'.[10] Operating within these highly varied contexts, Panti's cross-dressing performances did much more than play with gender and sexual norms. Rather, drag became the mechanism through which an extensive concatenation of transgressive practices and ideas could be re-signified and mobilized. Throughout her career, Panti has turned the celebration of a range of appearances, characteristics, behaviours, and modes of contact, normally understood as either oppositional or unthinkable, into an art form. Unique, given drag's hyperbolic tendency, Panti has offered herself as an uncanny matereal or matrixial figure who does not police desire by way of prohibition and guilt, but through a kind of conductible affectivity, licenses the development of a variety of queer positions among the 'nieces' and 'nephews' she fondly refers to as 'chickens'. [11]

Writing on clothes and mourning, Peter Stallybrass argues that the 'magic of cloth' is that 'it receives us'. Not just an expressive material, cloth 'receives our smells, our sweat, our shape even'.[12] Following on, we might press generalized theories on the subversiveness of drag to think about how clothes-conscious Panti might not only 'receive' the man beneath her garments, but be literally and conceptually imprinted by the life and times of those among whom she performs. In effecting and affecting the complex conditions in which she and other queers have found themselves for over a decade, I suggest that Panti does more than dress up as a woman. More radical than that, Panti embodies the trace of sub-jugated queer experience and performs those pleated histories along the fault-lines of public and counter-public spheres. In doing so, the border-crossing that drag involves is amplified beyond the material to register as symbolically highly significant. In performing queer politics as a mode of relationality, Panti has been a central force in mobilizing queer communities of feeling.

'A Triumph of Greasepaint and Gaffer Tape'

In furthering this discussion, I want to focus on Panti's most recent work. I do so not only because the performance pieces represent her most developed endeavours, nor even because they appear more significant for taking place in conventional theatre spaces during festival periods, but because they involve Panti reflecting on her own personal life and artistic practice. In May 2007, Panti staged *In These Shoes?* at the New Theatre as part of the *International Dublin Gay Theatre Festival*. Produced by *thisispopbaby* and directed by Philip McMahon, in being formally structured the piece marked a departure in Panti's normal mode of address. Playing on her persona as educator to the uninitiated, Panti assumed the role of lecturer in drag school. More specifically, she talked the audience through the blondes who inspired her – the 'triumph of greasepaint and gaffer tape' who stood before us – and from whom we might also draw wisdom. [Figure 1]

The performance was organized around separate modules, during which Panti schooled her students on a range of famous blondes mainly from Ireland. The lesson on Catherine Nevin (the woman convicted for conspiring to kill her husband in 1996) does not focus on whether or not the former landlady at *Jack White's Inn* was actually guilty of the crime, but on how much the media focused on her image during the trial. Nevin's appearance was subjected to more forensic examination that the case itself, we are led to believe. Panti reasons that, quite literally, Nevin's blondeness both made and unmade her. While the constructedness of Adele King ('Twink') is also foregrounded by comparing her to 'something *Macnas* made for St Patrick's Day,' the comic actress's facility to play that particular role, with and against public preconception, is equally celebrated. Brunette-turned-blonde news presenter Anne Doyle also figures in the lecture, used to prove the point that gender-play is by no means the preserve of drag queens, actresses, or latter day *femmes fatales*.

Of course, the show's premise is that all gender is a form of drag: a performative mode of expression that bears no direct relationship to biological sex. Then there is the emphasis on blonde women in particular, treated in a comic manner that nonetheless purposefully considers the contradictory associations of the much maligned look: ditsy, sexual, and powerful. Accrediting Darwin with the observation that 'all drag queens eventually go blonde,' Panti connects herself, other queer performers, and the audience to a very specific history that maligns certain forms of gendered presentation, while also analysing some of the fears that produces such stereotypes in the first place. While she humorously critiques a number of these figures, she does so not to slander the individuals, but to grate against the system that produces and perpetuates the categories and their associations. As she says herself, 'it's not a parody, it's an homage'. In so doing, Panti encourages a similar kind of playful cross-identification among her students.

Writing about performances by 'queers of colour,' José Esteban Muñoz has discussed the dynamics disidentification. This intersubjective process involves the recycling and resignification of culturally encoded messages: 'The process of disidentification scrambles and reconstructs the encoded message of a cultural text in a fashion that both exposes the encoded message's universalizing and exclusionary machinations and recircuits its workings to account for, include, and empower minority identities and identifications.'13 While Muñoz suggests that these practices indicate a move towards 'cracking open the code of the majority,'14 their greatest contribution is towards the production of alternative worlds.

Similarly, while the performance in question very much involves a critique of the blonde stereotype, the focus of the piece extends beyond discursive interrogation to affective accretion. While Panti indicates that future (imaginary) course topics will focus on Irish politician Liz O'Donnell, singer Doris Day, and the dog Lassie, the final subject of this event is the performer's own idol, Dolly Parton. Panti has never made any secret of her fascination with the singer, and at the AMI in 2007, a personalized message from Parton was screened at the show. What rendered Panti's discussion especially interesting here, however, was the way in which this interest was divulged at the intersection of O'Neill's and Panti's identities.

Suspending fiction for the most part, the vet's daughter from County Mayo revealed how she first heard Dolly on the radio in 1978 shortly after Dusty Springfield, her pet sheep, died. Thus began the life-long love affair, revealed here through fragmented tales of ardent fan worship. Other personal anecdotes are added too, that offer both a critical and emotional glimpse of life in Ireland in intervening years. These stories culminate with an account, complete with recorded footage, of Panti's invited appearance on the New York based *Maury Povich Show* in the 1990s. Masquerading as an Irish transvestite, under pressure from Catholic parents and a sister (performer Katherine Lynch) to dress more like a man, Panti is treated to a female to male make-over by the chat show's production team. After an hour of innumerable crossings, *In These Shoes?*, like the *Maury* episode in question, ends with Rory O'Neill standing on stage.

While disidentification implies a psychic rejection of symbolic logic, in the case of Panti's work in particular I would underscore the importance of the affective encounter to this process. Ann Cvetkovich has suggested that the most profound queer archive would be radically affective, arguing that 'an archive of sexuality, and gay and lesbian life ... must preserve and produce not just knowledge but feeling.'[15] As the interrogative tone of the play's title implies, *In These Shoes?* involves a certain questioning and disarticulation of identity, but its more urgent call is for empathic engagement with lived experience, and for the sharing and reproduction of those affective repertoires. Given that the Irish Queer Archives were handed over to the National Library in June 2008, this seems like a timely tacit proposal.

'Full Blown Woman'

In September 2007, only four months after *In These Shoes?* was first performed, Panti made a return visit to Temple Bar to stage *All Dolled Up* at the Project Arts Centre. Although a discrete piece in its own right, the performance developed and elaborated upon many of the strands suggested by the earlier venture. While the previous show was certainly reflective, *All Dolled Up* might be more readily understood as a memory play. The retrospective tone of the production was established with Panti's soulful rendition of Édith Piaf's 'Non, Je Ne Regrette Rien' at the outset. For Panti, lip-synching of this kind is a full-bodied act of channelling, 'a collaboration between the queen and the original artiste.' In this cross-identificatory vein, she proceeds to frame her show not as theatre in the traditional sense, but as a 'conversation' between her, the audience, and implicitly, the people she mentions along the way, who may or may not be present. Writing on the work of Luis Alfaro, Muñoz suggests that memory performances 'deploy affective narratives of self, ways of being from the past, in the service of questioning the future, a future without annihilating epidemics, both viral and ideological.'[16] By the same token, Panti calibrates this performance as an interactive, embodied journey through a lived Irish queer history in which identity, propriety, and relationality are all drawn into question. [Figure 2]

While Panti begins with a meditation on her own particular medium – 'Drag still retains its power to offend the easily offended, and that's part of the fun' – she moves on to account for some of her many involvements in queer culture throughout the 1990s. While the performer reckons that many audience members will know Sir John Rogerson's Quay in Dublin 2 as a nice middle-class neighbourhood with lots of new apartments, she knows it as the place where her fetish club Gag began. Referring to photographs and images projected on the back wall of the set, Panti describes some of the risqué acts she staged in the club, also recalling how she was invited to perform in fetish clubs in the United Kingdom. Most interesting, perhaps, is the account provided of the media's response at the time. Suspicious Breda at the *Irish Times*, we are told, would not advertise G.A.G. (as it was then spelled) until she knew what the acronym meant. She seemed satisfied with Gays Against Germaine Greer, even though it was a fabrication. This incident becomes representative of how sexual vernaculars, to use Cindy Patton's terminology – 'the identifying characteristics of liminal sexualities'[17] – are either misread, challenged, or rejected by normative discourse that distinguishes between the textual and the sexual. On the contrary, a sexual vernacular is *de rigueur* among queer communities. Taking the side of the moral majority, the *People* tabloid ran with the headline 'Dublin Sex Orgy Sensation' in a response that precipitated the eventual closing down of the venue.

'You don't have to pull something from your ass,' we are cautioned, 'to offend the easily offended.' Panti continues to tell of her recent invitation to take part in RTÉ's *Celebrity You're A Star*; an offer that was revoked when she said she wanted to make her donation to HIV charities. 'It was all a bit too gay,' is her assessment of the debacle.

Another story comes from the experience of taking part in the National College of Art and Design's graduate fashion show. When one tutor did not come on stage to receive flowers from Panti on behalf of her students, the performer approached the lady in the audience following the official ceremony. 'Fuck off. I am a full-blown woman and I have never been so insulted in all my life' was the lecturer's response. In recalling the incident, what fascinates Panti most is the invocation of 'the language of disease' to describe her womanhood; as if womanhood, like 'fully blown' AIDS was potentially fatal. Considering Panti's physical verisimilitude, the angered reaction might well point to deeper concerns of gender-passing. Yet, the implicit fear generated by a strange encounter with the embodied other points precisely to the anxiety of being infiltrated by that same figure. In turn, these phobias of dissolution, cannibalism, or non-identity lead to the production of affect aliens, as in Sara Ahmed's coinage, whose daily lives are policed by hatred, fear, and shame, rather than just legislation.[18] On the other hand, Panti's performances are undergirded by a drive to systematically undo this affective peripheralization. [Figure 3].

As with *In These Shoes?* the production takes on an even more personal twist when Panti describes how people feel they can tell her anything assuming that she, a cross-dressed man, will not judge them. Responding to this history of shared secrets, Panti tells those gathered that she is HIV positive, something she has never divulged in public before. While there is a reasonably well-established history of HIV performance art, much of which involves self-harm and bloodletting practices,[19] Panti does not follow this line of purgation. Instead, she talks through the original diagnosis, and describes her fears of dying, complete with an imagined rendition of 'Ding, Dong the Witch is Dead' at Glasnevin crematorium. She talks about attending HIV clinics through the years, and the shifting demo-graphic of clients: first the gays, then drug addicts and haemophiliacs, followed most recently by Black parents with their children. Delivered with comic relief, which included offering her glass of water to a spectator to drink from, the story gives voice to a greater history of untold experience, and marries a narrative of gender and sexual marginalization to a larger network of subaltern violence and social othering. Channelling 'that great philosopher Whitney Houston,' Panti ends with an affirmation of collectivity. Addressing the audience with outstretched arms, she announces: 'without you, I'd have nothing.'

What Panti Makes and 'Dos'

This chapter has foregrounded cross-dressing performer Panti as an accretive force in Irish queer culture. Panti does not only question the normative, but through a range of affective practices, she disidentifies with that culture and mobilizes queer communities of feeling. Panti enacts an *unheimlich* familial quality, that does not replicate the normative domestic structure that engenders literal and symbolic violence on so many queers, but she resignifies that peculiarity as all-embracing and life-giving. Queers respect her skill as a performer, her passing social observations, and her intelligent political commentary, such as what features in her annual Christmas address in GCN (*Gay Community News*) or her speeches during Pride. More than that, however, people are moved by her ability to touch in all manner of ways. Around Panti, gender ambivalence, sexual excess, social marginalization, illness, creativity, pleasure and joy mischievously intermingle in a manner that does not simply critique the status quo, but is regenerative of those lives excluded by the law of hetero-normativity.

Eve Kosofsky Sedgwick has observed that queer criticism has been dominated by paranoiac cultural observations that essentially involve the struggle to understand how homophobia and heterosexism work. The most obvious danger in this approach, she cautions, is the reification of a hegemonic way of knowing that does not give adequate address to affective, reparative intervention:

> The monopolistic program of paranoid knowing systematically disallows any explicit recourse to reparative motives, no sooner to be articulated than subject to methodical uprooting. Reparative motives, once they become explicit, are inadmissible in paranoid theory both because they are about pleasure ('merely aesthetic') and because they are frankly ameliorative ('merely reformist').[20]

Using camp as an example, Sedgwick highlights how although camp is most often understood in the context of deconstructive acts of parody, denaturalization, and demystification, its reparative impulse is equally important:

> To view camp as, among other things, the communal, historically tense exploration of a variety of reparative practices is to do better justice to many of the defining elements of classic camp performance: the startling, juicy displays of excess erudition, for example; the passionate, often hilarious antiquarianism, the prodigal production of alternative

historiographies; the 'over' – attachment to fragmentary, marginal, waste of leftover products; the rich, highly interruptive affective variety; the irresponsible fascination with ventriloquistic experimentation; the disorienting juxtapositions of present with past, and popular with high culture.[21]

While many queer cultural practices in Ireland may have reparative qualities, as a solo performer Panti's role is somewhat unique. Indeed, what Gilles Deleuze remarks about literature is perhaps especially true of performers who play to the (melancholic) queer audience: 'health as literature, as writing, consists in inventing a people who are missing. It is the task of the fabulating function to invent people.'[22] Panti's affective innovations of this kind are apparent not only in what she does (crossing gender; channelling divas; retelling stories of days gone by; invoking lives passed on; reminding us of someone, but no one in particular ...), but in her engagement with proximate (queer) others in the present, and her insistence that we do something too. While this approach inflects events such as the Casting Couch, the AMI, and the variety of lectures she has given, not to mention her frequent mingling with those in her vicinity, the strategy has become firmly established with the founding of her pub *Pantibar* in 2007. While the radical particularity of queer culture risks being neutralized by the kind of commodifying gesture that this branding might imply, it is important to recognize that access to commercial culture is very much part of the way in which marginal social groups have come to negotiate and manipulate cultural hegemony.[23] Since the venue's opening, Panti has broadened traditional conceptions of gay, pub, and indeed performance culture by scheduling a range of themed nights that might be more readily understood in the context of curated play. Indeed, the bar is referred to as a 'Homo Activity Centre' on the venue's website.[24] [Figure 4] To date, events have included screenings and discussions of significant queer films (downstairs in Panti's living room), a competition to become Panti's PA (Performing Assistant), and an ongoing weekly crafts night known as Panti's Make and Do Do. Each week, the assembled crowd are given art and craft tasks to complete, such as designing an ideal partner with plasticine and pipe cleaners, or making a coming-out card. After Panti talks through each piece of art, and announces a winner, individual works are displayed in an assigned cabinet, as proud parents might do with their children's efforts.

The performative tenor to these forms of queer sociality exemplifies Panti's commitment to a creative, reparative performance ethic. Gregory Bateson emphasizes the therapeutic dimension to play with:

> The resemblance between the process of therapy and the phenomenon of play is, in fact, profound. Both occur within a delimited psychological frame, a spatial and temporal bounding of a set of interactive messages.[25]

Although Bates discusses the therapeutic, neither he nor I do so to pathologize the encounters in question, but to stress their function in imagining communities into being.[26] Arguing for the need to consider the possibility of this kind of embodied intervention further, Dolan asks 'How might *queer* theatre become a kind of social ritual that *audiences* need for sustenance?'[27] As I understand it, the coming together of queers and the doing of queer do not just signify 'outward' oriented symbolic dissidence. Rather, I suggest that the associated acts of intimacy, engagement, and sometimes carnivalesque revelry to which I refer contribute to the cultivation of an 'internal' dynamic necessary to the personal, social, and cultural constitution or restitution of participating parties.

Dressed to Express

In Frank McGuinness's *Carthaginians* (1988), gay Dido crossdresses to direct his production of *The Burning of the Balaclava* in which, among other things, the artistic exploitation of the Troubles is examined. At the end of McGuinness's work, it is Dido who stands in a graveyard among the dead, reciting the names of those killed during Bloody Sunday. Mirroring his own interlocution, the drama ends with the imperative 'Play:' play as interrogative, play as reparative, play as preparation for an alternative way of life. [28] This creative imperative is given exemplary actuation in the performance tradition I have discussed here, especially in Panti's work. In the performances that emerge from this community based and community-identified artist queers are afforded the opportunity to rehearse the constitutive reiteration of individual and collective identities, while also enacting 'proactive resistance to, and defiance of, hegemony's own unending production of what does and does not constitute', in Judith Butler's phrase, 'bodies that matter'[29]. In this regard, we might even think about Panti's work and associated queer performances as examples of Dolan's utopian performatives that 'provide[s] a place where people come together, embodied and passionate, to share experiences of meaning making and imagination that can describe or capture fleeting intimations of a better world'.[30]

Iris Young understands touch as 'an orientation to sensuality' and maintains, following Luce Irigaray, that ' ... touch immerses the subject in fluid continuity with the object, and for the touching subject the object touched reciprocates the touching, blurring the border between self and other'.[31] In this chapter I have considered how certain unresearched queer performance practices in Ireland, in particular the work of Miss Pandora 'Panti' Bliss, counteract the production of affect aliens by blurring manifold material and symbolic borders between self and others, while rehearsing alternative forms of queer relationality through the production of affective communities. Writing against trends discernible in mainstream and gay culture that attach shame to the varied practices of queer communities, the essay focuses specifically on the fleshy activism inherent in the coming together of queer bodies in a variety of spaces in search of the pleasure that comes with opening up to other bodies. As in Ahmed's work, this too has political value: 'The hope of queer politics is that bringing us closer to others, from whom we have been barred, might also bring us to different ways of living with others.'[32] Elsewhere, following Muñoz, I have argued that 'any thorough investigation of queer performance practices that seeks to retrieve or account for marginal identities and performance traditions should not look solely at that culture's dissonances relative to the dominant, but also analyse that culture's discrete world-making'.[33] I reiterate this urgency here with the added insistence on distinguishing between identity and equal rights. If we think of the queer as a marginal (sexed) position assigned to certain figures within the social, we might also consider the impossibility of fully signifying that position. Instead of rushing to normativize the queer, as so many utopian strands of discourse on partnership, marriage, and adoptive rights suggest, we might revel in the queer itself, and the disorienting affect that so much queer performance effects on ours and others' lives.

---

[1] Jill Dolan, Introduction, *The Queerest Art*: *Essays on Lesbian and Gay Theatre*, eds Alisa Soloman and Framji Minwalla (London and New York: New York University Press, 2002): pp. 1-8, 6.

2 While these particular performances often take place within or adjacent to what is often referred to as gay culture, I consider them within the rubric of queer in their resistance to the hegemony of sanitation, commodification, and the active generation of other forms of social exclusion. Further, I understand the word queer to index a wider range of sexuated difference not always accommodated within LGBT categories.

3 Dolan, p. 5.

4 Tim Miller and David Román, '"Preaching to the Converted,"' *The Queerest Art: Essays on Lesbian and Gay Theatre*, pp. 203-226, 211.

5 Noreen Giffney, 'Quare Theory', *Irish Postmodernisms and Popular Culture*, eds Wanda Balzano, Anne Mulhall, and Moynagh Sullivan (Basingstoke and New York: Palgrave, 2008): pp. 197-207, 198.

6 Peggy Phelan, *Unmarked: The Politics of Performance* (London: Routledge, 1993): p. 101.

7 Judith Butler, *Gender Trouble: Feminism and the Subversion of Identity* (New York and London: Routledge, 1990): p. 175.

8 Here, 'home' signifies normative collectives and residences of kin.

9 Here, community is not monolithic but broadly defined and constituted through a variety of gender, sex, ethnic, national, etc., affiliations that are loosely bound through queer identifications.

10 Panti's description of the acts as offered in *All Dolled Up*.

11 Griselda Pollock, elucidating Bracha L. Ettinger's theory of the matrixial borderspace, considers the matrixial to denote subjectivity-as-affective encounter, Introduction, 'Femininity: Aporia or Sexual Difference', Brach L. Ettinger, *The Matrixial Borderspace* (Minneapolis, London: University of Minnesota Press, 2006): 2.1-37.8, 2.3.

12 Peter Stallybrass, 'Clothes, Mourning and the Life of Things', *Cultural Memory and the Construction of Identity,* eds Dan Ben-Amos and Liliane Weissberg (Detroit: Wayne State University Press, 1999): pp. 27-44, 28.

13 José Esteban Muñoz, *Disidentifications: Queers of Color and the Performance of Politics* (London and Minneapolis: University of Minnesota Press, 1999): p. 31.

14 Ibid.

15 Ann Cvetkovich, *An Archive of Feelings: Trauma, Sexuality and Lesbian Public Cultures* (Durham: Duke University Press, 2003): p. 241

16 Muñoz, pp. 227-246, 232.

[17] Cindy Patton argues that a theory of sexual vernacular makes no sharp distinction between 'sex' and 'text', but views sexual performance, sexual identities, and sexual networks as constructed in and as language. See Cindy Patton, 'Safe Sex and the Pornographic Vernacular', How do I Look: Queer Film and Video, eds Bad Object Choices (Washington: Bay Press, 1991): pp. 31-64, 45.

[18] Sara Ahmed, Introduction, *Strange Encounters: Embodied Others in Post-Coloniality* (London and New York: Routledge, 2000): pp. 1-17.

[19] For example, as in the work of the American performance artists Ron Athey.

[20] Eve Kosofsky Sedgwick, *Touching, Feeling: Affect, Pedagogy, Performativity* (Durham and London: Duke University Press, 2003): p. 144.

[21] Ibid, pp. 149-150.

[22] Gilles Deleuze, *Essays Critical and Clinical*, trans Daniel W. Smith and Michael A. Greco (London: Verso, 1998): p. 4. I refer to 'the (melancholic) queer' after Judith Butler, who has theorised subjectivity as an effect of melancholy whereby homosexual desires become gendered identifications. In 'Melancholy Gender/Refused Identification' (published in *The Psychic Life of Power: Theories in Subjection* (Stanford: Stanford University Press, 1997), Butler argues that heteronormative culture prohibits primary homosexual attachments. Yet these repressed attachments are continually grieved by being encrypted inside the subject to constitute the repudiated ground of gendered identity, p. 135. In Butler's neo-Freudian account, the burial ground of homosexuality is the shaky site on which heterosexuality is erected, and homosexuality is the ghost that perpetually haunts it: 'The straight man *becomes* ... the man he "never" loved and "never" grieved', and 'the straight woman *becomes* the woman she "never" loved and "never" grieved', p. 147.

[23] Many strands of queer theory bemoan the commercialization of gay culture. But if capitalism enables if not defines hegemonic culture, perhaps we should pay closer attention to even the subtlest dialogues, resistances and contradictions established by certain practices/subjects rather than blankly deeming associated parties as apolitical sellouts.

[24] See. http://www.pantibar.com/menu.html. Viewed 18 August 2008.

[25] Gregory Bateson, 'A Theory of Play and Fantasy', *The Performance Studies Reader*, ed. Henry Bial (London and New York: Routledge, 2004): pp. 137-151,150.

[26] In *Imagined Communities: Reflections on the Origin and Spread of Nationalism* (London and New York: Verso, 1983), Benedict

Anderson argues that national communities are imagined into being by those who perceive themselves to be part of that group. While all communities are imagined into being at some level, certain communities, such as the kind I address here, are constituted through face-to-face encounters.

27 Dolan, p. 8.

28 Dido speaking in 'Carthaginians,' *Frank McGuinness: Plays 1* (London and Boston: Faber and Faber, 1996), p. 375.

29 Miller and Román, p. 223.

30 Jill Dolan, *Utopia and Performance: Finding Hope at the Theatre* (Ann Arbor: University of Michigan Press, 2005), p. 2.

31 Iris Young, *On Female Body Experience* (Oxford and New York: Oxford University Press, 2005), p. 69.

32 Sara Ahmed, *The Cultural Politics of Emotion* (London and New York: Routledge, 2004), p. 165.

33 Fintan Walsh, 'Shirley Temple Bar at the Abbey: Irish Theatre, Queer Performance and the Politics of Disidentification', *Irish Theatre International* 1 (Spring 2007), pp. 53-72.

6 | Edward Martyn's Theatrical Hieratic Homoeroticism

Michael Patrick Lapointe

> No other Irishman, in the various movements which together may be generally described as the 'Irish Revival'—between the eighteen-nineties and the establishment of the Irish Free State in 1921—occupies the same prominent place as Edward Martyn as a connecting link between so many intellectual activities.
>
> Denis Gwynn, *Edward Martyn and the Irish Revival* (1930) 13.

> What drove him to those long prayers, those long meditations, that stern Church music? What secret torture?
>
> William Butler Yeats, *Dramatis Personae* (1953) 235.

> Did you hear Miss Mitchell's joke about Moore and Martyn? That Moore is Martyn's wild oats?
>
> James Joyce, *Ulysses*, 1922, (1986) 9.306-8.

An incongruent mystery exists between Denis Gwynn's assertion of Edward Joseph Martyn's position as a founding member of Ireland's national dramatic movement and Yeats's and Joyce's questioning of the playwright's private life. The public image of Martyn's involvement with a myriad of Ireland's most significant cultural activities contrasts with the muted exclusion of *homoeros* in shaping the writer's austere celibacy, suggestively inscribed not only within the literary portraits of Martyn by fellow Irish Revivalists George Augustus Moore and Yeats, but also within his own writing for the theatre. Martyn's dramatic work and his life story convey an ironic, yet fitting, case in point for *The Heather Field* (1899), as one of the premier productions of an Irish national theatre introduces ciphers of *homoeros* into the modern Irish theatre at its inception. The question is not whether one can prove the *truth* of Martyn's sexuality, an elusive and futile venture, but rather the salutary effects of others' perceptions of Martyn's work. Adrian Frazier, the only critic to significantly engage Martyn's 'queerness', states that 'Moore provided a way to read Martyn's plays as involuntary coming-out stories'.[1] This serves two purposes: first, to flesh out the ways in which the writings of Moore and Yeats as well as that of biographers and literary critics consciously colour their re-presentations of Martyn with suggestions of closeted homo-sexuality; second, to contend that this textual construction of the author enables a crucial understanding of how *homoeros* operates in his plays, particularly *The Heather Field*, within the cultural nationalist enterprise of the Irish Literary Theatre. For Martyn's principal characters, torn by thinly concealed queer desires, suffer comparable sacrificial fates for the sake of Ireland in one formulation or another.

According to Frazier, 'cultural nationalism was an offshoot of London 'Decadence' as much as of the Dublin 'Irish Party'; begotten by an inflow of Wilde upon an upwelling of John O'Leary'.[2] The artistic incursion into the Irish movement was known to men like D.P. Moran, who spoke disagreeably of the 'effeminate character of the new Irish literature' with its lisping and crooning poets.[3] This acknowledgement of queer elements circulating within the Literary Revival by Moran and others, may be considered an instance of what Eve Kosofsky Sedgwick labels the 'epistemology of the closet' and its complement the 'privilege of unknowing'; '"Closetedness" itself is a performance initiated as such by the speech act of a silence.'[4] Frequently, coming out of the closet confirms others' suspicions and intuitions which may have existed for years. 'After all, the position of those who think they *know something about one that one may not know oneself* is an excited and empowered one,' writes Sedgwick.[5] In these circumstances, the closet operates as if made of glass where individual sexuality becomes an open secret; with Martyn, one discerns the Irish Renaissance's own instance of the epistemology of the closet. Perhaps, as his critics and the Revivalists suggest, everyone *knows* about Martyn's sexual yearnings even before he does, reflecting the transparent structure of the closet and the crucial role ignorance plays in identity construction. Martyn's intense piety can be read as a compensatory reaction to the horror of his own alterity and the very real fears of degeneracy, effeminacy, and sin so much embedded in the Victorian mind through a combination of the spectacular falls of Parnell and Wilde in the 1890s, and the restrictions of Roman Catholic doctrine.

Amidst the cultural veil of knowing silence however, abundant references in memoirs, biographies, collections of letters, pages of literary criticism, theatre reviews, and in Martyn's own hand, reveal a consistent and provocative pattern of *homoeros*.[6] Typically, Martyn's dramas are marked by overwrought, suggestive dialogue between male figures, sexually ambiguous diction, and the presence of inverted love triangles, whereby the woman ceases to be the desired object vied for by male rivals but becomes the impediment between two men's ties with one another. Homosocial/erotic desires register in the disembodied symbols of the heather field, *An Enchanted Sea*'s Greek marble statues and the sea, and, even, the ethereal always off-stage Prince of the hoar dew from *Maeve*.[7] Specifically, in Martyn's texts a double movement unfolds whereby characters valorize a philosophy of aesthetic idealism, specifically coded as masculine/male, in contrast to the traditional con-figuration of the Irish national ideal as feminine/female, while simultaneously shunning direct engagement with this idealism's homoerotic ramifications. Restrained desire functions as a source of torment that haunts the quotidian lives of the playwright's protagonists. This oppositional tension between passion and asceticism or, *hieratic homoeroticism*, underwrites the topos of the conflicted interaction between religious belief and the demands of the flesh, epitomizing Martyn's dialectical dance of (homo)sexuality and cultural nationalism within Ireland's embryonic theatre.

Along with Lady Gregory, Yeats, and, later, Moore, Martyn founded the Irish Literary Theatre[8] (1899-1901), contributing three plays and substantial finances to the fledgling venture. In the movement's initial days, a struggle for artistic direction as fought out in the Irish Literary Theatre's journal *Beltaine* ensued: What types of plays should be produced? Which representations of *Irishness* would be most efficacious in developing a cultural renaissance as the country increasingly assumed a distinct national consciousness? A stalwart champion of the dramatic realism of Norwegian playwright Henrik Ibsen, Martyn opposed Yeats's vision of producing only heroic, folk, or peasant pieces for the new theatre informed as it was by Yeats's inveterate rejection of the emerging bourgeois Catholic culture; conversely, Yeats was hostile to Ibsen's social politics and disliked modern drama.[9] Common ground lay in the belief that 'authentic Irish experience might be cast as vision, the dream of an alternative reality', finding expression in both Yeats's and Martyn's symbolist-poetic dramas.[10]

Politically, both nationalists and constructive unionists agreed that 'an Irish national theatre was a highly desirable sign of modernization'[11] which addressed the need for Ireland to demonstrate the existence of a civilized public sphere associated with a respectable theatre and an opportunity to present the Irish character in a popular and favourable light.[12]

In contrast to his public persona, Martyn's personal life involved a celibacy practised with an ascetic vigour, displaying an aversion to physical comforts. The playwright's bedroom resembled a bare white-washed cell with a narrow bed and no upholstery according to George Moore[13]; more significantly, however, commentators register the fact that Martyn was afflicted lifelong with some unexplained psychological anguish.[14] Martyn's perplexing and enigmatic personality persuades Yeats to posit a conflict between the man's spiritual life and his bodily desires. In his memoirs, Yeats observes that

> Martyn has a good intellect, moderate and sensible, but it seems to me that this intellect has been always thwarted by its lack of interest in life, religious caution having kept him always on the brink of the world in a half-unwilling virginity of the feelings imaging the virginity of his body. He had no interest in women, and Moore would accuse him of a frustrated passion for his own sex.[15] 'I believe,' he said to him once, 'you think sexual intercourse between men more natural than between women'. I wonder if Moore invented the answer, 'Well, at any rate it is not so disgusting.'[16]

Well-known as a misogynist[17] and critic of marriage, Martyn 'hat[ed] all women with an instinctive, almost perverted antipathy'[18] as Denis Gwynn phrases it, steadfastly refusing female company in spite of his mother, Annie Martyn's (*née* Smyth) attempts to find a wife for her son by inviting young women to the Tillyra estate.[19] Out of Martyn's voluminous lifetime correspondence, he preserved only one woman's letters belonging to his cousin, a Benedictine nun living in Worcestershire, who wondered where he had inherited his 'monastic tastes'.[20]

Given Martyn's privileged position, his celibacy is not easily explained away as yet another instance of Irish Catholic familism that circumscribed the life of tenant farmers. His socio-economic status allowed Martyn the freedom to marry whichever woman he had wished, but he consciously chose not to, preferring the company of men[21] – to what degree exactly will probably never be known. For Martyn's private unpublished papers, accumulated over thirty years and arranged prior to his death, to which he had given the prospective title 'Paragraphs for the Perverse', were entrusted to the Carmelite Order in Clarendon Street and allegedly have been lost or destroyed during the Nazi *blitzkrieg* of London.[22] Before this, the Order had Gwynn write a biography published in 1930, 'sanitized of names, dates, and, as much as possible, facts'.[23]

Sister Marie-Thérèse Courtney designates Martyn's chronic struggle as a conflict between what she terms his religious faith and his Hellenic aesthetic theories acquired at Oxford – a site of the 'uncanny convergence of Catholic and homosexual interests late in the century'.[24] During Martyn's time there, the presence of Walter Pater was keenly felt through his admiration for Catholic ritual and 'the celebration of Greek ideals of male beauty and Greek relations between men'.[25] At Oxford, Martyn also began a close friendship with Count Stanislaus Eric Stenbock, an Estonian homosexual and fellow student, which lasted until Stenbock's death in 1895. Martyn toured Greece, collecting replicas of Greek statuary, and waxed lyrically that Greek was the most beautiful of the world's languages.[26]

In 1885 Martyn burnt his collection of poems fashioned after Greek models and written over a period of years because the writer considered them 'dangerous to faith and morals'.[27] Martyn's ensuing cancellation of newspapers and magazines that possibly contained material contrary to Catholic teachings and his application to his bishop to read works banned under the *Index Expurgatorius* indicated his new adherence to doctrine.[28] As Martyn remarks to Moore in *Hail and Farewell* (1911), '[i]f it hadn't been for the Church, I don't know what would have happened to me'[29]; nonetheless, Frazier interprets the incineration of the poems virtually as evidence that 'he tried to burn himself at the stake: the good celibate Catholic punished the bad homosexual pagan'.[30]

Throughout George Moore's career, his various statements concerning homosexuality and his portraits of his cousin construct Martyn's sexual abstinence as an index of repression. Numerous critics link Moore's and Martyn's fictional creations to biographical and autobiographical materials, a practice common to the writers involved in the Irish Revival.[31] The veracity of the portraits of Martyn and Moore in each other's work remains problematic, and they cannot represent the authors themselves without qualification. As Moore tell us in his ruminations on bachelorhood, 'there is a tendency in us all to look askance at the man who likes to spend the evening alone with his book and his cat',[32] instead of pursuing the charms of women. Frazier asserts, however, that 'Moore was famously indiscreet: he left behind confession after confession, in which he outed himself, then outed Martyn, and finally made intriguing insinuations about Yeats.'[33] The relationship amongst Moore, Yeats, and Martyn is one of homosocial and homoerotic desire according to Frazier, where artistic rivalries and jealousies surface as an imitation of each other's texts and an emulation of each writer's 'male' style; '[l]ove of the man led to imitation of the work: the imitation revealed to the beloved one's love'.[34] Martyn, for instance, collects Degas and Corot as Moore had done, and then composes plays after Moore has written for the stage; conversely, Martyn reciprocates by teaching his cousin about music and taking him to his first Wagner concert.[35]

In Moore's satirical masterpiece *Hail and Farewell* (1911)[36], Martyn declares, 'as you well know, my interests are in public life. I have no private life', to which Moore quips, 'Oh yes, you have, Edward; I'm your private life.'[37] Apparently, one of Martyn's favourite long-standing jokes with Moore involved the repeated uttering of the French pun *'Mon ami Moore, Mon ami Moore!'*[38] The life of 'dear Edward', as Moore affectionately and condescendingly refers to Martyn throughout *Hail and Farewell*, is too ripe an opportunity for Moore not to tacitly question Martyn's sexuality:

> The oddest of all animals is man; in him, as in all other animals, the sexual interest is the strongest; yet the desire is inveterate in him to reject it; and I am sure that Christ's words that in heaven there is neither marriage nor giving in marriage have taken a great weight off Edward's mind, and must have inspired in him many prayers for a small stool in heaven. If by any chance he should not get one (which is, of course, unthinkable) and finds himself among the damned, his plight will be worse than ever, for I suppose he will have no opportunity for correcting his natural disinclination, and I believe no theologian has yet decided that the damned do not

continue to commit the sins in hell which they were damned for committing on earth.[39]

Since celibacy is not considered sinful nor a 'natural dis-inclination,' Moore, thus, strongly insinuates that the cross Martyn must bear pertains to homosexuality. One of Moore's early bio-graphers, Susan L. Mitchell, is critical of what she terms Moore's 'malicious portrait' of Martyn, fashioning him into a 'scapegoat for his own personal antipathies, castigating him for sins he never sinned'.[40] No doubt Moore's satirical treatment of his cousin is highly prejudiced, but Mitchell's assurances aside, Moore introduced Martyn to his decadent circle of erotically-ambiguous artists living in London and Paris: personalities including Arthur Symons, Max Beerbohm, Villiers de l'Isle Adam, Henry James, Walter Pater, and Aubrey Beardsley.

Yeats further incorporates a notion of a circulating open secret when he imputes a degree of psychosexual irregularity between the two cousins in his allusion to Moore and Martyn in *The Cat and the Moon* (1924). In the notes accompanying Yeats's revised 1926 version of the play, he explicitly states the two beggars' discussion of the voyeuristic connection shared by the holy man and the old lecher was 'meant for Edward Martyn and George Moore, both of whom were living when the play was written'[41]:

> **BLIND BEGGAR.** Do you mind what the beggar told you about the holy man in the big house at Laban?[42]
> **LAME BEGGAR.** Nothing stays in my head, Blind Man.
> **BLIND BEGGAR.** What does he do but go knocking about the roads with an old lecher from the county of Mayo, and he a woman-hater from the day of his birth! And what do they talk of by candle-light and by daylight? The old lecher does be telling over all the sins he committed, or maybe never committed at all, and the man of Laban does be trying to head him off and quiet him down that he may quit telling them.
> **LAME BEGGAR.** Maybe it is converting him he is.
> **BLIND BEGGAR.** If you were a blind man you wouldn't say a foolish thing the like of that. He wouldn't have him different, no, not if he was to get all Ireland. If he was different, what would they find to talk about, will you tell me that now?[43]

The beggars' dialogue, situated within a framework of gossip, implies that the lecher and the holy man remain dependent upon each other for their own abnormal functioning and are duplicitous in constructing one another's ineffectual camouflage of both the pious abstainer and of the Don Juanesque paramour.

Turning to Martyn's dramatic work, one senses that a private conversation operates underneath the dialogue between the men on-stage: a language striving to settle some unarticulated dilemma, or a palimpsest where Martyn's encoding of psychosexual relations remains overlaid with Irish nationalist themes and rhetoric. Martyn's plays attempt to elucidate the life of the bachelor by rending its problematic status from any suspicion of deviance as a technique of interpreting his own experience. Granted the sexually repressive streak within Catholicism, masculinist nationalism's own homosociality, the Revival's fascination with hypermasculine heroes; all combined with the formidable psychological mechanisms of denial, shame, and projection, a more plausible reading of the unconventional features of Martyn's writing necessitates an understanding informed by the dynamic operations of the closet. This idea of passion held in check accounts for the indirection, the coded subtexts, and the layers of sexual suggestion within many scenes. Although none of Martyn's characters is explicitly construed as a dandy, his representation of male relationships remains reminiscent of those in Wilde's *The Importance of Being Earnest* (1895) and *The Picture of Dorian Gray* (1891); furthermore, Gothic elements tint Martyn's texts with madness, remote overpowering landscapes, mystery, obsession, the supernatural, ghosts, and hints of incest in the unsettling homosocial triangulation amongst Kit, Miles, and Ussher, revealed in Carden Tyrell's melding of their identities.[44]

The charged emotional dynamics between Martyn's men predictably produce a tragic melancholic atmosphere. The writer's desire to depict psychological realism, dramatizing to varying degrees the battles within the male psyche, poignantly results in revelations of weakness, vulnerability, despair with the material world, and emotional disturbance; in other words, the male protagonists suffer from symptoms strikingly similar to late nineteenth-century conceptions of 'feminine' hysteria. In these diagnoses, the apparent reversal of gender inscription suggests that repressed erotic desire is an avenue to understanding the characters' self-destruction, melancholy, and alleged charges of madness.

Along with Yeats's *The Countess Cathleen*, Martyn's *The Heather Field* inaugurated the first season of the Irish Literary Theatre in the Antient Concert Rooms in Dublin on 9 May 1899. Because of his technical and practical experience in the theatre, Moore had overseen the rehearsals of both plays, changing cast members and stage managers[45]; moreover, Moore later commented to Yeats that he had 'told Martyn what was to go into every speech'.[46] Taking cues from Ibsen's dramaturgy, Martyn eschews spectacle but instead crafts scenes where the subtle problems of characters' psychology, emblematic of the contest between illusion and reality, are explored on-stage. The playwright essentially situates *The Heather Field* within the world of realism, the standard genre that dominates twentieth-century Irish drama, rather than modernist or more experimental modes. Generally, the realist form tends to be 'ideologically restrictive' in maintaining notions of fixed identity and preventing a more far-reaching interrogation of nationality and gender although Martyn's plays demonstrate some resistance to this tendency in the inversion of gender stereotypes.[47]

As Martyn exercised relentless discipline over his own body, he rigorously controlled how he wished his plays to be performed through his writing. In the published introduction to the play, Moore claims Martyn wrote plays that are 'perfectly constructed; they could be acted as they are written'; furthermore, Martyn composed 'with strict regard for the stage, because it is impossible to write good plays without the actors and actresses who will [...] interpret them'.[48] Moore points out the 'strange irony ... that the plays which lend themselves to interpretation are the plays which are neglected on the stage and cherished in the study'.[49] Moore's counter-intuitive comments overturn the notion that more literary closet dramas are failures on the stage in comparison to dramatic texts which lend themselves to performative interpretation.

Martyn saturates *The Heather Field's* script with precise stage directions explaining how the actors are to punctuate their lines with the frequent action of 'looking', which is a substitution for all that is not being articulated: '*with a frightened look*', '*with a baffled look*',[50] '*averts his look*', '*with dejection*',[51] '*with a swift shy glance*',[52] '*with anxious intensity*',[53] '*with a penetrating look*',[54] '*looking at her with a sort of wonder*',[55] '*looks significantly*',[56] '*with suppressed anger*',[57] '*looks at her for a moment with vague alarm*',[58] '*a quick look at Tyrell*',[59] '*looks out in reverie*',[60] and '*with a look of humiliation and despair*'.[61] What's more, Tyrell frequently stares out the glass doors at the heather field in the distance.[62] All of this 'eye-play' remains indicative of the intense emotional barriers between the performers within their roles and is symptomatic of hieratic *homoeros*.

Martyn's friends felt *The Heather Field* was an original drawing-room drama, even exotic, very unlike plays then being produced in London.[63] Theatre reviews and the reaction to *The Heather Field* were generally laudatory. The play was well received in the nationalist *Freeman's Journal*, *Independent*, and *United Irishman*, and there were no objections from the audience to the drama's preoccupations with the troubles of the Ascendancy class.[64] While watching the play, Yeats curiously claims to have thought of Martyn's personal life; 'Mrs. Martyn's attempts to find a wife for her son came into my head,' notes the poet.[65] James Joyce also liked *The Heather Field* for its unique Ibsenesque qualities and, later in March 1919, Zurich's English Players would revive it.[66] Joseph Holloway, Dublin's eccentric theatre commentator, wrote in his journal an enthusiastic review of the performance:

> A more absorbing play ... I have not witnessed for a long time ... One cannot give any idea of the amount of pathos and tenderness the dramatist has worked round the incidents leading up to the tragedy of this dreamer whose mind gives way ... His love for his brother, son, and friend were beautifully indicated, and his utter hopelessness in trying to make his wife understand him one little bit was also admirably hit off.[67]

In an unsigned review of another one of Martyn's plays in *Sinn Féin* (3 February 1912), this pathos which Holloway refers to comes under criticism: 'We tire ... of Mr. Martyn's weak men and strong women ... Martyn can do large things in drama, and does not do them because he lets a little devil compounded of perversity and sentimentality run away with him.'[68]

Courtney comments that Ussher's 'reprehensible' inability to dedicate himself to idealistic philosophy indicates that 'something evil, therefore, must be at the heart of it, an evil of which he is aware, and this idea was not lost on spectators outside of Ireland, some of whom sensed that "a certain sort of unhealthy pathos pervades the whole"'.[69] The day after the premiere *The Freeman's Journal* mentioned, 'here ... is a play that reveals a tragedy of social and domestic life although there is *not the remotest suggestion in it from beginning to end of the disordered eroticism* which is responsible for so many stage successes in London and Paris during recent years' (emphasis mine).[70] The rhetorical strategy of containment with this manoeuvre of indubitably asserting what is not suggested on-stage remains even more suspect, while ostensibly assuaging any hint of sexual 'immorality'; after all, this production remains part of the launching of an *Irish* theatre for an *Irish* people.

Martyn utilizes a single setting throughout the production – Tyrell's library/study situated in the West of Ireland in 1890. The setting generates an atmosphere of increasing confinement, metaphorically similar to that of the closet, as Tyrell's world falls apart in the course of events, especially in Act Three when Tyrell is imprisoned inside his home because of the threat of angry evictees.[71] Act One, however, opens with a visit from bachelor and close companion, Barry Ussher, to Tyrell's estate; ostensibly he has come to discuss Tyrell's land reclamation project[72] and to offer financial advice.[73] On the surface this visit remains entirely comprehensible, but the bulk of the act is a prolonged discourse by the players on the subject of Tyrell's estranged marriage and nostalgia for his days as a bachelor. This extensive digression, as it were, achieves a stereotypical gender reversal where Ussher and Tyrell's younger brother, Miles, gossip about the personal affairs of another man in contra-distinction to the male world of politics, sport, and other subjects associated with public life:

> **USSHER.** ... [Grace] would probably have made an excellent wife for almost any other man; but for your brother – well, it might have been better if he had never thought of marriage at all.
> **MILES.** What? Surely he might have found someone to suit him. Why should you say such a thing?
> **USSHER.** [*with a frightened look*] Why?
> **MILES.** Yes, Ussher. But what is the matter with you?
> **USSHER.** [*quickly recovering himself*] Oh, nothing, Miles, nothing. I merely meant to say that it would be very difficult for anyone to suit Tyrell. He is a person so much of himself, you know.
> **MILES.** Ah, it is certainly a great misfortune he ever met Grace. And their estrangement is so extraordinary, for he once used to be so fond of her.
> **USSHER.** Yes, they generally begin that way. I remember just before he became engaged he told me that he thought till then he should never marry, but that at last he had found real happiness. They all say that, you know.[74]

This odd exchange between Miles and Ussher produces an interesting question: Does an open secret operate within the play?

The scene proceeds with the revelation that ten years prior to the opening of Act One, Ussher attempted to convince his friend not to marry, suspecting that Tyrell's feelings were not genuine nor lasting. Ussher defends his interference by claiming,

> Tyrell and I have been intimate so long ... I understood him better than anyone. The sudden overturning of all his ideas at the time seemed to me strange and unnatural. He was like one bewitched. A man's whole nature somehow does not change in a moment.[75]

Ussher sets himself up as the informed insider who is privy to the innermost workings of his friend's heart; for example, in Act III Ussher tells Tyrell that he knows the 'pain of loss'[76] but also seems to express a certain amount of jealousy in criticizing Grace's influence:

> Oh, he always did so fascinate and interest me. What poetry he put into those days of my youth – the days that are dead. [*pause*] Then to see him suddenly changed, grown even prosy under the power of her influence – it made it impossible for me to consider this attachment of his genuine or likely to endure.[77]

Ussher proceeds to characterize Tyrell, synonymous with the heather field, as possessing a disposition 'too eerie, too ethereal, too untameable for good, steady, domestic cultivation ... whose latent, untameable nature was not to be subdued'[78]; furthermore, the 'first sign of revolt against suppression'[79] involves Tyrell's reclamation scheme. Ussher's diction echoes the Freudian lexicon that was emerging in the 1890s, for, in effect, Ussher theorizes sublimation – in this case: the massive undertaking of land reclamation that dominates Tyrell's waking life.

Afterward, Tyrell and Miles discuss Ussher's advice against marriage, the incompatibility of the couple, and Grace's efforts to fashion Tyrell into a typical member of his social class. Tyrell's musings veer philosophically to the subject of idealism so central to Martyn's own intellectual and artistic interests:

> **TYRELL.** ... your true idealist can only be a man. Alas! Had I known that then, my fate would have been different. I thought others were easy to find, in whom I could confide as in Ussher.
> **MILES.** Do you consider him an idealist?
> **TYRELL.** I should think so indeed – a true idealist – only he is in a way so drilled and careful, that he will never let himself go. But he is such a friend, and understands everything! Isolation only began with my marriage, which led me out into a lonely

world. Oh, it was a great misfortune. And I have no one to
blame but myself.

Overtly gendered as masculine, Tyrell's idealism, nonetheless,
simultaneously disavows the flesh and blood of this philosophy.
Tyrell briefly associates ideal beauty with Grace's allure but almost
straightaway overturns such attraction as a sham. Ussher, who
Tyrell declares can perceive the 'truly beautiful', resists such
feminine distractions. The language of classical Greek idealism
provides a vehicle for the codes of hieratic homoeroticism,
emblematizing Tyrell's inner struggles.

In the erotic love triangles that frequently occur in Martyn's
plays, women such as Grace Tyrell, Rachel Font, and Millicent Fell
are cast as interlopers in the homosocial relationships between
Irishmen. In *The Heather Field*, Grace's entrance shatters the all-
male world and the 'great peace' of her husband's mind[80] indicated
not only by the shifts in conversation but also by the tenor of
language; Grace's appearance precipitates a dramatic change from
poetic sentimentality, evidenced by Tyrell's plea to Miles, 'You will
not leave me if – if ever I should stand helpless and alone,'[81] to the
pragmatic world of Grace and her demand for domestic order. Tyrell
repeatedly interpellates Miles into the subject position of the
conventional lover/spouse rather than Grace, raising the spectre of
paedophilia.[82] Moore writes that 'the play resolves itself into a duel
between husband and wife, and one of its merits is that although all
right and good sense are on the wife's side, the sympathy is always
with Tyrell,'[83] in part, due to Martyn's uneven treatment of his male
heroes and female antagonists.

In the final act, Ussher and Tyrell discuss their feelings of
sadness and loneliness, their desire for escape, and the pain of their
mutually understood idealism. The knowledge of ideal beauty
haunts the men due to the tremendous challenge in accessing and
connecting with this *phantom*, this 'lost paradise',[84] which appears
only to be experienced temporarily from a distance:

> **TYRELL.** Well then, have you ever seen on earth something
> beautiful beyond earth – that great beauty which appears in
> diverse ways? And then you have known what it is to go back to
> the world again?
> **USSHER.** [*sadly*] I know, I know – the pain of loss –
> **TYRELL.** Is it not misery? But you have seen great beauty,
> have you not? Oh, that immortal beauty – so far away – always
> so far away.

USSHER. Yes–yes, our ideal beauty that forever haunts and eludes us through life. [*with a movement of resignation*] But let us not speak of it any more.
TYRELL. Why, Ussher?
USSHER. Because, as you say, it makes one so miserable in the world, and it is such a hopeless phantom after all.
USSHER. [*cautiously*] Hush, Tyrell, I do not know.
TYRELL. [*laughing bitterly*] There–just like you, Ussher, careful never to let yourself go.[85]

This philosophical rambling, central to the play's themes and significance, resembles a worldview shared by people living in the closet: self-denial, dissembling, and chronic fear, generated by the radical division between individuals' inner cognizance of themselves and the social conventions of the outside world. Martyn's dialogue attests to both the joy and the despair of desires that are forbidden open acknowledgment.

In *The Heather Field*, Tyrell's unequivocal masculine idealism underpins the play's two major topoi: aesthetics and land reclamation. Irish Revivalists and nationalists traditionally imagine the symbolic sacralized land of Ireland as a feminine body. In romantic and revolutionary Irish nationalism, there is an attempt to reclaim the material body of that land and, metaphorically, of the woman whether through the use of the gun or the pen. Seamus Deane explains that land is more than just a civic and economic unit of territory, for it also comprises the soil – a metaphysical cultural and communal reality.[86] 'The romantic-nationalist conception of the soil, its identity with the nation, its ownership by the people, its priority over all the administrative and commercial systems that transform it into land,' writes Deane, 'is the more powerful because it is formulated as a reality that is beyond the embrace of any concept.'[87]

Tyrell's failure to suitably possess or to reclaim the heath, metonymically, is a failure to reclaim a masculine body. The heather field, with its young grass of 'matchless Irish green',[88] functions as a type of unconscious repository of all that is most ideal, poetic, and beautiful; the land enchants Tyrell, offering him freedom and individual singularity, yet it threatens his mental health. Tyrell's 'infatuation'[89] with the mountain propels his desire to achieve his ultimate goal of 'buying up and reclaiming or re-afforesting every inch of waste land in Ireland',[90] and thereby, sacrifice the well-being of his family. The many forms of development associated with modernization and economic independence, nevertheless, smack of colonization creating an ideological quandary for nationalists.[91] *The Heather Field* remains uneasily poised between, on the one hand, the Romantic stereotype of the wild and unspoiled countryside which inspires nationalist dreams of ending British rule and, on the other hand, the constructive unionist agenda which holds that fulfilling the need for modern industrialization and land reform will preserve the Union and secure the position of the Ascendancy in a volatile socio-political situation.

The heath serves as a displacement of Tyrell's sublimated desires; he admits to hearing voices out in the heather field, which he claims, 'keep telling me I am not what I am ... They often call me back to my real life ... the life before I wandered into this dream'.[92] These voices of Tyrell's unconscious mind, which return with a vengeance along with the heather when *madness* erupts, signify his own disavowals. Ussher had cautioned earlier that 'if heather lands are brought into cultivation for domestic use, they must be watched ... else their old wild nature may avenge itself'.[93] This warning of nature's vengeance upon Tyrell's blueprint for uprooting the land represents a central irony at the heart of the play.

The text signals the return of these repressed desires through the omnipresent symbol of the budding heather field as a masculine body-as-homeland in need of reclamation. Martyn strives to generate sympathy for his landlord's ambitious plan despite violent resistance by Tyrell's own evicted tenants. Tyrell's reclamation of the field through the destruction of the native heather exposes the imaginary fantasy of both romantic nationalism's and, ironically, the Ascendancy's assertion of its own origin or *rootedness* in, or justifiable claim to, the land. Ussher's and Tyrell's idealization of the male body traverses these other fantasized archetypes operating in the text, culminating in the sacrificial punishment of Tyrell's madness instigated by his attraction to the beauty of the land and his obsession with reclaiming it. Martyn's fascination with this ruinous, inviolable realm of beauty signifies his importation of a strain of Romanticism situated within nationalism's *homoeros*.

The interaction between Martyn's biography, representations, and dramatic invention oscillates as Patricia McFate argues:

> In Carden Tyrell and Barry Ussher we find partial portraits of George Moore and Edward Martyn ... The characters are never simple imitations, of course, but rather combinations and permutations. Jasper Dean combines qualities of Yeats and

Moore; Ralf Kirwan recalls both AE and Martyn. Aspects of
Martyn are found in both Carden Tyrell and Barry Ussher. The
companionship of Carden and Miles Tyrell is a fusion of
Moore's past relationships with his brother and his cousin.[94]

If one hypothesizes that Martyn was not himself queer, then it
must be said that particular facets of his plays seem very *queer*
indeed.

Wayne Hall remarks that Martyn succeeded in 'establishing a
correspondence between his own lifestyle and that of his major
literary characters',[95] and Ellis-Fermor states that 'Edward Martyn
is a hard man to understand ... [I]t is easy to draw a series of
portraits, but hard, to the verge of impossibility, to see the man.'[96]
Part of the reason for this ambiguity lies with Yeats's
marginalization of Martyn and his dismissal of the man's
contribution to the development not only of Irish theatre but also of
cultural nationalism. For many years in Ireland, according to Jerry
Nolan, Martyn was the sole voice pushing for modern, cosmopolitan
drama informed by an interaction with Europe.[97] Additionally,
Nolan objects to Yeats's writing off of Martyn and his work based on
the poet's recourse to psycho-sexual theories, but then Nolan fails to
offer any clear explanation or reasoning for his criticism of Yeats's
observations of Martyn.[98]

In spite of Martyn's awkward treatment of traditional Celtic
themes, his melodramatic, wooden dialogue; shoddy, static characterization; and his attempts at introducing a drama of ideas into the
numerous theatre projects that he was involved with in his lifetime,
Martyn inscribes homosocial and homoerotic desires consistently
across his texts. Romantic longing is displaced into philosophical
discussions of beauty personified by male figures, and thereby
functioning as an open secret. Martyn's explicit connection between
beauty and male youth and its metaphorical association with Ireland
via the enchanting fields or waves of the sea as enunciated by Tyrell,
Mask, and Maeve highlights the demands for Irish redemption in
the form of masculine love. The sacrificial end game for all of
Martyn's sensitive souls involves death through murder, suicide, or
madness, all entangled with *homoeros* in nationalist identification;
ends that for decades, as Nicholas de Jongh states, were common in
homosexual representations.[99] The sexualized or, for that matter,
desexualized construction of Martyn in the commentary of Irish
Revivalists and other critics subsequently opens a critical horizon in

Martyn's writing, disclosing a pattern of hieratic homoeroticism with its concomitant contradictions.

As Gwynn attests, Martyn achieved singularity in many of his country's most significant cultural movements over the course of his life. Martyn's plays remain significant to the history of the Irish dramatic movement, foremost because his work, perhaps unintentionally, ruptures nationalist myths of Irish identity on several levels. Suffering from a strain of misrecognition, Martyn's disembodied, 'non-representation' of *homoeros* haunts the playhouse through its homosocially-coloured ellipsis, connotations, and ambiguities. Perchance one cannot help but hear the sounds of Wilde's and Joyce's sympathetic laughter at the quirky ironies of such a singular and contradictory Irish bachelor as Edward Martyn being responsible for one of modern Irish culture's originating moments.

---

[1] Adrian Frazier, 'Queering the Irish Renaissance: The Masculinities of Moore, Martyn, and Yeats', *Gender and Sexuality in Modern Ireland*, eds Anthony Bradley and Maryann Gialanella Valiulis (Amherst, MA: University of Massachusetts Press, 1997), p. 27.

[2] Frazier, 'Masculinities', p. 9.

[3] Ibid.

[4] Eve Kosofsky Sedgwick, *Epistemology of the Closet* (Berkeley: University of California Press, 1990), p. 3.

[5] Ibid, p. 80.

[6] I am not dealing here first and foremost with sexual acts, but, instead, with a plurality of sexual categories, of expanded, yet often vexed, notions of love and male friendship, and of emotional and spiritual yearning for another member of the same sex. These relational discourses, sometimes marked by an intimacy or intensity usually associated with most standard configurations of heterosexual romance, are also, at other times, marked by anxiety and hostility. I have grouped all these phenomena under the term *homoeros*.

[7] Edward Martyn, *Maeve: A Psychological Drama in Two Acts*, 1900, *Selected Plays of George Moore and Edward Martyn*, Introduction, David B. Eakin and Michael Case (Gerrards Cross, UK: Colin Smythe, 1995), p. 294.

[8] In 1899, Patrick Pearse was severely critical of Yeats, Martyn, Moore, and Gregory for establishing the Irish Literary Theatre as he wrote

in a letter that the new theatre was 'more dangerous, because glaringly anti-national, than Trinity College ... Let us strangle it at its birth. Against Mr. Yeats personally we have nothing to object. He is a mere English poet of the third or fourth rank, and as such he is harmless. But when he attempts to run an "Irish Literary Theatre", it is time for him to be crushed.' Séamas Ó Buachalla, ed., *The Letters of P.H. Pearse* (Gerrards Cross, UK: Colin Smythe, 1980), p. 9. However, Pearse later cozied up to Martyn in 1908, soliciting financial support for St. Enda's through a series of letters. See Ó Buachalla, pp. 121-24.

9 Jerry Nolan, 'Edward Martyn's Struggle for an Irish National Theatre, 1899-1920', *New Hibernia Review/Iris Éireannach Nua* 7:2 (Summer 2003), pp. 90, 92.

10 Christopher Murray, *Twentieth-Century Irish Drama: Mirror up to Nation* (New York: Manchester University Press, 1997), p. 3.

11 Lionel Pilkington, *Theatre and the State in Twentieth-Century Ireland: Cultivating the People* (New York: Routledge, 2001), p. 9.

12 Pilkington, pp. 15-16.

13 George Moore, *Hail and Farewell*, ed. Richard Cave (Gerrards Cross, UK: Colin Smythe, 1976), p. 186.

14 Una Ellis-Fermor, *The Irish Dramatic Movement* (London: Methuen, 1964): p. 118; Sister Marie-Thérèse Courtney, *Edward Martyn and the Irish Theatre*, 1956 (New York: Vantage Press, 1969), p. 49; Gwynn, pp. 83-84.

15 The typescript version of Yeats's *Dramatis Personae* includes the following additional sentence in this passage on Martyn: 'He once said the majority of lost souls are lost through sexuality, had his father's instincts through repression or through some accident of birth turned, as Moore thought, into an always resisted homosexuality.' W.B. Yeats, *Memoirs: Autobiography – First Draft Journal*, ed. Denis Donoghue (London: Macmillan, 1972), pp. 118-19, n.3.

16 Yeats, *Memoirs*, pp. 118-19.

17 Madeleine Humphreys argues that the charge of misogyny against Martyn can unfairly be traced back to Moore's representation of 'dear Edward' in *Hail and Farewell*. In his later years, Martyn's respectful friendships with women such as Maud Gonne, Helen Mitchell, Sarah Purser, Grace Gifford, and Lady Gregory grew and matured. Humphreys, pp. 204-06.

18 Gwynn, p. 18.

19 In her distress, Martyn's mother turned to the local priest to persuade Edward to marry and to continue the family name. Martyn responded by declaring that he would rather become a monk than marry. 'And

you know well,' he added, 'how much I would hate to be one.' Gwynn, p. 84. During this period of maternal matchmaking, Martyn, in a possible case of sublimation, threw himself into the hiring of architects – sparing no expense – to design a spacious modern mansion adjoining Norman-built Tillyra Castle. Gwynn, p. 49.

20 Gwynn, pp. 51-52.

21 'What is sufficiently interesting and worthy of study,' suggests Frazier, 'is the way in which Martyn took pleasure in travelling with men, in having men of a certain kind pay long visits to Tillyra, in listening to opera with men, [and] in collaborating with men on plays about his own frustration of desire.' Frazier, 'Masculinities', p. 37, n.63.

22 Courtney, p. 167; Gwynn, p. 30. In 1992, Jerry Nolan interviewed Father Anselm Cooney of Kensington Church Street, who claimed that the bomb damage to the Carmelite Order was very minor, restricted to the roof of the church. Nolan feels that the hypothesis that cleaning staff threw out Martyn's papers is the most satisfactory explanation for their disappearance. Jerry Nolan, *Six Essays on Edward Martyn (1859-1923), Irish Cultural Revivalist* (Lampeter, UK: Edwin Mellen Press, 2004), pp. 191-92. However, Madeleine Humphreys suggests that perhaps Cyril Ryan of the Carmelite Order in Dublin destroyed the documents because of their revelations of sexual desire or paganism. Humphreys, p. xiii.

23 Frazier, 'Masculinities', p. 12.

24 Jack Morgan, 'Queer Choirs: Sacred Music, Joyce's "The Dead", and the Sexual Politics of Victorian Aestheticism', *James Joyce Quarterly* 37.1-2 (Fall 1999/Winter 2000), p. 133.

25 Frazier, 'Masculinities', p. 23. In his biography *George Moore 1852-1933*, Adrian Frazier quotes John Addington Symonds on the 'dangers' of a classical Oxford education where boys discover that the basis of Greek higher culture was homosexuality – 'not a crime but a cultural ideal'. Adrian Frazier, *George Moore 1852-1933*, (London: Yale University Press, 2000), p. 100.

26 Frazier, 'Masculinities', pp. 23-24.

27 Frazier, 'Masculinities', p. 25.

28 Courtney, pp. 46-47.

29 Moore, *Hail*, p. 596.

30 Frazier, 'Masculinities', p. 25.

31 Patricia McFate, 'The Bending of the Bough and The Heather Field: Two Portraits of the Artists', *Éire-Ireland* 8.1 (Spring 1973): pp. 52-61; Ann Saddlemyer, 'All Art Is Collaboration? George Moore and Edward Martyn', *The World of W.B. Yeats: Essays in Perspective*, eds Robin Skelton and Ann Saddlemyer (Victoria, British Columbia: Adelphi

Bookshop, 1965), pp. 169-88; Helmut E. Gerber, ed., *George Moore in Transition* (Wayne State University Press, 1968), pp. 44-45; W.B. Yeats, *'Dramatis Personae', The Autobiography of William Butler Yeats* (New York: Macmillan, 1953), p. 251.

32 Moore, *Hail*, p. 144.

33 Frazier, 'Masculinities', p. 11.

34 Frazier, 'Masculinities', p. 25.

35 Frazier, 'Masculinities', p. 21.

36 'The greatest outrage of the volume is not that Moore lied, but that he told unseasonable truths, not that he was inaccurate but that he was indiscreet and thus unkind.' Frazier, *Moore*, p. 364.

37 Moore, *Hail*, p. 336.

38 Moore, *Hail*, p. 337.

39 Moore, *Hail*, pp. 160-61.

40 Susan L. Mitchell, *George Moore* (Dublin: Talbot Press Limited, 1916), p.94.

41 William Butler Yeats, *The Cat and the Moon: The Variorum Edition of the Plays of W.B. Yeats*, ed. Russell K. Alspach (London: Macmillan, 1966), p. 808.

42 In alternative dialogue listed in the variorum edition of the play, the Blind Beggar asks the Lame Beggar: 'Did you ever know a holy man but had a wicked man for his comrade and his heart's darling?' Yeats, *Cat*, p. 797.

43 Ibid.

44 Edward Martyn, *The Heather Field: A Play in Three Acts*, 1899, *Irish Drama Series*, Introduction, William J. Feeney, vol. 1 (Chicago, IL: De Paul University Press, 1966), pp. 25-6, 39, 63.

45 Moore, *Hail*, pp. 92-96.

46 Frazier, *Moore*, p. 245.

47 Margaret Llewellyn Jones, *Contemporary Irish Drama & Cultural Identity* (Bristol, UK: Intellect Books, 2002), p. 117.

48 George Moore, Introduction, *The Heather Field: A Play in Three Acts* and *Maeve: A Psychological Drama In Two Acts* by Edward Martyn (London: Gerald Duckworth, 1899), p. xxvii.

49 Moore, 'Introduction', p. xxviii.

50 Martyn, *Heather*, p. 19.

51 Ibid., p. 20.

52 Ibid., p. 21.

53 Ibid., p. 26.

54 Ibid., p. 30.

55 Ibid., p. 31.

56 Ibid., p. 44.

57 Ibid., p. 50.

58 Ibid., p. 51.

59 Ibid., p. 54.

60 Ibid., p. 56.

61 Ibid., p. 60.

62 Ibid., pp. 27, 56.

63 Jan Setterquist, *Ibsen and the Beginnings of Anglo-Irish Drama, II: Edward Martyn* (New York: Oriole, 1973), pp. 28-40; Gwynn, pp. 119, 142-44.

64 Pilkington, p. 19.

65 Yeats, 'Dramatis', p. 253.

66 James Joyce, *The Critical Writings*, 1959, eds Ellsworth Mason and Richard Ellmann (New York: Viking, 1989), pp. 68, 251-2; William J. Feeney, 'Edward Martyn', *Irish Playwrights 1880-1995: A Research and Production Sourcebook*, eds Bernice Schrank and William W. Demastes (London: Greenwood Press, 1997), p. 207.

67 Joseph Holloway, *Joseph Holloway's Abbey Theatre: a selection from his unpublished journal, Impressions of a Dublin playgoer*, eds Robert Hogan and Michael J. O'Neill (Carbondale, IL: Southern Illinois University Press, 1967), pp. 8-9.

68 Quoted in William J. Feeney, *Drama in Hardwicke Street: A History of the Irish Theatre Company* (London: Associated UP, 1984), p. 171.

69 Courtney, p. 86.

70 Robert Hogan and James Kilroy, eds, *The Irish Literary Theatre, 1899-1901, The Irish Theatre Series*, 6 (Dublin: Dolmen Press, 1975), p. 46. Adrian Frazier views the comments by the *Freeman's Journal* as 'ridiculous', incredulous that no one noticed how saturated the play is with homoeroticism, and Madeleine Humphreys acknowledges that Tyrell and Ussher's sexuality is 'problematic'. Frazier, *Moore*, p. 271; Humphreys, p. 65.

71 Martyn, *Heather*, p. 56.

72 According to Katie Trumpener in *Bardic Nationalism: The Romantic Novel and the British Empire* (1997), experiments in irrigation, bog reclamation, and cultivation techniques utilizing tenant labour were believed to be the best route to economic progress that would alleviate agrarian discontent and produce peaceful relations between classes. 'Bog drainage synecdochically represents the project of Enlightenment land reform: the creation of arable, profitable soil out of its former uselessness, by bringing it into the light of day, out

of primeval ooze that now covers it,' writes Trumpener. Katie Trumpener, *Bardic Nationalism: The Romantic Novel and the British Empire* (Princeton, NJ: Princeton University Press, 1997), p. 42. Landlords attempted to secure their hold on the land by transforming the surface of Ireland into their own image; however, for nationalists, the bog was significant as a material and discursive site. Trumpener, pp. 43, 46. On account of the outlines of the past embedded within the landscape that denoted historical memory – the scars of conflict and the remains of Gaelic civilization – nationalists wished the topography to remain unmolested; subsequently, agrarian resistance to reclamation schemes was common. Trumpener, pp. 52-53.

[73] Martyn, *Heather*, p. 18.

[74] Ibid., pp. 18-19.

[75] Ibid., p. 19.

[76] Ibid., p. 57.

[77] Ibid., p. 19.

[78] Ibid., p. 20.

[79] Ibid.

[80] Ibid., p. 28.

[81] Ibid., p. 26.

[82] Frazier, *Moore*, p. 271; Humphreys, p. 117.

[83] Moore, Introduction, p. xxv.

[84] Martyn, *Heather*, p. 26.

[85] Ibid., p. 57.

[86] Seamus Deane, *Strange Country: Modernity and Nationhood in Irish Writing since 1790* (Oxford: Clarendon Press, 1997), p. 70.

[87] Deane, p. 77.

[88] Martyn, *Heather*, p. 27.

[89] Ibid., p. 44.

[90] Ibid.

[91] Ben Levitas, *The Theatre of Nation: Irish Drama and Cultural Nationalism 1890-1916* (Oxford: Clarendon Press, 2002), p. 47.

[92] Martyn, *Heather*, p. 46.

[93] Ibid., p. 20.

[94] Patricia A. McFate, '*The Bending of the Bough* and *The Heather Field*: Two Portraits of the Artists', *Éire-Ireland* 8.1 (Spring 1973), pp. 57, 61.

[95] Wayne E. Hall, *Shadowy Heroes: Irish Literature of the 1890s* (Syracuse, NY: Syracuse University Press, 1980), p. 112.

[96] Ellis-Fermor, p. 117.

[97] Nolan, 'Struggle', pp. 90, 105.

[98] Jerry Nolan, ed., *The Tulira Trilogy of Edward Martyn (1859-1923), Irish Symbolist Dramatist*, (Lampeter, UK: Edwin Mellen Press, Ltd., 2004), pp. 22-23.

[99] Nicholas de Jongh, *Not in Front of the Audience: Homosexuality on Stage* (New York: Routledge, 1992), p. 3.

7 | The International Dublin Gay Theatre Festival

Brian Merriman

The idea of the International Dublin Gay Theatre Festival had been germinating throughout my Master's Thesis process as a new direction for a theatrical career that had both elements of theatre and social equality at its core. I had already premiered the role of Zaza/Albin in *La Cage Aux Folles* (as no other actor would do it in 1993!) and then went on to play Oscar Wilde in 'A Chelsea Affair' in 2000 – the centenary of his death. When an unexpected gap came in my theatre schedule, I established the Dublin Gay Theatre Festival in January 2004. My first calls were to promoter John Pickering and performer Eddie Devoy to come on board, and they did. The company never looked back and attracted lots of volunteers from all walks of life. Soon Senator David Norris and Emma Donoghue became our patrons, joined in 2008 by Terrence MacNally, renowned playwright. Later we formed a 'not for profit' company limited by guarantee, and built a highly talented and committed volunteer base. I am now the Artistic Director and Executive Chairman of the International Dublin Gay Theatre Festival, Ltd.

Within three months of those first phone calls in 2004, we staged eleven productions in May of that year (including one from the UK), and extended the Festival to sixteen companies the following year (including two from the UK). In 2006 we decided to expand substantially and go fully international; 66% of our programme came from abroad and we began a unique dialogue of Irish and international gay culture through theatre as an art form in Dublin.

The political, artistic and social importance of what we want to achieve through theatre is deliberately planned. That is, using the cultural dynamic of theatre as an essential catalyst for change in society, through acknowledging our identity as a legitimate culture. The recognition of gay theatre as an art form motivates us, in conjunction with our premier desire to identify, develop and encourage gay art and artistry through theatre as an art form in Ireland and abroad.

We launched the third festival in the Mansion House in 2006 – the home of the Lord Mayor of Dublin. We were next door to the meeting place of the first Dáil (Irish Parliament) in the month of the celebration of the 90th anniversary of the 1916 Rising – a revolutionary event which had at its core, equality for all citizens. Padraig Pearse, one of the Proclamation's signatories, as historians debate, was probably gay, as was the martyred Sir Roger Casement. As a new Republic we still had kept some of the cherished traditions of the British Empire we were seeking to overthrow close to our newly liberated hearts. The progression of a full Republic for all citizens has never exorcized those who have done many diverse things to protest their true Republican spirit and conviction. Convenient or selective Republicanism is at best a more generous description of what we have been put through as a nation for the past ninety years.

One of the reasons we have an International Dublin Gay Theatre Festival is to unwrap the seclusion and exclusion of gay life, which has remained obscured from public view for centuries in Ireland. Ireland has long been constructed as a society that conceals it differences. One such ongoing exclusion accommodates the notion that prohibiting gay couples from formalizing their natural relationships, in some way enriches a democratic society or underpins the moral or religious values that sustain heterosexuality and protect the family. This narrow and flawed perspective ensures that differences are created and maintained in order to diminish the value of specific lifestyles and cultures. The works presented in the gay theatre festival are an appropriate response to that barren philosophy. There are different standards at work.

Irish theatre has challenged concealment and discrimination effectively in the past by discussing these issues through an artistic construction like when being Irish was accorded a lesser status of citizenship by Imperial powers. Gay theatre can hopefully contribute something similar in the liberation of gay people today.

The International Dublin Gay Theatre Festival presents gay life and culture for what it is to the widest possible audience in the most accessible way in a variety of programmes welcoming to many. When citizens are perceived as being different, then society can utilize this difference to discriminate. When such difference is deliberately constructed, what chances have the discriminated? One must take on those who insist on the negative stereotype and exploit that fear of difference to the advantage of the truth. One must present the 'feared' culture with confidence, professionalism and skill. Theatre enriches a civilized society. It is a forum where life can be portrayed and understood from its many diverse perspectives. It is a forum that informs and creates a space which allows the audience to make up its own mind.

Society can enable validation of marginalized identity by offering the supports granted to the mainstream lifestyles. The role of national arts and cultural funding bodies is crucial if citizenship, diversity, freedom of expression, communication and human rights are to be embedded in the core of a society – especially one which seeks to follow the values and human rights so eloquently and fairly set out in the Proclamation – namely, to cherish and treat all its citizens equally. The only principle should be the merit principle – the bedrock of equal opportunity – that will ensure good art.

The International Dublin Gay Theatre Festival has looked to national arts and cultural funding bodies to assist us in fulfilling our art form, our citizenship and our valid cultural expression to little avail. In 2006 in the anniversary month of 1916, I was very pleased, however, to acknowledge the only partnership we got from the arts and cultural institutions operating in Ireland that year and that was the generous support received from the British Council. This is not wholly unprecedented, as it was the British Council who helped establish the international reputation of the Edwards and Mac-Liammóir Productions by funding its European tours before World War Two. The Festival honours their contribution today by awarding the best male performance and best aspect of a production in their distinguished names.

Our task in this artistic visibility endeavour is not only to honour Oscar Wilde, Hilton Edwards, Micheál MacLiammóir, Eva Gore Booth, Patrick Murray, Aiden Rogers and others, but to create a channel where new artistic endeavour can thrive, inspire and enlighten. We seek works by gay authors, or that have a gay character, theme or relevance. We examine issues of gender identity, masculinity, and feminism to name a few.

The Festival is inclusive, accessible and great value. Men and women, old and young, regardless of their sexual orientation, are taking part. The audience is local, national and international. Sixty-four different nationalities attended Festival 2008. It is great that many foreign nationals see the inclusivity of gay culture as a welcoming place in a new country, be they straight or gay. Difference enriches us. With this Festival we seek to build bridges between Irish and international theatre practitioners and locally between gay people and mainstream audiences. We place ourselves firmly in the context of artistic value. Our founding 'catchcry' has been 'don't attend because it is gay theatre – attend because it is good theatre'.

This Festival is for anyone who wants to see, or be part of a modern, pluralist and accessible event. Not only do we endeavour to add to the already rich cultural arts landscape in Ireland, but hopefully we will entertain and help more people realize that difference enriches and fulfils the arts and a democratic society. A truly functioning arts sector in any democracy is one where all citizens can realize their human right and responsibility to participate openly, freely and generously. Our presence helps give a meaning to that noble concept too often consigned to print but more rarely realized in the delivery of national artistic planning.

The context for the fifth Festival was very clear – the President of Ireland very kindly sent us a message of support. President McAleese said, 'The Festival since its establishment in 2004 has served to build important bridges of cultural understanding across Irish society and to offer a fuller picture of cultural life on our island.' We are honoured, grateful and inspired by her insight and kindness. The contribution this event made to the European Year of Intercultural Dialogue in 2008 is also unique. The Festival will continue to facilitate and to inform the dialogue by gay people within Irish society. It will not censor or inhibit the freedom of expression, which when respectfully presented in good theatre, is so necessary to build understanding, and to open the closed minds, which so often condemn without ever listening, hearing or knowing what is being said.

The European Year of Intercultural Dialogue was a valid context for the Fifth International Dublin Gay Theatre Festival – one that embraces the challenge, along with many others, to dialogue with wider society and to explain who we are. It was appropriate that The European Year of Intercultural Dialogue is not narrowly defined or confined to visible diversity such as race or ethnic origin. It was an opportunity to give space to many diverse aspects of the cultures that co-exist on this Island. That is what this Festival does well. In Dublin City Council we met a willing partner.

We engage mainstream Ireland in a 'standards driven arts dialogue' which presents our culture and explores and discusses its characteristics, value and relevance through theatre as an art form. We have made a significant breakthrough in defining ourselves in 2008. At the 2008 Festival launch I spoke about our common culture – an argument made much more profoundly by Harry Hay as far back as the 1950s. The first Government Minister to launch our event, Eamon Ryan, TD, contributed to this affirmation as did Dublin City Council (DCC). With its modest resources Dublin City Council's arts policy, through Jack Gilligan and the Arts Committee, is a driving dynamic for accessible theatre. In July 2008, DCC's Declan Hayden went on to present a storytelling theatre production (The Intercultural Kitchen) to celebrate the year and included my own short work 'The Gentleman Caller' in the programme – the first time sexual orientation was included as a recognized culture in their intercultural dialogue. DCC also significantly sponsored a new Intercultural dialogue award which was won by 108 Productions from Los Angeles for their production of Terrence MacNally's *Corpus Christi* – which provoked an interesting religious dialogue during the Festival!

In the Festival we use the term gay as part of the concept of completing the whole identity of the artist. I am fully aware that there are gay artists, administrators and people who don't like, or are not comfortable with what we do – emphasizing the whole identity of the valuable contribution gay and lesbian people make to arts and society – clearly in the cultural context here, through theatre as an art form. They don't want to be included under that identifiable tag. Internalized and externalized homophobia, developed as a result of witnessing discrimination, is ongoing and deeply felt in Ireland.

The quality and richness of the art presented will help combat that barren homophobia, while entertaining and informing and challenging our diverse and growing audience. I hope too, that to bring the great success of brilliant artists who are also gay, might act as a positive role model for young people, who may yet live to see gay members of Aosdána's complete identity being included and recognized in the deserved laudatory acclamations and honours bestowed on them. It is not acceptable for society to laud the art and 'loath' the artist. This is the ongoing challenge of gay theatre.

This Festival and many other great gay community initiatives, are the best response to such learned negativity. I also run Mr Gay Ireland and Mr Gay Northern Ireland competitions as the Theatre Festival's charitable/civic/social initiative. This has been internally controversial and often dismissed as trivial. It supports HIV/AIDS while promoting self esteem amongst gay men. This event is a HIV/AIDS awareness and gay rights awareness raising initiative amongst a generation that never had a youth or educational service tailored for the needs of their emerging sexuality. It has raised over 90,000 euros in four years for gay and HIV causes and brings urban and rural communities together North and South to present positive and attractive images and voices of young gay men out and active in Irish society. Local newspapers like the *Sligo Advertiser* and the *Monaghan Post* have given their local Mr Gay great support by running ads and positive newspaper articles on the winners. Young gay isolated men and boys in rural communities read these positive articles which may help in replacing even one of the obituary notices of happy young men who inexplicably go missing or take their own lives, which happens far too often, especially – though not exclusively – in rural Ireland.

The winners of Mr Gay Ireland and Mr Gay Northern Ireland have gone on to achieve a spectacular record of success in Mr Gay Europe and Mr Gay International in the United States. These young men confidently represent gay Ireland abroad, often to disbelieving audiences about how much Ireland has actually changed! The fun event is a novel and lucrative way for the charities to engage this generation in gay rights and of course to raise significant sums and awareness for HIV/AIDS. There are few positive visual images of young gay Irish people – so we produce a charity calendar each year featuring the contestants. There are very few unmasked images of gay Ireland – even in visual art exhibitions of gay culture – the mask remains a key and colourful distraction or defense. Many of our masks as gay men are feminized by drag or colour. The Theatre Festival is clearly unmasked, happily including the drag and the colour!

The International Dublin Gay Theatre Festival has a motivation many other art activities do not – a passion and a necessity to succeed. As many non-theatre people as theatre people have stepped up to volunteer their services to run this huge event – 216 performances over 16 days in 2008 by companies from four continents. Change is controlled by the denial of resources, when 'permission' is vested in the chosen few. We challenge that denial by replacing the financial resource with the power and passion of those who are determined that change will triumph. That challenge is eventually drained by the denial of the resources for the event to expand and embed. The 100% volunteer element of the Festival has been the biggest earthquake for the 100% grant-aided sector to contend with, as our talent and commitment overcomes many obstacles put in our way – even deliberately by those threatened on two fronts – we challenge the societal norms in presenting and naming our culture and arts norms in presenting our art publicly. We did it because we wanted to, and we didn't seek permission from the establishment to offer a new art form to Irish theatre and to make a contribution to completing Ireland's cultural identity. There are some important quarters where we remain to be forgiven for such audacious innovation.

The Festival has had a very frustrating and unfruitful relationship with the Arts Council. On our 897th performance, a senior member of the Arts Council finally accepted the invitation of a friend and attended one of our events. Up to that time, their Council members had relied on 'insightful recommendations' about where taxpayers' money should be wisely spent from those who declined our invitations to attend. Gays and lesbians are the most highly taxed in our community, as we are entitled to fewer pension or welfare benefits than straight people get for the same tax contributions. Civil partnership will 'cost' the Exchequer the most conservative minimum of 25,000,000 euros a year – there is no mention of compensation for us having been forced to absorb that cost for the past century.

The arts continually help define the Irish as a nation and a race. Gay arts can do likewise. Theatre has a wonderful capacity to educate, inform and discuss issues, raising the veils on cherished taboos or unexplained norms, and enriching pluralism and diversity within society. Theatre as an art form is a key to liberating silenced voices, to encouraging emerging voices, to recognizing the capacity we have to contribute and the value of the contribution in a civilized society. It's a challenge that oils the wheels and drives forward our actions in this unique Festival of world theatre.

Our priority – new writing – this Festival's core value is a major contribution to the art form. It is not economically sensible to present 35 Irish premieres, but we have made it work. Each year we find a space for new playwrights. We have prioritized women writers/contributors as well. Katherine O Donnell from UCD, who brilliantly presented at our Seminars on Lesbianism and the arts, describes it as something that exists in the shadows of our society. We now have a space to help bring that contribution out of the shadows.

The Festival, thanks to contributions from Katherine, Sonja Tiernan, Naoise O Reilly, Vickey Curtis, Suzanne Lakes and Americans Carolyn Gage, Kerric Harvey and Kathleen Warnock amongst others, is willing to help turn the lights on for this important yet still inaudible voice. Lesbian theatre has the additional hurdle to overcome – one which keeps women artists and voices down, and the other which keeps gay artists down. We are proud of the work and effort we put in to encouraging new writing and of course in staging new works. All but one of the 35 plays staged in Festival 2008 had never been seen before in Ireland.

In 2008, if we had had the resources, and if we had accepted all submissions, we would actually have been bigger than the great programme presented each year by our good friends in the Dublin Fringe Festival. I had to 'stop counting' after receiving the 130th submission for 2008. We had submissions from Ireland, the UK, the US, Canada, Brazil, Mexico, Estonia, Germany, Italy, Netherlands, Senegal, Republic of South Africa, Israel, Cyprus and Australia. This is staggering for an event so young and so poorly financially resourced. This is wonderful for theatre, gay theatre, and audiences in Ireland. Within a month of the end of Festival 2008, we had already received our first submissions from Japan, Germany and the Czech Republic. Later Iran and Zimbabwe sent in proposals. They were amongst the thirty-six submissions to arrive within ten weeks immediately following the festival, and before we had even launched our submissions campaign for 2009.

Hundreds of authors and actors from around the world join in this discourse here in Dublin or across the worldwide web. All make great sacrifices to come to Dublin and present their work. Work premiered here is then brought to other countries. The number of repeat applications is most encouraging. They, along with our growing audience, are our shareholders – they are this Festival. The Festival has prompted great new theatrical activity in Ireland.

Outhouse, the gay and lesbian resource centre, proudly unveiled their new performance space in 105 Capel Street for this year's festival. We are delighted to have theatrically commissioned this project and helped them assist this wonderful initiative at a time when performance space is at a premium in the city.

In celebrating five years we were also celebrating our essence, that in these very self-centred times there are still people who will volunteer, or write and work passionately to create a better understanding of the true diversity that makes up the arts and every society. That is active citizenship. Many of us might and do achieve good things on our own, but we are truly great when we do it together, with and for our community, contributing to respect for all cultures and lifestyles in our wider pluralist society. In that, the contribution of straight people to this Festival is one of the healthiest dynamics that fuels the passion for this event and allows the full exploration of issues like sexuality, feminism, masculinity and gender identity. This Festival was never conceived as only a gay event – it was and has succeeded in becoming a mainstream event in the Irish arts calendar. The Festival and its gifted artists reach out and welcome all who want to hear our voice and who might value the incredible, but often invisible contribution, of gay artists to the arts and to society, past and present.

It is from that acknowledgement that artists and role models will emerge giving much needed guidance, inspiration and purpose to the future generations of young gay people – replacing the damage of homophobia in behaviour and policy, with a goal, purpose and acknowledgement of the special gift that every individual's sexuality and ability to love brings, when expressed fully and without fear, and acknowledged and respected equally in and by every person. It is from that that new voices will be encouraged and heard and new quality art presented.

The Festival and our artists will continue to work on and to challenge those who will not listen. Our mere presence does that, but the quality of the work presented is the key to getting the attention of narrowed minds. The denial of better access to arts funding is yet another barrier to overcome. We will continue to create the space for gay people and our many friends to express themselves in the arts, because we all are entitled to ownership of, and to contribute to, theatre as an art form. The contribution of straight people is one of the healthiest dynamics that fuels the passion for this event and allows the fuller exploration of issues like sexuality, feminism, masculinity and gender identity.

We will continue to encourage new writing, new companies, new stories, new performances and new voices – gay and straight, on subjects important and relevant to us and to society. We will continue to insist on playing our role as full and equal citizens and, by doing so, we will challenge those who actively undermine our human rights and our citizenship. This is still necessary in a country that in many ways is a shining beacon of growing respect for gay people, but which still struggles with our right to love, cherish and honour our chosen partner and to care, nurture and provide decent, safe, healthy and loving environments for our children.

The President of Ireland has said the Festival has served to build important bridges of cultural understanding across Irish society. It is our determination in building those bridges, that we now encourage everyone to join us in crossing those bridges, to participate and benefit from what the President has so generously described as our offer of 'a fuller picture of cultural life on our Island'. The International Dublin Gay Theatre Festival has modestly reached out across five continents to give a space to a voice that has struggled to be heard in many countries and is still not heard in many others today. The fact that we in Ireland can hear that voice further contributes to the real meaning of diversity in expression, perspective and experience in the arts in Ireland.

The Festival not only entertains our audiences but also informs them and equips them to contribute knowledgeably to the rights debate so frequently staged by the media and conservative moral ideology. They apparently represent middle Ireland when it is clear middle Ireland supports equality of rights to marriage and parenting. In sections of the media it is apparently an 'extreme' to want to get married in Ireland and one whose opinion can only be 'balanced' in a debate by those who believe gay people should be prohibited from marrying and should endure discrimination in legal rights, status and respect, in our pluralist democracy.

There are those who wish to continue to conceal our existence with the trite remark 'you are all legal now so what's the problem?' That problem is even presented to us by gay artists who lack the confidence to place their total and complete identity in their work. I hope this event also assists in the self-esteem and confidence-building necessary to overcome this internalized homophobia still evident in the Irish gay and artistic community.

Hilton Edwards and Micheál MacLiammóir certainly brought the notion of male partnership into Irish discourse, though in those days it was the business element of their joint work that primarily allowed people to give their lifelong relationship some, though not legal, recognition. The absence of, or the difficulty of tracing, other gay contributions to the Irish arts scene is a symptom of the Ireland of concealment that so suited religious and political agendas in the previous centuries. The Festival is trying to identify these contributors, such as the late great set designer and dance advocate from Cork, Patrick Murray, the late Shakespearian expert and professor of Drama at St Patrick's Teacher Training College, Dr Aiden Rogers, and scion of the revolutionary Gore-Booth family in Sligo – Eva, sister of Countess Markiewicz. We would like very much to hear of gay artists, living and long forgotten so that we can affirm them and their contribution to the arts today in some small way.

Unconstrained theatre allows you to present what you wish. An audience can choose to attend. We dim the lights and you can take in what you want, uninterrupted, for an hour or two. You will be entertained, you may learn, enjoy, connect, relax, laugh, cry, be reassured, enlightened or just survive it! Your thoughts are your own and you have the freedom to bring as much or as little as you wish from the theatre into your own life. This International Gay Theatre Festival is as liberating as that. It is not happening elsewhere in the world in such a specific internationalized format. It is driven by strong artistic standards, ambitions, and goals. Its increasing and diverse audiences ensure that this emerging space is sustained for the continuation of the opportunity to address and contribute to meeting the full challenge of the identification and recognition of gay culture and of its value to the arts and society.

An exclusionary 'vision' of the arts has allowed all arts spaces to fall to developers of apartment blocks, switched off audiences, and forced artists to become successful and skilful grant applicants, rather than creators of new innovative art. It would be incurable, but for the few brilliant people who see the dynamic of arts administration as the enabler of a struggling sector, despite all the obstacles put in their way by those who seek 'value' only through a monetary lens or peer reaffirmation. Happily we have been encouraged and inspired by some of these 'enablers' whose role in the arts world is invaluable and greatly appreciated by novice grant applicants like ourselves.

A key to the lack of challenge to this discretionary based policy is that many arts decision makers are all from the same class and the same circle. Ireland is a lot more than the view from the front room of the opulent Merrion Square, where diversity too often resides in the art form rather than the artist. Those set up to develop the arts and to protect it, presided over a decline of huge proportions, particularly in Dublin at a time of unprecedented economic growth. Those levels of resources may not be available in years to come. What did they achieve? Some arts administrators need to get out from their Georgian surroundings and accelerate their thought processes into the multicultural, diverse community that is Ireland today and to assist in new innovative ways to secure resources for the things we do well in the arts in Ireland. Otherwise what is their value?

The job goes beyond the responsibility to preserve our artistic heritage. It includes identifying new forms of artistic expression that reflect the new Ireland, a step beyond the old repertoire, done by the heavily long term grant-aided institutions and to secure resources for us all. No matter how many times that door is closed, Festivals like ours are a constant reminder to the blind eyes and laziness that we will be heard – and we all need to be heard if the arts in Ireland are to have a new sustainable dynamic.

The International Dublin Gay Theatre Festival fulfils the standards and criteria for arts funding – it's about time we got it in a meaningful and enabling way. Our experience to date with the Arts Council has been distasteful, lacks transparency and contributes to our development at a level of schoolyard gossip. Here is my brief understanding of the mixed messages we have been receiving to date. We were told in our third year that we were 'too new' to get funding. When we cheekily pointed out that their failure to fund any recognized gay art form might be misconstrued as 'homophobia' they promptly funded a new gay company, in a different genre, less than three months in existence! The IDGTF ticks many of their policy boxes: we create new audiences, we have a new vibrant volunteer base, we encourage and develop new writers, we create new space for new voices, all our companies are paid from the box office creating real employment, we network nationally and internationally. We long to have the resources to improve. We didn't get the grants or the attention – those who write the reports to Council have yet to make it to one of our 897 performances – you can make your own assessment about that!

In 2007, we had another long good meeting with them and they agreed it was in order to apply for revenue funding and a specific figure was discussed. The subsequent 'recommendation' to Council was on the lines that we were not suitable for revenue funding but that we were being funded under another scheme. The recommendation was that they should meet us and explore this! We had done the meetings – followed the advice and had never been previously funded. To this day, polite correspondence remains unacknowledged.

Our Arts Council funding, received on foot of an erroneous report to the Council in 2007, is 5,000 euros. It has remained static in the face of enormous growth in our event. It cost us 5k to meet their accounting requirements in the first year! There has been some 'regime change' in this body and we hope for a more productive hearing as we enter our second five years. It is important to note the consistent greater support received from Dublin City Council and Faílte Ireland through Dublin Tourism since our inception – in fact I like to think we have been instrumental in encouraging Dublin Tourism to have a gay-specific page on their website. The support of the Theatre Forum, the Dublin Theatre and Fringe Festivals, the Project Arts Centre, Smock Alley, The INTO and our other venues has been very encouraging.

Happily, this lack of perspective as to who makes up this nation does not exist everywhere but it is part of the international struggle for gay artists. We are being heard in five continents, in the embassies (e.g., Israel, Italy) and arts organizations (Governor Of Illinois Arts Fund, British Council, Artscape New Writing Programme South Africa), in production companies, in the output of playwrights in five continents, in our own city, just ... not properly in the national arts funding organization. I believe that also has a somewhat negative effect on Irish companies participating in the festival when they see it being accorded such a low value by a portion of the arts establishment.

Our participating companies have been aided by their own cultural institutions in every country except Ireland. These foreign institutions examine our track record, our output, our standards, and to our delight, recognize their value. They offer financial support to people in their own country to travel to Ireland to participate in this unique event in the birthplace of Oscar Wilde. Frequently the financial aid given to visit us for one week far exceeds the total given to us locally to run the event for a year.

Foreign arts bodies clearly see the value of this event, even from such a distance, many even travel to attend and learn more, and we gratefully acknowledge that. Such interaction enriches our work in so many ways.

But we cannot criticize too much – the arts are a tight, closed circle where grace and favour are often as legitimate a currency as artistic merit and value. In finding ourselves continually without meaningful State arts assistance, this has impacted on our ability to present even higher standards of work from more diverse regions including within Ireland. We had five applications from Australia in 2007 and, with even modest support, some would have been on our programme. I say modest because the commitment of all the participating companies is the main driving force for their participation in this unique event. They see the dynamic, appreciate the standards, are excited by the intercultural learning and networking, are open to new perspectives, are inspired by new writing, informed by our educational programme, and appreciated by our audiences – hence they make a financial sacrifice to participate too.

Every year, men and women of all ages and cultures, straight and gay, tell me the festival is valid and worthwhile. Every year they come back in increased numbers. We survey our audience and over 3,500 forms have been filled in each year giving the Festival productions an 87% excellent rating (5/5). It is in their defence that I reject the exclusionary attitudes of those who look into their own hearts and see Ireland. None of us can afford that outdated analysis today.

Most importantly, as long as we create a valid artistic channel and continue to inspire generous volunteers, we are here and are here to stay. We will drive forward this event because we have something of value to give to the arts, to our living, to diverse democracy, to our own community, to the society to which we contribute an enormous amount, and to you. We do so out of a passion, a commitment and a drive that would infuse and re-energize many an arts event. We have reached out way beyond our country and our community and we have inspired an international response which we have spared no physical effort to accommodate. That is art. This is a living culture. The International Dublin Gay Theatre Festival is a cultural event that will bring people together to define and to present Irish and international gay theatre in the years to come, which will inform debate and assist those who strive to change cold hearts and closed minds. Join us for the first fortnight in May every year in Dublin. www.gaytheatre.ie

8 | Sexuality and the Dysfunctional City: Queering Segregated Space.

Niall Rea

In this chapter I look at an emergent gay sexual identity in Belfast twenty years ago at the height of the conflict in Northern Ireland. I will cast a 'queer' eye backwards to this particular time and place, basing the study primarily on the script of an unstaged community play and its location within contemporaneous theatrical practice. Through interviews with the playmakers and others on the circumstances surrounding this play's construction, its eventual non-performance and their memories of war-torn Belfast, I will detail a hidden moment in the queer history of Ireland and its wider repercussions on a particular dysfunctional society and place.

In 1988 Belfast Community Theatre (BCT), a populist and successful Nationalist theatre company based at Conway Mill, West Belfast, began work on a new production, *Ecce Homo*. Ostensibly taking as its theme gay liberation, this could be seen as a surprising change of direction for the company, given the Nationalist aims that had underpinned their work up to this point and the conservative, Catholic background of its audience demographic. The then theatrical collaborator of the company and future academic, Bill McDonnell, deals briefly with the circumstances of this planned production in his article 'A Good Night out on the Falls Road: Liberation Theatre and the Nationalist Struggle in Belfast 1984-1990', noting that the play 'could not have been more alien to its community's belief system, or more apparently marginal to the overall Nationalist struggle'.[1]

In further examining Belfast Community Theatre's praxis, the impetus that led to the company tackling the production of *Ecce*

Homo and its position in their body of work, identity politics and
the realization of a civil rights agenda emerge as the through-line
that follows from the earlier productions into this seemingly 'queer'
direction for the company. The emergent gay identity of the 1980s
in Belfast can be understood through the methodology of queer
theory, specifically the concepts of 'queer space' and 'queer
memory.' The word queer is employed here as meaning that which
works contra to heteronormative perspectives. In the dysfunctional
urban geography of segregated communities, the formation of a
'queer space' in the centre of Belfast had an important desegregating
effect. The formative use of the desegregated city centre space, as
alluded to in the script of *Ecce Homo* itself, by both the queer
community and other desegregated identities, notably the punks, is
central to my argument. A comparison is drawn between this
desegregated space along with its associated alternative identities,
and the affluent space of middle-class identity in south Belfast.

My approach is framed within the notion of queer memory: what
is to be achieved as a queer historian looking back twenty years on
at this community play that, at the last minute, the company
decided not to stage? Further, why exactly was the production of the
play abandoned and does that really matter? David Cregan posits
that 'Queer historians, by identifying and uncovering previously
hidden gay and lesbian experiences, have initiated a type of cultural
revolution by juxtaposing queer memory with heteronormative
histories.'[2] While its non-performance was hidden, uncovering this
play's existence reveals a key convergence of theatre, community,
geography and queer identity in Northern Ireland in the 1980s and
by placing it alongside the 'straight' history of the time this study
seeks to provide a 'queer' perspective on that history.

Belfast Community Theatre flourished for a few years in the late
1980s, at a time when 'The Troubles' in Northern Ireland were going
through one of their worst phases. Tony Flynn, one of the main
members of BCT, describes Belfast as 'a powder-keg waiting to go
off – a cauldron'[3] of sectarian tension and political strife. Bally-
murphy, where the theatre company was based, is the heart of West
Belfast geographically; to its north is part of the longest 'peaceline'
in Europe dividing it from a loyalist/Protestant area. In this
economically deprived area of the city, BCT was a politicized,
interventionist community theatre that was absolutely embedded in
its locale, at a time when its community members were caught up in
all-out armed conflict. Beyond this localized frame, it was also

aligned to the practices and principles of the radical community theatre of mainland United Kingdom of the 1970s and 1980s, Baz Kershaw elucidates:

> The companies making this theatre aimed to combine art and action, aesthetics and pragmatics. Often they were dealing with material – stories, documentary information, images and so on – inscribed with questions of fundamental importance to their audiences. Always their starting point was the nature of their audience *and its community*. The aesthetics of their performances were shaped by the culture of their audience's community.[4]

Belfast Community Theatre's radical and culturally incisive methodology was born out of their long-standing practice as community workers in West Belfast.

Joe Reid, community activist and founder member of BCT, is adamant that theatre has a role in exploring ideas central to the community's concerns and highlighting any important issues: 'The Troubles' were the main issue at the time and, to break away from the feeling of being powerless, theatre meant you had a voice.'[5] In exploring the use of this voice, Reid and the group consciously presented the community not as a homogeneous monolithic nationalist/Catholic identity but rather stressed that it was made up of a continuum of identities of various political viewpoints within its segregated construct. He insists that 'you must have an awareness that your voice is full of your own contradictions'.[6] Reid's point is confirmed in a recent sociological and spatial examination of Belfast's 'segregated communities' by Peter Shirlow and Brendan Murtagh who suggest that:

> it could be argued that highly segregated communities contain diverse populations that reject/partly reject or accept symbolic representations and discursive hegemonies that are related to wider ethno-sectarianized discourses.[7]

Within the company and its artistic collaborators, there was an extreme degree of variation in republican sympathies, from mild nationalist tendencies, through Marxist socialism, to actual IRA volunteers: volunteer Mairead Farrell, a key advisor to the company during their production of *Sign on the Dotted Line* in 1987 (Figure 10),[8] was later shot dead in 1988 by members of the British SAS in Gibraltar.[9] For Reid, their empowering, political and community-based approach was a tool for the examination of the plurality and contradictions of identity within this localized, segregated culture;

and crucially of the civil rights of *all* these identities. Reid's vision for the transformative power of this kind of theatre is absolute: There is no such phrase as waiting for freedom, justice, equality. These phrases are given to us by those who would have us wait. Take what is ours! Theatre is our weapon![10]

The immediate and local effects of this intervention were felt in the powerful and intimate plays that they toured around many working class venues in Belfast and beyond – mostly in bars and social clubs. David Grant, lecturer in Drama at Queen's University Belfast and then editor of *Theatre Ireland*, reviewed one of their most successful productions, Ulick O'Connor's *Execution,* in 1988. He commended the company saying that 'to craft so attention holding a production of so difficult a text ... was a considerable achievement.' and noted that 'this was an exceptional experience' after which 'the room erupted in enthusiastic discussion'.[11] The subject matter of O'Connor's play was the execution of four IRA men in 1922, by the fledgling Irish government, in reprisal for the assassination of one of its ministers. The struggle among the various factions of nationalism during the birth of a nation and this bloody resolution would have struck home resoundingly in the minds of their besieged West Belfast audience, creating public discourse about the ongoing, intense and sometimes violent disagreement amongst the various factions of republicanism both north and south of the border. This kind of interventionist community theatre, at its most powerful, seeks to affect its audience's ideas, attitudes and their future actions. The 'enthusiastic discussion' described by Grant adheres to the aims outlined by Kershaw:

> By tailor-making performances for known audiences these companies hoped to change those audiences in some way, however marginally. Not only that: if a number of audiences in similar types of community, in a specific sub-region, could be changed by such a show, there might be a wider effect.[12]

It was not surprising that this theatre was largely unreported by mainstream media at the time. Its oppositional cultural practices were fundamentally challenging to contemporaneous hegemonic discourses and Grant's review marks a rare appearance by the company in the theatrical press.

One might initially suppose that to move on to a 'gay liberation' play from this successful production about the bloody birth of the Irish state was a startling change of direction. Actually, there was a clear progression through the previous productions that leads directly to *Ecce Homo*. For example, the production before *Execution, Sign on the Dotted Line,* examined women's rights using the subject matter of strip-searching at the local women's prison. For the company it was clear that all the issues they dealt with were issues of civil rights and the infringements of them. Marie McKnight, a founder member of the company, clarifies their decision to work on a gay rights theme:

> We had been looking at people who were marginalized and we decided to look at gay issues because a number of our group were gay and had been doubly marginalized because of this. We had raised the 'unraiseable' before, so we felt we were in the best position to tackle this issue.[13]

For BCT gay liberation was one issue that could not be separated out from a general liberation agenda. They used the coming out experiences of two of their main actors, Tony Flynn and Gerard Mc Laughlin to construct a script supporting these performers' civil rights within their own republican community. This company was part of a politically very sophisticated community and as Mc Donnell points out:

> At this time you were beginning to get an important rethinking of republican views on gay rights, women's rights, gender politics more generally, led by male and female IRA prisoners in Maghaberry and the Maze prisons. So the BCT work was not an isolated gesture but part of a wider intellectual/cultural revaluation by important formations within republicanism.[14]

Reid goes further, saying categorically that this was *not* a gay liberation play but a play about 'rights, entitlements and dignity'.[15] Given that their productions were intensely debated among the group, and would have been shown in rehearsed readings to the wider Nationalist community at Conway Mill, including members of Sinn Fein, then this new production was an important symbol of this 're-valuation'. Martin Lynch, the well-known Belfast play-wright, described this quiet *volte-face* that the republican move-ment and Sinn Féin in particular were undertaking during this period.

Through the 1970s and into the 1980s they [Sinn Féin] were conservative and right wing in their leadership, but in the late 1980s their liberalization and political evolution were mirrored by the rows on women's rights and abortion in the Ard Fheis.[16]

The Sinn Féin party of the 1970s was far removed from their perceived current position as the most pro-gay rights political party in the north of Ireland (see their landmark 1996 document on gay rights *Moving On: A Policy for Lesbian, Gay, Bisexual Equality*). This radical shift is illustrated in their response to the fledgling gay rights movement, which had approached various members of the first Stormont devolved government for support:

> It sent circulars to members of the ill-fated power-sharing assembly in 1974; 63 did not reply, and of the 14 that did, only two alliance members appeared mildly sympathetic but said they felt 'unqualified to act'. A Sinn Féin spokesman asserted, 'There has never been a homosexual republican.'[17]

This fallacy was later to be exploded spectacularly by the foremost Northern Irish gay rights activist of the time, Jeffrey Dudgeon, in his book *The Black Diaries of Roger Casement* (2002). It was Dudgeon who successfully took the NI office to the European court of human rights in 1981, resulting in the legalization of homosexuality in the province in 1982. His was also the case cited in the successful David Norris v Ireland human rights judgment which took place in 1988; the same year BCT were working on *Ecce Homo*. The wider republican movement would have been aware of the Norris case and it was also in the background of the minds of the BCT theatre-makers themselves.

After the 1981 legal watershed there had been examples of homosexual characters on the Ulster stage,[18] but their sexuality was not central to the themes of the play. A reticence remained about the tackling of themes of gay liberation directly – rather homosexuals were at best just headline-grabbing incidental characters. There was a scandalous case the year before work on *Ecce Homo* began, when a large section of the Lyric Theatre audience walked out *en masse* from a preview of Robert Glendinning's play *Mumbo Jumbo,* which featured a graphic homosexual encounter between two teenage schoolboys. Against this context BCT approached gay sexuality not as sensational but to propose a radical alignment between the rights of gay individuals as equal in consideration to all other civil rights issues. This was the central purpose of *Ecce Homo.*

The BCT play tells the story of a young gay man, Emanuel, struggling with the idea of coming out to his family. He has a secure relationship with his boyfriend and they are trying to move to a new flat together. His mother initially assumes that he wants to 'live in sin' with his punk 'girlfriend' whom she also assumes to be pregnant. She is devastated when she learns the truth and she turns to her local priest for support. When Emmanuel eventually comes out to his father he is disowned completely. *Ecce Homo* is a powerful title, and is thematically and structurally at the heart of the play. The phrase 'ecce homo,' or 'behold the man' can be interpreted as equating the struggle of the gay man ('homo') with that of any oppressed man (*homo*). That these are the words of Pontius Pilate presenting Christ in crown of thorns to a hostile crowd before his crucifixion becomes a way of thematically challenging the 'belief system' of the community. A harrowing, arguably blasphemous, image of Christ as a victim of homophobic attacks is presented by the main character.

> **EMANUEL**. I saw the crucified Christ three days ago. He did not hang by the cross, but lay instead on a Belfast street. There were no nails in His limbs, no crown of thorns, no open wounds. The Queer-bashers had left nothing. But a gaping gash upon His head. And He did not cry: 'Forgive them, Lord;' but only lay there, gazing at the rain-filled sky.[19]

There follows a strong structural build, through scenes of rejection and defiance, towards an ending in which the gay men at the centre of the play are placed in front of the audience, with the challenge to set them on fire with a match; a direct rewriting of the idea of throwing the first stone or shouting 'crucify them'. Rather than the audience being asked to feel sympathy for the central protagonists, they are asked, powerfully, to examine their own complicity in the image of this homophobic attack.

Further following this biblical allusion the script subtly references narratives well known to Catholic audiences. The names of the characters reinforce the close integration of religious imagery and theatrical thematics: Emanuel, the protagonist, who 'comes out', is the son of 'Mary' and 'Joe'. In some interpretations, the name Emanuel refers to the Messiah, Jesus or 'God amongst us'. His lover in the play is Simon, whose name is interpreted in a wide variety of ways, including 'there is sin', in reference to a type of (sexual) relationship that rabbinical sources regard as sinful. Other characters include Emanuel's punk friend Veronica and his two workmates on the building site, Peter and Thomas. All these character names would have referenced gospel narratives in their expected audience demographic. But religious imagery out of context was not as blasphemous to the audience as one might first think. It had been used extensively by republican activists in its portrayal of the hunger strikers in the early 1980s on wall murals and in graphic media (Figure 11).

This use of biblical names is part of a cohesive dramaturgy resulting in what comes across most strongly in the play: anger directed at the (Roman Catholic) church, along with the pusillanimity of a community that continues to hold on to beliefs and social systems that do not support the inclusion of alternative lifestyles and choices. In fact, *Ecce Homo* reads as a socialist passion play, in which the decision for the ending of whether to 'crucify' the 'man' is thrown open as an active challenge for the audience, rather than the passive re-enactment of a well-known plot with the expectation that the audience will follow the prescribed outcome. This imperative demands that the audience think beyond mythologized narratives. It is a 'coming out' story, but 'coming out' as a political, as well as personal, act. It is a narrative belonging very much to a stage in gay liberationist struggle founded in identity politics, and formulated within a particular political theatre dramaturgy, based on the methodologies of Brecht and Boal. Typical narrative interruption devices are used to prevent illusion such as the use of the narrator, direct audience address, the use of song/music, and short scenes separated by blackouts. In Reid's introductory notes he marks the play as a Brechtian *Lehrstück*:

> This text should be seen and performed for what it is; a learning play based on the experience of working class people in Belfast, Ireland. Wherever possible no opportunity to involve the audience should be missed, and at all times no illusion allowed to be created.[20]

In interview both Reid and Mc Knight stress that the epic theatre format of the script was the important change of direction for the company, not the subject matter. At no point did they want the audience to feel sorry for the characters, but rather 'it was important to explore a non-naturalistic style and the resultant empathy and engagement rather than sympathy'.[21] In using the day-to-day experiences of their gay actors, they also followed the Boal technique of breaking repression by relating the actual lived oppression of an individual to the oppression of the larger group. The individual civil rights issues tackled in *Ecce Homo* were crucially aligned, by the company, to the civil rights of everybody in the community.

The civil rights marches of the late 1960s and their brutal suppression were the spark that had ignited 'The Troubles'. Indeed the pursuit of civil rights and entitlements was the mortar that held together the multiplicity of nationalist identities, of whatever persuasion, regardless of their preferred methodologies for achieving these rights. But to what extent could the rights of an emerging gay identity in the north of Ireland have been accepted by the two monolithic segregated identities of British loyalism (majority Protestant population) and Irish nationalism (minority Catholic population)? Holding an identity that was seen as removed from this atavistic binary was problematic. As Shirlow and Murtagh explain: 'The construction of sectarianized affiliation casts those who do not accept cultural affiliation and repetitive ethno-sectarian discourses as both deviant and treacherous.'[22]

The 'treacherous' position of having non-segregated affiliations outside of the monolithic cultural identities was taken up by queers and, amongst others, punks. And this alternative identity was also geographically constructed within the city. There was, throughout Belfast, the notion of spaces outside one's known ethno-sectarian boundaries being estranged and dangerous. This was most clearly made manifest by the British government's imposed solution of the 'Ring of Steel'. An area of around a square mile of commercial and office buildings in the city centre was cordoned off using high steel fences with heavy-duty revolving pedestrian gates and patrolled security barriers. Apart from the area around the university, and the ironically titled 'golden mile' of Great Victoria street that ran between the two, this was the main place where bars and clubs remained completely outside the segregated norms that had been established elsewhere in the separated communities. Once the shops and offices in this area closed, the ringed off city centre was quickly vacated. There was a certain *frisson* of danger attached to the exploration of the deserted space within the steel barriers themselves that intensified the experience. To occupy defiantly the estranged, vacated space 'between segregation' was a punk statement and, within a contemporary understanding of 'queer' as an anti-normative strategy, could be seen as a 'queering' of that space. This estranged spatial notion is, I believe, central when considering an emergent queer identity during the conflict.

The suspicion of space outside the regulated sectarian boundaries is dealt with implicitly in *Ecce Homo*. The mother of the central character, Emanuel, is unhappy about her son frequenting the centre city venues. Speaking at a point in the story when her son has not yet come out to her, she frets:

> **MOTHER.** I wonder where he's away to now. One of them
> clubs in town I suppose ... I don't like him going into that
> town.[23]

And the mother's worries about her son are later confirmed when
he is confronted by a squad of homophobic UDR[24] men, patrolling
the security barriers around the infamous 'Ring of Steel'. The few
gay venues were either within or just outside its security barriers. A
direct route from whichever neighbouring community to these
venues would take you through this ring and avoid the 'other' ethno-
sectarian community's area. The UDR ask Emanuel and his friend
which bar they are coming from, and when the answer is a known
gay venue they react viciously.

> **UDR-MAN.** Up against that fucking wall nancy Boys ... Now
> spread them, oh I forgot you'd know all about that ... You're
> both experts I bet ... (*Manoeuvres Gun Between Legs of
> Emmanuel/Simon*) I bet you love that don't you? You perverts
> fucking disgust me ... Now don't be getting all worked up
> boys... there'll be no frisking tonight, too risky ... I don't want to
> get infected now do I? I'm sure the Special Branch will be
> interested in two closet queens ... opens up all sorts of
> possibilities for them so to speak. Doubtless you'll be getting a
> wee visit in the near future ... After all I am sure you'd both be
> very co-operative in ensuring that no-one finds out your little
> secret. Night, night Boys ... [25]

Contemporaneous theatrical practice reveals other examples of
characters crossing these ethno-sectarian boundaries, where theatrical space and scenography tackle the issues of segregation of
identity. The geographical embodiment of this 'treacherous' position
between the two identities is perhaps illustrated by the isolated
house in Stewart Parker's most successful play *Pentecost*, which had
had its premiere production by Field Day theatre company in 1987.
The theatre practitioners of BCT were familiar with this remarkable
production performed the year before work on *Ecce Homo* began.
Here were four characters, two Protestant, two Catholic, of different
backgrounds finding a way to exist together in an abandoned house,
in a derelict street, at a flashpoint in the imploding city. Civil rights
are crucially fore-grounded by the returning of the exiled
(Protestant) character Peter in the last scene, as the 1974 riots rage
around him.

> **PETER.** Six years ago, I was standing in a human chain
> encircling a building. It was in America ... a university. Black

students had seized the building and had smuggled in guns, the police were lined up in their hundreds, ready to storm it. Me and a few score of other white liberals had put our bodies in between, holding hands with each other, armed blacks behind us and armed cops in front ... it was scary as hell.[26]

Parker was intentionally refocusing attention on the roots of the conflict – the civil rights marches of the late 1960s. The four characters in this abandoned house are occupying the space between the two communities that had been closed down as the two factions distanced themselves from one another. This middle-ground position of the mixed city space had been gradually estranged and disabled by the conflict. 'The neighbours leaving one by one, blind houses blocked up behind them, the street gradually silenced.'[27] This deaf and blind house is the last refuge of these variously damaged human beings but is also in the end their succour and life-giving home. Parker is pointing us to the rediscovery of the place between the monolithic Northern Irish identities as a way forward and an attention to our shared civil rights as the methodology for this: an ambition shared by BCT. This rediscovered place made concrete, in the disabled centre city, among empty and abandoned buildings was becoming occupied in the 1980s by the queer community; most notably in the abandoned dance halls of an earlier era.

For Reid and BCT this alignment with international civil rights causes was a crucial introduction to the subject of gay liberation, and they drew the audience's attention to this with the most simple of spatial solutions. In the introduction to the script of *Ecce Homo*, Reid outlines the segregation of the audience seating area with signs saying niggers, queers, Jews, women, lesbians, Irish. The individual spectator's act of choosing a position was a political act, and its consequences had to be carefully considered. The dangerously scary position of 'put[ting] our bodies in between' two warring factions, that Peter outlines in Pentecost, was echoed by the prominent nationalist Belfast politician Gerry Fitt when he said, 'If you stand in the middle of the road you will get knocked down.'[28] Fitt was alluding to the position 'in the middle' of reconciliation that he tried to occupy politically in the mid 1970s.

To leave one's segregated area in order to occupy this position 'in the middle' was a difficult road to travel, but was crucial to the world building practices of the newly emerging gay community. The other community that marched out of their segregated areas and reclaimed this city space were the punks. The strange appearance of Emanuel's punk 'girlfriend' Veronica is described by his suspicious mother:

> **MOTHER**. She's a bad egg that'n ... All that coloured hair and her clothes ... Jesus she ... [29]

Martin Lynch points out that being a punk was an extremely anti-sectarian position and not just in its day-to-day practicalities but also 'extreme punk identity was stronger here and lasted longer here, they [punks] were saying 'We don't like what we see here. We don't like this sectarian shit. Fuck that.' Punks deliberately and conspicuously marched out of their own districts.[30] Whereas in the rest of the UK and the US the alienated cultural space that briefly fostered punk was closed down by commercial absorption, in Belfast this alienated space that punks (and queers) occupied, was the space that was defiantly re-constructed outside of the segregated binary by subsequent alternative generations.

Marching out of one's own ethno-sectarian area could often be problematic. In the confrontation between Emanuel and Simon with the soldiers at the security checkpoint, as well as touching on issues around the fear of AIDS, the UDR man also hints at the darker side of living as a homosexual in a war zone. The homophobic soldier warns the two unfortunate gay men that they can expect a visit from the Special Branch (the elite detective squad of the British Police concerned with political security). Homophobic blackmail at this time in Belfast was used not as a tool for the extortion of money from the unfortunate gay man or woman, but rather as a method of gaining information about the activities of one side or the other in the conflict. Marie Mc Knight talks of the idea that 'even though homosexuality had been decriminalized several years earlier, the murky world of homosexuality being used against someone still existed dependent on your family background. There was still the notion of leaving your sexuality at the door.'[31]

At this point it is important to re-address the notion of the desegregated queer space in the centre of Belfast. Although it did provide an area where the gay community could come together, it also provided a locus for homophobic hate crime. There was perhaps a sense that the ideologically abject is made material by this geographical sectioning, in the creation of a 'gay ghetto,' but, as Tony Flynn recounts, there was a fervent desire to get into the town and attend these illicit venues. When the English director John

Goodchild, from the Sheffield community group Theatreworks who often collaborated with BCT, visited in 1988 he was shocked by this determination. One night, around the time of the rehearsal period for *Ecce Homo*, he shared a taxi down the Falls road in West Belfast. This second-hand London black taxi was one of many that are a primary public transport option along the most troubled roads. The taxi steered in and out of roadblocks and abandoned vehicles. As they reached the bottom of the Whiterock Road hill a burning vehicle came hurtling down towards the taxi. The driver sped up and the burning car just missed them, passing behind. He couldn't understand why the journey was continuing. But John's companions in the taxi were five recently out young gay men and nothing was going to keep them from their night out, which, as Flynn points out, 'says an awful lot about growing up in a place like that. That it takes an awful lot to stop you going out and doing what you want to do.'[32] In the pursuit of this dangerous marginal world-making enterprise, this alternative queer identity was adopting what queer theorist Jose Esteban Muñoz describes as,

> The strategies and rituals that allow survival in such hostile cultural waters, and in turn feel a certain compulsion to try to articulate and explicate these practices of survival. These practices are the armaments such children and the adults they become use to withstand the disabling forces of a culture and state apparatus bent on denying, eliding and, in too many cases, snuffing out emergent identity practices.[33]

I would go further and suggest that in Northern Ireland the formation of this emergent identity and its associated geographies was an example of a positive desegregated identity as opposed to the negative desegregated identity of the affluent middle classes of south Belfast.

It had long been the case that leaving Northern Ireland was the primary strategy of those wishing to escape the conflict. Exit could be in a number of ways, emigration to US, moving to mainland Britain or relocating south of the border. There was also an exit strategy within the city itself, to the affluent area around and to the south of the university. But these options were open primarily to educated members of society and the employed. This led to the process, as later perceived by Shirlow and Murtagh, of a 'hollowing out' of the middle ground politically in the segregated areas left behind, as those remaining were the less educated, the less well off and were more likely to hold a more extreme political position. This 'hollowing out' could often leave a more segregated community behind – as if only the polar opposites remain in the economically more deprived areas of the city. And further, in the more socially affluent parts of the city the concern of the middle-class desegregated identity is 'driven more by the collective protection and enhancement of property prices and less by atavistic ethnic claims'.[34] This apparently separatist attitude and lack of concern in well-to-do south Belfast, notably the very wealthy Malone Road, during the conflict had been lampooned in a famous socialist poster in the 1970s (Figure 12).

Queer (and punk) identity construction was a cross-community enterprise, and to be punk or gay was not the privilege of the educated or affluent classes. The everyday performance of these identities crossed over the atavistic structures and assaulted the binary monoliths of Northern Irish identity but yet they remained embedded, to a large extent, in their own communities. As subordinate group identities they subverted from within. The subversive quality of this identity was harnessed by *Ecce Homo* in its questioning of the conservative republicanism of the 1970s and early 1980s as embodied by the character of the father recently released from prison where he had been interned without trial.

> **EMANUEL.** And why were you interned Da? As I remember it you called yourself a Freedom Fighter … Were you fighting for the freedom of all or just yourself?
> **FATHER.** That's not the point …
> **EMANUEL.** But that's exactly the point … who were you fighting for?[35]

Reid and BCT are adamant that the republican Nationalist movement, with which their company was intimately linked, should not marginalize any identity within itself as this risked undermining their own legitimacy as based on the bedrock of universal civil rights and entitlements. In his examination of cultural contestation in ethnic conflict Mark Howard Ross underlines the performance of identity as crucial to the tenuous position that these sub-groups held.

> Dominant and subordinate groups that feel threatened can use performance to communicate identities that define boundaries between themselves and outsiders and can make it more or less difficult to become a group member or hold multiple identities.[36]

The fact that in the end *Ecce Homo* was never staged is perhaps less important than the fact that the company decided to work on it at all; researching the ability to hold multiple identities and promoting the rights of a doubly marginalized sub-group. There were two main reasons for the lack of a final performance. Firstly Reid and McKnight both felt that the non-naturalistic format was problematic and needed more work before a successful staging. Up to this point the company had been used to a more realistic documentary style of performance. Secondly, Tony Flynn, one of the main performers, got a professional acting job in Dublin and Reid felt strongly that the play could not have been recast, but had to be performed by the original company on whose lived experience the script was based.

When the wider field of extra-theatrical performance studies is applied, however, the performance that actually did happen that year was extraordinary: that of a crucial Republican funeral procession that ended in tragedy. This funeral can, perhaps, be examined using performance related methodology, alongside an examination of cultural identity. As Janelle Reinelt proposes: 'In particular, I am convinced that many aspects of what we have considered extra-theatrical experience can be grasped in terms of, understood by reference to, made intelligible through performance paradigms.'[37]

In march of that year Flynn and fellow BCT actor Gerard Mc Laughlin had carried a wreath for one of the Gibraltar three; Mairead Farrell, a consultant on *Sign on the Dotted Line*. It was at this funeral that grenades were thrown into the crowd of mourners by the loyalist paramilitary Michael Stone, killing three and wounding many. At the time of these tragic incidents there was a vocal censorship ban in place on Sinn Féin from mainstream media. Images could be seen of Gerry Adams and other republicans but they were unable to speak directly to the camera or the microphone. The visual and performative power of the mass demonstration/funeral was a crucial public face of the Nationalist republican community.

The crowd that followed the three coffins was immense, and silent. It included many elderly people, women and young children. Black flags lined the route, and hundreds of people stood silently waiting to join the cortège, many red-eyed from weeping, and some openly in tears ... the silence was shattered by the thud-thud-thud of grenades. Terrified mourners dived for cover.[38]

Tony and Gerard were representatives of a community that felt under siege in a rapidly deteriorating war zone where cultural conflict was spiralling out of control.

The very public representation of a community arts group by two gay men at such a large demonstration should be seen as an important moment in local queer history and may be examined as a queer cultural performance in and of itself. Even if the crowd did not realize that they were gay, their sanctioned appearance here was groundbreaking, if only for the fact that the actors felt the confidence to represent their community. Within the cultural performance of the funeral procession – the acceptance and public display of this queer identity marked a shift and perhaps an acceptance of the need for change within the dominant group Republican identity. This fragile acceptance, though, was shattered by the events that followed in the cemetery. This community under attack understandably retrenched its fundamental positions and fractured subordinate identities were passed over.

In remembering this seemingly minor part of a much larger politically and socially devastating event, this research seeks to affirm the place of queer identity within that community at that time and its wider social effect. As the current post-conflict situation now gradually stabilizes and historical conclusions are drawn, it is important to follow David Cregan's arguments that:

> Queer memory is transformative as it seeks to destabilize the solidification of any particular version of the past. It offers a self-reflective and socially challenging voice in the midst of memory formation, queering marginalized memory as well as the memory of the dominant.[39]

How should we remember BCT's praxis in the midst of that turbulent year? They were saying to their audience: 'Behold the man, behold the gay man, behold their place within our community, behold our common civil rights.' And in turn this emergent queer identity was saying to the dysfunctional society: 'Behold the disabled place in the middle that you have forgotten – that you have abandoned – this is where we can meet to resolve our differences.'

A few years later another community theatre group, Derry Frontline, produced a play called *Time Will Tell*, which, while not a gay liberation play as such, featured the prominent character of a lesbian daughter. Although the process did not go completely smoothly, it did reach performance. The part of the daughter had to be recast a number of times as three young actresses faced family pressure to withdraw; the group were based in a staunchly republican neighbourhood. The resultant production, however, broke many taboos and was symptomatic of the seismic shift that had taken place in Republicanism. The production director Dan Baron Cohen speaks poetically of the new 'queer' space metaphorically opened up on the first night production:

> The community centre had been transformed into a new space of empathy by an uncontrollable laughter which transgressed centuries of prohibition. Republican guerrillas and gay activists passed through the checkpoints together that marked the frontiers of their ghettoes.[40]

The queering of segregated space then was both symbolic and physical in that it occupied an abandoned area of the city and established perhaps a theoretical place of communion between segregated identities.

---

[1] Bill Mc Donnell, 'A Good Night out on the Falls Road: Liberation Theatre and the Nationalist Struggle in Belfast 1984-1990', *Radical Initiatives in Interventionist and Community Drama* (Bristol: Intellect Books, 2005), pp. 25-54. See p. 46.

[2] David Cregan, 'Queer Memory', from a paper delivered at Queens University Belfast, November 2007.

[3] Tony Flynn, in interview with the author, 8 March 2008.

[4] Baz Kershaw, *The Politics of Performance: Radical Theatre as Cultural Intervention* (London: Routledge, 1992), p. 5.

[5] Joe Reid, in interview with the author, 21 April 2008.

[6] Ibid.

[7] Peter Shirlow and Brendan Murtagh, *Belfast: Segregation, Violence and the City* (London: Pluto, 2006), p. 25.

[8] This remarkable production was partly constructed using scenes written by republican prisoners in the Maze and Maghabery prisons and smuggled out on cigarette papers. It also toured to socialist community venues in England – including Sheffield.

[9] The unarmed IRA volunteers Mairead Farrell, Dan McCann, and Sean Savage were shot dead in Gibraltar by the British SAS on Sunday, 6 March 1988.

[10] Joe Reid, Introduction, *Ecce Homo*, unpublished script, Belfast Community Theatre, 1988.

[11] David Grant, review of BCT's production of *Execution*, *Theatre Ireland* 16 November 1987, p. 47.

[12] Baz Kershaw, *The Politics of Performance: Radical Theatre as Cultural Intervention* (London: Routledge, 1992), p. 3.

[13] Marie Mc Knight, Interview with the author, 20 April 2008.

[14] Bill Mc Donnell, emailed interview response from the author, April 2008.

[15] Joe Reid, Interview with the author, 21 April 2008.

[16] Martin Lynch, Interview with the author, 7 April 2008.

[17] Diarmaid Ferriter, 'On Thursday' column, *Irish Examiner* (Cork), 2 August 2007.

[18] Martin Lynch's play *Crack Up* (1982) had a prominent gay character called Nipper, who in coming out to his brother's friends at their wedding party precipitates a violent confrontation. Frank Mc Guinness's *Observe the Sons of Ulster Marching towards the Somme* (1985) featured a gay narrator, Piper, through whose eyes the tragic events unfold.

[19] Joe Reid and BCT, *Ecce Homo*, unpublished performance script, 1988.

[20] Ibid.

[21] Joe Reid, Interview with the author, 21 April 2008.

[22] Peter Shirlow and Brendan Murtagh, *Belfast: Segregation, Violence and the City* (London: Pluto, 2006), p. 25.

[23] Joe Reid and BCT, *Ecce Homo*, unpublished performance script, 1988

[24] The Ulster Defence Regiment (UDR) was an infantry regiment of the British Army which became operational in 1970, formed on similar lines as other British reserve forces with the operational task of countering armed guerilla-type attacks, replacing the Ulster Special Constabulary ('B-Specials' in assisting with security duties within Northern Ireland. Recruiting from the (mostly protestant/loyalist) local community at a time of intercommunal strife, it was often accused of sectarian attitudes and collusion with loyalist paramilitary organizations.

[25] Joe Reid and BCT, *Ecce Homo*, unpublished performance script, 1988.

[26] Stewart Parker, *Pentecost*, *PLAYS 2* (London: Methuen, 2000), p. 216.

[27] Parker, p. 209.

[28] Peter Shirlow and Brendan Murtagh, *Belfast: Segregation, Violence and the City* (London: Pluto, 2006), p. 25.

29 Joe Reid and BCT, Ecce Homo, unpublished performance script, 1988.

30 Martin Lynch, Interview with the author, 7 April 2008.

31 Marie Mc Knight, Interview with the author, 20 April 2008.

32 Tony Flynn, Interview with the author, 8 March 2008.

33 José Esteban Muñoz, *Disidentifications: Queers of Colour and the Performance of Politics (Cultural Studies of the Americas)*, vol. 2 (Minneapolis: University of Minnesota Press, 1999), p. 37.

34 Peter Shirlow and Brendan Murtagh, *Belfast: Segregation, Violence and the City* (London: Pluto, 2006), p. 103.

35 Joe Reid and BCT, *Ecce Homo*, unpublished performance script, 1988.

36 Mark Howard Ross, *Cultural Contestation in Ethnic Conflict* (Cambridge: Cambridge University Press, 2007), pp. 21-22.

37 Janelle Reinelt, 'Witnessing Change: Public Life and Performance in These Times', *Irish Theatre International* 1.1 (April 2008), p. 5.

38 'Gibraltar/Milltown 20th Anniversary Supplement', *West Belfast News* March 2008, p. viii.

39 Cregan, 'Queer Memory'.

40 Dan Baron Cohen, *Alfabetização Cultural: a luta íntima por uma nova humanidade* (São Paulo: Alfarrábio, 2004), pp. 114-115.

9 | Gender as performance in the works of Glasshouse Productions, Dublin

Samuele Grassi

Irish theatre has recently been criticized for its tendency to overlook gender and sexuality in favour of national identity.[1] Although some contemporary dramatists such as Marina Carr and Frank McGuinness have successfully worked against this tendency, it is no coincidence that drama remains a form that women find difficult to access or identify with. Dublin's Glasshouse Productions (active 1990-1996) was the first company to offer women a space of their own in the theatre of the Republic, following the path initially laid down by other leading independent theatre companies such as Rough Magic. Other People Arts and Muted Cupid were also interested in new and out-of-the-mainstream productions.[2]

This chapter attempts a queer reading of Glasshouse's commitment to feminist issues by looking at women as subjects on the Irish stage through Eve K. Sedgwick's notion of periperformativity. In her *Touching Feeling: Affect, Pedagogy, Performativity*, Sedgwick questions the 'temporal terms' of performative (speech) acts defined by British philosopher of language J.L. Austin which are at the core of queer gender theory. She then calls for a reconsideration of 'the spatial register' stating that although periperformative acts are not themselves performatives, 'they are about performatives and, more properly, ... they cluster around performatives'. The proximity of the periperformative to the performative is such that 'Like the neighborhoods in real estate ads, periperformative neighborhoods have prestigious centres (the explicit performative utterance) but no very fixed circumferences; yet the prestige of the centre extends unevenly, even unpredictably through the rest of the neighbour-hood.'3

The effect of periperformative (speech) acts is made explicit by their ability to 'invoke (if not participate fully in) the force of more than one illocutionary act' (Sedgwick 78) – an act performed *when* saying something.4 Sedgwick then discusses the topos of marriage as slavery in Victorian literature. By focusing on the idea of marriage as an exemplary performance she analyzes the (performative) acts around it and compares them to the acts which have instituted and maintained slavery in the United States. Following this example of performativity, I will now look at the legal exploitation of women as sanctioned by the text of the Irish constitution of 1937. Written under the influence of the Catholic Church, it assigned to men and women role positions specifically bound to support the Nation. Marriage thus became a way of expressing devotion to the Nation, to religious observance, and to the male-oriented legacy of Irish Nationalism. These aspects have repeatedly been performed on the Irish stage, where the figuration5 of the Cathleen helped secure women's dutiful role(s) as supporters of home and Nation. By the time Glasshouse emerged, the conditions of women had improved due to Ireland's entrance into the European Economic Community (now the European Union). Amendments to the constitution achieved through referendum in the period 1937 – 2004 included the recognition of specified religions (1972 Fifth Amendment, signed into law in 1973), which remove the special position occupied by the Catholic Church.6

A further consideration should be made regarding same-sex relationships. In June 2008 proposals of civil partnership were published in the Heads of Bills, but, as Kiernan Rose argues, they 'do not provide for legal recognition of the many same-sex couples, particularly women, who are parenting children together, leaving these parents and their children outside the protection of the State'.7 Kiernan's comment stressed the unbalanced conditions faced by women. How women can achieve full equality is an ongoing debate in contemporary global Ireland. In 1996 the Fifteenth Amendment of the Constitution granted divorce, but abortion is still not legal. This proves that the 1937 constitution has left its imprint on the present marginalization of women.

Debates carried out by feminists throughout Ireland had con-tested Article 41 of the constitution, primarily in that it claimed:

2° The State ... guarantees to protect the Family in its constitution and authority, as the necessary basis of social order and as indispensable to the welfare of the Nation and the State.

2. 1° In particular, the State recognizes that by her life within the home, woman gives to the State a support without which the common good cannot be achieved./2° The State shall, therefore, endeavour to ensure that mothers shall not be obliged by economic necessity to engage in labour to the neglect of their duties in the home ...

It is, however, in the 'preamble' of the constitution that we find State and Catholic Church empowered as conjunct authorities:

In the Name of the Most Holy Trinity, from Whom is all authority and to Whom, as our final end, all actions both of men and States must be referred,/We, the people of Éire,/Humbly acknowledging all our obligations to our Divine Lord, Jesus Christ, Who sustained our fathers through centuries of trial,/Gratefully remembering their heroic and unremitting struggle to regain the rightful independence of our Nation.[8]

Early in the twentieth century, the figure of the Cathleen had dominated as the embodiment of the yet-to-be-formed Irish Nation, as evidenced, for instance, by W.B. Yeats's *Cathleen* written at the time of the Revival. As supporter of the male armed struggle for an Irish free state, the Cathleen secured women's position within the home, and set up their relegation to the 'backstage'. In her reading of the traditional Cathleen, Victoria White highlights the shaping of a national identity in the theatre where women are objects to be ignored yet deified. She argues that: 'It is ... partly due to the fact that the fashioning of national identity and the simultaneous ignoring and deification of women have become intertwined that there are so few Irish women playwrights of real merit (which has a knock-on effect for directors and, particularly, actresses).'[9]

Marriage can be considered a founding institution of a hetero-normative State based on laws made by the fathers of the nation; this relational structure was traditionally supported in early modern Ireland by women through their (domestically) productive and reproductive role, embodied by the normative icons of 'Cathleen' and 'Mother Ireland'. We can say that marriage is nation in that marriage performs nation through a legal illocution producing new citizens; it is however a periperformative in that it also produces a series of even and uneven collateral acts such as the objectification of women described by Victoria White.

In 2003 the Irish Theatre Institute undertook the project of archiving plays produced in Ireland since 1904. As Research and Playography Director for 2004-2006, former Glasshouse co-founder Caroline Williams co-edited the *Findings Report of the Irish Playography 1904-2006* which provides a glimpse of women's difficulties in accessing the theatre. A 'playwrights by gender' analysis indexes 189 plays written by women in the period 1904-2006, accounting for 24% of the total – Lady Gregory's *Spreading the News* (1904) being one of the first plays produced in Ireland. The period 2000-2005 registered only a minimal increase, with a percentage of 29% (115 plays), as opposed to 281 written by men. Lady Gregory again features in pole position of the 49 playwrights with 10 or more new plays and/or adaptations on the 'professionally produced plays' chart. Former Charabanc Marie Jones has 24 plays compared with the 36 of Gregory, and despite her international success Marina Carr is fifth to last with 10 plays. A survey shows, on the other hand, that recent years have witnessed a consistent overall increase in plays staged at venues such as the Project Arts Centre which has always paid attention to out-of-the-mainstream, fringe material.

This paper will examine plays produced by Glasshouse Productions, such as *Out of My Head* by Trudy Hayes, and *I Know My Own Heart* and *Ladies and Gentlemen* by Emma Donoghue in order to show how contemporary Irish women's performance may operate in relation to the 'marriage as Nation' periperformative. My reading is based on the assumption that periperformativity can work as a productive political strategy to dismantle any dominant discourse. To talk of periperformativity here is to assume that marriage as a performative act produces a series of acts that allow an anti-essentialist understanding of its effects. By disengaging from the temporality of a performative (act), periperformativity reveals the extended effects of marriage generally concealed by dominant representations.

The 1980s opened a new phase of Irish feminism, in which 'feminist energies tended to focus on educational, cultural and creative projects'[10] – such was the background for Glasshouse's two-fold re-invention of Irish theatre from women's perspective. A programme note reads:

Glasshouse Productions play a vital role in the promotion of Irish women's writing for the stage. We are interested in new writing, and in fostering emerging writers, through advice, improvisational workshops and through production. In addition to new writing, we engage ourselves in valuable research and reclamation of Irish women dramatists, whose work is gradually disappearing from history.[11]

When Clare Dowling, Katy Hayes, Siân Quill and Caroline Williams set up the company, Belfast-based Charabanc Theatre Company had been touring Ireland for some time as the only all-women's theatre company with a political agenda.

By contrast, England had witnessed the challenging and often provocative work of highly successful feminist or co-feminist companies with a different experience of women's movements and feminism. According to Katy Hayes in an interview, 'We had never had the upsurge in political drama that had emerged in the UK in the Seventies and Eighties, the neo-Brechtian yawp that produced voices like Howard Barker, Caryl Churchill and Sarah Daniels, and companies like Trouble and Strife and Joint Stock. This is an aesthetic environment, which provides a natural home for feminism.'[12] Using work-shopping as devising method, Glasshouse started their activity on a profit-share basis. In the latter years of the company they received funds from the Arts Council and Dublin Corporation, and always retained a substantially co-operative scheme, similar to a collective undertaking, but with no 'formal decision-making structure'.[13] Despite the company's reliance on the fringe, Glasshouse was ambivalent towards the situation of independent theatre in the 1990s, 'grossly underfunded, ... reliant on blind commitment, unpaid labour, and a measure of luck'.[14]

The group's 'hallmark of fresh, provocative work'[15] had trouble finding a voice in the all-male establishment of theatre criticism. As women and feminists, the group really had a very cold iron to strike. In an interview on the company, Dermot Bolger discussed this point with actor and co-founder Siân Quill, who argued that: 'there was a belief out there that plays by women were for women, and that a play which explored women's sexuality, pornography, eating dis-orders ... was marginal because it was not about men. Such resistance to our work didn't discourage us, on the contrary we found it proof positive that presenting plays by women about women was an important and radical act' (Bolger, 137). In the same interview, Clare Dowling lamented 'a great lack of intelligent critical comment on the type of work that the company was doing' (Bolger,

140). For Mary Elizabeth Burke-Kennedy, Deirdre Hynes and Marina Carr, collaborative experience with companies made it possible for new women playwrights to emerge, as in the case of Glasshouse's co-founders Clare Dowling and Trudy Hayes, and also of Emma Donoghue.[16]

   The company debuted with two productions of Eve Lewis's *Ficky Stingers* at Andrews Lane Theatre in November 1990, and Clare McIntyre's *Low Level Panic* at the same venue in June 1991. Trudy Hayes's *Out of My Head* was their first new work. The play was premiered at the City Arts Centre in November 1991 and nominated for the Stewart Parker Theatre Award. It tells the story of twenty-year-old Lisa, an alcoholic actress who drinks 'to forget the future'[17] and has a relationship with Tim, an actor in his thirties. The play focuses both on the theme of women and alcoholism and on their being unable to choose a better life; it also deals with domestic violence in that Lisa cannot free herself from her violent partner. She finds relief in a strong female bond with her actress friend June, who repeatedly tries to help her without succeeding; this friendship contributes to the motif of female communion and mutual support which backgrounds the play.

   Out of My Head addresses a substance abuse problem common to many women in Ireland at that time, although alcoholism, mostly due to sex role conflicts, tended to remain hidden within the domestic walls.[18] Lisa is observed at various stages of her addiction problem. She can neither drop the bottle, nor can she leave Tim, and as a result she can neither take a part in a play nor take hold of her own life. The first scene introduces Lisa and Tim quarrelling over the issue of what makes a woman 'natural':

> **TIM.** My God. You're a most unnatural woman. (1)/It's natural for a woman to have these sexual urges.'

It then shifts to his requests to marry her so she can take on the role of dutiful wife/mother:

> **TIM.** Seriously Lisa, I'd like to marry you. We could buy an old shack and do it up and you could cook and clean for me and satisfy my sexual whims. Marry me (2).

And later on:

> **TIM.** Don't be bothering your brain with that play. You should devote yourself to satisfying me' (28).

Lisa struggles vainly to master the situation, attempting to make Tim jealous by pretending to have flirted with other men, or searching for help, though not June's. Her condition is dramatized by a series of hallucinations and nightmares which are introduced on stage by a change of lighting; by using this technique, Hayes breaks the conventions of realism and establishes a complicity with the audience, 'flung into the horrors of an alcoholic gaze, as a woman' (Williams, 7).

The nature of Lisa's relationship with Tim is shown on stage many times as the play goes on to shift from the pair's plea for a 'saner' rapport to (Tim's) violent and (Lisa's) dreadful, sometimes disturbing reactions. Act II, scene 7, is the scene of extreme male violence, when Tim grabs Lisa by her hair and tells her 'You're nothing. You're nothing' (29); she leaves but while she is out has other hallucinations, collapses to the ground surrounded by men ridiculing her, then is nearly raped. As in other episodes in the play, the issue of men abusing women for their appearance is dealt with here. Eventually, Tim rescues Lisa, carries her home and later attempts to strangle her (31). The scene ends with her facing the audience as she confesses: 'I'm out of my head all the time ... I don't know how things went so wrong. But I love my boyfriend. I need him as much as I need drink ... If anyone here can help me' (33).

Later in the play, Lisa has left Tim and started a new relationship with Mark, which she seems to enjoy, but she soon feels that it does not suit her:

> **MARK.** We'll have to train you in so if you're going to move in (36).

After meeting Tim in a pub she realizes that she wants to go back to him. The play ends with them kissing. Fade out is on Lisa's voice-over:

> **LISA.** Hello my name's Lisa and I'm an alcoholic ... I drink at night while my boyfriend lies there ... I fight with him – constantly. Sometimes I think I hate him. One minute I'm lying laughing in his arms and then ... (39).

A production note depicts the two actors frozen, in 'drunken abandon', as if to interpellate again the (women) spectators. Trudy Hayes sees the play as a story of the relationship between a woman of 'low self-esteem' and an 'emotionally dysfunctional male' who nurtures 'her destructive down-ward spiral' through his violent behaviour. This may finally lead to considering domestic violence a *collateral* act of marriage that encloses women in 'violent and abusive' relationships, while at the same time upholding the founding heterosexual norm of the nation endorsed by marriage.

I argue that Glasshouse's articulation of women's experience is grounded in the concepts of compulsory heterosexuality and heteronormativity. Compulsory heterosexuality abhors and censors same-sex desire. As defined by Adrienne Rich, it conceives of desire 'as if, despite profound emotional impulses and complementarities drawing women toward women, there is a mystical/biological heterosexual inclination, a 'preference' or 'choice' which draws women toward men' (637).[19] Compulsory heterosexuality is rehearsed and performed through reproduction as the end product of heteronormativity. Gayatri C. Spivak's concept of reproductive heteronormativity refers to the extent to which heterosexuality is justified and enforced as society's survival norm and *raison d'être*. While reproductive heteronormativity 'is accepted as the currency to measure human dignity', it also grounds gender inequality in local realities.[20] In Hayes's play, gender inequality is measured against Lisa's addiction to alcohol and her abusing love story.

Hayes's *Out of My Head* was also given a reading during *There are no Irish Women Playwrights! I*. This was the first episode of two distinct performances 'designed to disprove the title'[21] which the company devoted to promoting new writers for the theatre and retrieving the lost tradition of women playwrights in Ireland. Devised by Williams and directed by Katy Hayes, this first edition featured extracts from Anne Devlin's *Ourselves Alone*, Geraldine Aron's *A Galway Girl*, Trudy Hayes's *Out of My Head*, Emma Donoghue's *I Know My Own Heart*, Sheila Flitton's *For Better or Worse*, Clare Dowling's *Burns Both Ends*, Deirdre Hynes's *Howling Moon, Silent Sons*, and Marina Carr's *Low in the Dark*. The first production of the show, at the City Arts Centre, consisted of a series of other readings and panel discussions on the state of women's writing for the stage. In March 1992 the company had prepared Women Centre Stage, a day of events 'celebrating women's achievements in Irish theatre'.[22] The second part of the collection, *There Are No Irish Women Playwrights! II*, also devised by Williams, featured twelve extracts from playwrights of the period 1920-1970 and included Edna O'Brien's, Jennifer Johnston's and other playwrights' one-act plays.[23] This second edition formed part of *Acts and Reacts: a festival of drama and dialogue*.[24]

In August 1992, Clare Dowling's *Burns Both Ends* was staged at the Project Arts Centre. The theme of the play was women in an urban context, and tells the story of two women friends, Martina and Trish, who lose their jobs and set up in business together. Anna McMullan and Caroline Williams have commented that Dowling's

> theatrical presentation is highly contemporary in its form and settings. She uses high energy scenes set in everyday Dublin locations – a chip shop, a rock concert, a football pitch, an unemployment exchange – and harnesses the rapid action of television to reach a new audience (McMullan and Williams, 1243).

The play was reviewed as 'boisterous and up-beat, sharp and insightful, a hilarious exploration of success, who gets it and who needs it anyway!'[25] It earned Dowling the recognition necessary for a production of her second play. *Leapfrogging* was presented as a lunchtime performance at *Acts and Reacts Festival* in association with the Project Arts Centre and the Irish Writers' Centre. It casts 'a comic look at gender, power and desire, both past and present, a case of *can't live together* and *can't live apart*'.[26] Reviewed as 'a sustained skit on gender roles' in which role reversal 'reveals the eejityness of both, to hilarious effect' and with Katy Hayes's 'skilful direction',[27] it is set in the Dublin of today, where Private Eye Phil tries to solve the gender war following Jack and Jill's journey which had begun with the bite of the apple.

Hayes's play presents domestic violence as a legally justifiable, unpunishable side effect of marriage repeatedly performed within domestic walls. As a collateral act of marriage, domestic violence is thus legitimated by the very idea of Nation; in other words, the disempowerment and subjugation of women sustains marriage as the founding institution of the (Irish) nation. In this case, peri-performativity refers to/is 'tangent to' yet 'different from' explicit performatives (Sedgwick, 5). In other words, periperformativity allows us to look beside hegemonic representations of marriage, and offers embodied alternatives that exist alongside yet in opposition to it.

A similar approach based on periperformativity could be used to explore how relationships that exceed normative heterosexuality function in the proximity of marriage, re-mapping the idea of nation and/or the ideology of Nationalism . However, it is to be pointed out that, in a contemporary context such as Glasshouse Productions, nationalism involves attitudes and behaviours sustained by dominant cultural norms. Contemporary notions of citizenship and national identity look beyond the confines of the term 'Nation' as it was conceived of in the early twentieth century. Sedgwick insists that, since the periperformative depends on spatiality, it may untie 'that fateful reliance of explicit performativity on the exemplary, on the single example – which so often has meant ... the exemplarity of the marriage act itself'. The plays here considered share this same concern in portraying the 'periperformative struggle to displace and remap the theatrical space of marriage' (Sedgwick, 79-80) both in its figurative-political and in its literary meaning.

I will now examine the performance of lesbianism and lesbian relationships in terms of what is 'tangent to, yet different from' marriage in two lesbian plays produced by Glasshouse Productions. *I Know My Own Heart* first opened as a one-act, lunchtime show in April 1993 at the Project Arts Centre, and was later staged there in its current, two-act published version. It came out of a workshop organized by Glasshouse and Donoghue who then started a co-operative playwriting/company which commissioned her second play three years later. 1993 was a year of major social changes in Ireland when homosexuality was decriminalized. Such progress in homosexual rights revealed, however, problems related to lesbian (in)visibility, still well below that of gay men. This was partly due to the prevailing heterosexual orientation of the women's groups where lesbians were active but also relatively closeted, despite the support given by women to the rights of gay men since the 1970s.[28] *I Know My Own Heart*, a lesbian play by an openly lesbian writer, invited the audience to identify with its protagonist, the aristocratic Anne Lister. A programme note by Donoghue reads:

> In Dublin 1993 it delights me that modern audiences can identify so easily with Lister and her friends across the gulf of almost two centuries. But it also makes me draw the saddening conclusion that too little has changed across that time. The financial, religious and social pressures on women to marry men; formulaic notions of 'femininity'; the almost total invisibility of lesbians; the closet with its real and imaginary bogeys of exposure and loss – these are as familiar to many of us today as they were to Anne Lister.[29]

She then confirmed in interview that 'of course I was drawn to Anne Lister's story, her sense of being the only one in the world, because I felt much the same in 1980s Ireland'.[30]

I Know My Own Heart, subtitled 'Regency Romance', deals with gender and class as themes where sexual and social awareness overlap. The play, focusing on the 'uncompromising intimacy'[31] of the real Anne Lister (1791-1840) and her diaries, is based on 'the choices of a woman trying to understand and express herself, in a society based on codes and conventions'[32]. Donoghue seems to appropriate certain motifs of the romance novel to tell the (autobiographical) story of upper-class, would-be-heir of her uncle's fortune Anne Lister and her relationship with lower class Marianne. Caught between her attraction to Marianne and the rules her status demands, Anne writes in her diary: 'Considering her low station in life, Miss Brown is quite wonderful',[33] while Marianne is seduced by 'her manners ... softly gentlemanlike' (105). But Anne also addresses Marianne as an 'impertinent little baggage' (109), and after meeting her for the first time she recounts:

> **ANNE.** I offered Miss Brown my arm at the bottom of the
> High Street. I regretted it the moment I did it. Think what
> damage this acquaintance might do to my dignity, my social
> standing. I offered her my arm; a slight readjustment of the
> muscles, no more. Such a small gesture to bear so much weight
> (107).

This seems to pose the question of what matters most, sexuality or class.

Is it the sexual deviance of lesbianism that prevents Anne from enjoying a relationship with Marianne, and vice-versa? Or is the play foregrounding their difference in status? The core of the performance is provided by Donoghue's skilful play on gender and characterization, with both Anne and Marianne holding to traditional notions of masculinity and femininity only to subvert them. Anne is nicknamed 'Gentleman Jack' by the townspeople, and her manners appear, as mentioned above, 'gentlemanlike'. At times Anne becomes Marianne's 'wife' and Marianne becomes Anne's 'Mistress Lister' (119), at others Anne is characterized as a 'female-*Don Juan*'. Soon after Marianne has married a man in order to elevate her status to match Anne's – thus becoming 'one man's wife, and one woman's ... beloved' (131) – Anne takes to bed her friend, Tib (a woman of 'independent means') and Marianne's little sister, Nancy.

It has been stressed that Anne's dress code 'appropriates the masculine', while she enjoys solely the company of women (*manca indicazione bibliografica*, 43). The one cross-dressing episode enhances the play on gender suggested by Anne's masculine behaviour and appearance:

> **ANNE.** This morning before breakfast I locked the chamber door and tried on my new waistcoat and braces over my drawers. The effect was striking, if I say so myself. Spent half an hour in foolish fancies about dressing entirely in men's clothes, driving my own carriage, being my own master (113).

Gender troubling is also evident from the way characters address each other; Marianne feels the need to call Anne by a masculine name, Freddy. Anne wants Nancy to call her 'Master' (141). The reversal of gender conventions is best evident when Anne flirts with all the other women as a Don Juan would do. By the end of the play, each of them is aware of having become one of Anne's 'ladies' (149). The play anticipated the company's concerns about the condition of women that was to become its distinctive feature, and also shared in the growing debate on sexualities evidenced by the upsurge of gay and lesbian activism.

References to the Anne Lister's real diary written in code are important in the play. This intimate literary form available to women hints of feelings and experiences hidden and secretly shared by the characters,[34] for lesbianism is always a 'sweet intercourse [which] must be the best kept secret in the history of womankind' (117). In his review of the Andrews Lane Theatre production, Fintan O'Toole, while gladly acknowledging Donoghue's avoidance of 'the principal subject of Irish writing ... Ireland', comments that:

> What makes it [the play] fascinating is that its implicit rejection of one imagined community – 'Ireland' – is accompanied by a search for another. The very act of the play itself ... is an effort, not to awake from the nightmare of history, but to invent an alternative history in which a young Irishwoman can place herself. Stepping outside of one set of allegiances, it assumes another. Gender and sexuality replace nationality as the forces that constitute the play's characters.[35]

Donoghue's debut as a playwright carries the hallmark of much of her later work where she uncovers the lost histories of women in order to offer alternative contemporary narratives of the Nation. In this regard she seems to move towards Rich's notion of lesbian existence 'as a reality, and as a source of knowledge and power available to women; or with the institution of heterosexuality itself as a beachhead of male dominance' (633). Implicit in Donoghue's play is an attempt to deal with an experience which 'suggests both the fact of the historical presence of lesbians and our continuing creation of the meaning of that existence' (648). Anne Lister's story is developed to occupy a 'tangent' location to the reproduction of normative heterosexuality.

After having produced an adaptation of two Angela Carter short stories by Katy Hayes (*Vampirella* and *The Company of Wolves*, presented at the Project Arts Centre on 18 January, 1995), Glasshouse Productions commissioned a new play from Emma Donoghue. Her interest in the 'idea of digging up what has been buried, giving voice to what has been censored'[36] is also at the core of her latest play to date, and Glasshouse's final production, in 1996, *Ladies and Gentlemen*. This play is about British vaudeville star Annie Hindle (born 1847) and draws on 'the music hall, vaudeville and variety act format to both entertain and foreground issues of performing gender ... .'[37] Gender roles are subverted, and sexuality is seen less as something assigned by a (heterosexual) norm than as a series of positions which may be freely occupied. In the play Donoghue experiments with temporal sequences. Set in 1891, the action shifts back to 1880 and forward to 1881, juxtaposing Annie's two comebacks to the stage. The first one occurred after she had been deceived and beaten by her husband, the second after her lover, Irish 'exiled' Ryanny, had died. Most of the play is set in the New York vaudeville theatre, but Annie (a male impersonator), Gilbert (a queer female impersonator), and Ella (Annie's ex-lover, a stage dresser and then male impersonator) perform and deconstruct genders both on and off the stage. In one scene we see Annie cutting herself with a razor in an attempt to encourage the growth of a moustache.[38]

In her analysis of female cross-dressing, Marjorie Garber has spoken of the third 'term' which it posits in contrast with binary gender oppositions. But, she continues, 'the third term is not a term. Much less is it a sex ... The 'third' is a mode of articulation, a way of describing a space of possibility. Three puts in question the idea of one: of identity, self-sufficiency, self-knowledge.'[39] This is assimilated in Donoghue's play by the theatricality of Annie's cross-dressing, a way to perform and identify with 'a space of possibility' which the vaudeville stage allows her. She explains what it means to her to wear men's clothes:

> **RYANNY.** Why do you pretend to be a man?
> **ANNIE.** I don't pretend anything. I impersonate men, which is far more demanding than just being one.

RYANNY. But do you like wearing men's clothes?
ANNIE. They're only called that because men got a hold of
them first. You bet your sweet life I like 'em; they've got pockets
for everything (22).

The background message of the play is the liberating potential of
theatre: a 'world of one's own' where everything can be performed,
and thus can be. The stage offers an opportunity to perform, to give
reality to what must not or cannot be real, as in the marriage scene
at the end of Act I, when Annie gives Ryanny the ring her husband
had given her:

> then [they] assume the formal pose of a Victorian husband-and-
> wife photograph; ... RYANNY turns and tosses her bouquet over
> her shoulders into the audience (65).

Like *Out of My Head*, this play addresses the often violent nature
of traditional husband-wife relationships. In this regard a further
application of Adrienne Rich's theories and her notion of 'male sex-
right to women' would indicate that the domestic violence
performed in Hayes's play is justified as a collateral act of marriage;
'male sex-right to women' sustains women's exploitation at home by
'defending sexual slavery within the family on the basis of 'family
privacy and cultural uniqueness' on the other' (645). When Ryanny
asks Annie about her black eye, she replies:

> **ANNIE.** No no, it was me who kept misunderstanding. I'd look
> in the mirror and see two great black eyes and ask myself,
> 'Annie, did your distinguished thespian husband raise his fist
> to you last night? Why no, he couldn't have, he's the people's
> darling. I must have walked into a wall.' Come think of it. I
> must have walked into two walls, every Saturday night (40-41).

Ladies and Gentlemen is interspersed with songs. The use of
songs, employed to emphasize a given message with political intent,
is a recurrent strategy in feminist drama. The play draws, above all,
from the tradition of female-male impersonators in the vaudeville,
where songs were also used to express serious themes. Donoghue
comments on her use of songs less as 'a Churchillian/Brechtian
device than a consequence of the fact that I was writing about
vaudeville stars'.[40] For some things there are no songs, as for
Annie's relationship with Ryanny: 'Where am I to get the words?
There aren't any songs about things like *this*' (49). But at the very
end of the play, when Annie makes up her mind to go back to the

stage, she sings *A Real Man*[41]: in Donoghue's plays, women always manage to find their own voice.

In less than ten years, Glasshouse Productions managed to explore feminist issues putting on stage the oppression of women from women's perspective, and experimenting with possibilities of gender in performance. This undertaking necessarily questioned the traditional masculinist concept of the Nation. McMullan and Williams have pointed out that 'many of the male playwrights of Irish theatre tradition have contested [the] dominant concept of both masculine and national identity, but their critical canonization has left little space for those whose imaginative world, stories or audiences fall outside the boundaries of what has become recognized as the national tradition of Irish theatre' (McMullan and Williams, 1237). The women of Glasshouse have contributed to re-writing this tradition in two ways, by focusing on the new and by recovering what had been lost, forgotten or simply, deliberately, left out.

This analysis has attempted to show how one of the most relevant all-female experiences in Irish contemporary theatre has contested, deconstructed, and replaced notions around the pre-existing framing of women within the strict, hetero-normative notion of adherence to the values of nation and state demanded, and perhaps sustained by the historical dominant ideologies of patriarchy and the Catholic Church that linger below the surface of the cosmopolitan Ireland of today. In particular, a queer reading based on the notion of periperformativity has been adapted to the 'marriage as Nation' trope in Ireland as first established by the constitution of 1937 and applied in order to show Glasshouse Productions' pioneer attempt to bring to the Irish stage alternative (gendered) representations which women could specifically re-cognize and identify with. In her interview with Bolger, Clare Dowling argued that 'the facts are that women are still not writing for the Irish stage in an equitable number. And given that most of the audience on any given night in any theatre in Dublin will be women, this is a debate that should continue' (Bolger, 142). A recent communication confirmed this view.[42] Irish women are still waiting to take their position 'centre stage' on a more permanent basis.

---

[1] Karen Fricker and Brian Singleton, 'Irish Theatre: Conditions of Criticism', *Modern Drama* 47.4(2004), p. 565.

[2] For a review of *Muted Cupid and Other People Arts*, see Victoria White, 'Other People Arts', *Theatre Ireland* 26/27 (1992), pp. 82-83;

Éibhear Walshe, 'Voices Beyond the Margin', *Theatre Ireland* 26/27 (1992), pp. 38-39.

3 Eve K. Sedgwick, *Touching Feeling. Affect, Pedagogy, Performativity* (Durham, NC: Duke University Press, 2004), p. 68. Subsequent references are cited in the text.

4 Sedgwick is questioning British philosopher J.L. Austin's theorization on speech acts as a form of action, which focused on an analysis of how saying something is actually to perform an action. Austin's *How to do things with words* (Oxford: Clarendon, 1962) has been and still is a work which queer criticism debates.

5 I refer here to Donna Haraway's use of the term 'figuration' as a political trope that can be embodied, or rather as a 'theory of representation that critiques the literal realism of science, scientistic thinking, and 'secular Christian Platonism', and offers an alternative in self-conscious troping, or embodied, performative images. See Donna Haraway, *Modest Witness@Second Millennium. FemaleMan Meets OncoMouse: Feminism and Technoscience* (New York and London: Routledge, 1996), and Rosi Braidotti. *Nomadic Subjects: Embodiment and Sexual Difference in Contemporary Feminist Theory* (New York: Columbia University Press, 1994). Lidia Curti has also dealt extensively with figurations in her *Female Stories, Female Bodies – Narrative, Identity and Representation* (London: Macmillan, 1998) and more recent published work.

6 A list of constitutional referenda in the Republic of Ireland is available at: <http://www.referendum.ie/home/>.

7 Kiernan Rose is included in 'Press Release' 24 June 2008; available at: <http://www.glen.ie/>.

8 See http://www.taoiseach.gov.ie/index.asp?docID=243.

9 Victoria White, 'Cathleen Ni Houlihan is Not a Playwright', *Theatre Ireland* 26/27 (1992), pp. 26-29.

10 Ailbhe Smyth, 'The Women's Movement in the Republic of Ireland 1970-1990', *Irish Women's Studies Reader* (Dublin: Attic Press, 1993), p. 266.

11 *I Know My Own Heart*, programme, p. 1.

12 Dermot Bolger, 'People in Glasshouse: An Anecdotal History of an Independent Theatre Company', *Druids, Dudes and Beauty Queens: The Changing Face of Irish Theatre* (Dublin: New Island Books, 2002), pp. 134-35.

13 See Victoria White, 'Glasshouse', *Theatre Ireland* 26/27 (1992), pp. 40-43.

14 Caroline Williams, 'This is One for the Sisters', *Theatre Ireland* 30 (1993), p. 7.

15 *I Know My Own Heart*, programme, p. 1.

16 Kay Sheehy, 'Few curtains rise for women', *The Irish Times* 11 May 1994, p. 11.

17 Trudy Hayes, *Out of My Head*, unpublished play. Subsequent references are cited in brackets.

18 See Art O'Connor, 'Female Alcoholism in Ireland', *Irish Journal of Psychiatry* (Spring 1987), pp. 13-16.

19 Adrienne Rich, 'Compulsory Heterosexuality and Lesbian Existence', *Signs* 5.4 (1980), pp. 631-60. Subsequent references are cited in the text.

20 Gayatri C. Spivak, 'Ethics and Politics in Tagore, Coetzee, and Certain Scenes of Teaching', *Diacritics* 32, 3/4 (2002), p. 21. See also her 'What is Gender? Where is Europe? Walking with Balibar' conference paper given at the *Fifth Ursula Hirschmann Annual Lecture on Gender and Europe*, European University Institute, Florence, 2006.

21 *The Irish Times* 27 June 1992, p. 32. See also Victoria White, 'There Are No Irish Women Playwrights', *The Irish Times* 1 July 1992, p. 10.

22 Glasshouse Productions.

23 See Williams.

24 *The Irish Times* 6 March 1993.

25 From programme notes provided by Caroline Williams.

26 From press release, programme notes provided by Caroline Williams.

27 Victoria White, review of *Leapfrogging*, by Clare Dowling, *The Irish Times* 25 March 1993 p. 10.

28 See Kiernan Rose, *Diverse Communities: The Evolution of Lesbian and Gay Politics in Ireland* (Cork: Cork University Press, 1994).

29 Emma Donoghue, in *I Know My Own Heart*, programme, p. 1.

30 Communication with the author.

31 Anne Fogarty, *I Know My Own Heart*, programme, p. 1.

32 Emma Donoghue, Afterword, *I Know My Own Heart*, *Seen and Heard: Six New Plays by Irish Women*, ed. Cathy Leeney (Dublin: Carysfort Press, 2001), p. 160.

33 Donoghue, p. 104. Subsequent references are cited in brackets.

34 Programme notes provided by Caroline Williams.

35 Fintan O'Toole, review of *I Know My Own Heart*, by Emma Donoghue, *The Irish Times* 13 November 1993; reprinted in *Critical Moments: Fintan O'Toole on Modern Irish Theatre*, eds Julia Furay and Redmond O'Hanlon (Dublin: Carysfort Press, 2004), pp. 118-21.

36 Communication with the author.

37 Anna McMullan, 'Gender, Authorship and Performance in Contemporary Irish Women Playwrights: Mary Elizabeth Burke-Kennedy, Marie Jones, Marina Carr, Emma Donoghue', *Theatre Stuff: Critical Essays on Contemporary Irish Theatre*, ed. Eamonn Jordan (Dublin: Carysfort Press, 2000), pp. 34-46.

38 Emma Donoghue, *Ladies and Gentlemen* (Dublin: New Island Books, 1998), p. 15. Subsequent references are cited in brackets.

39 Marjorie Garber, *Vested Interests: Cross-Dressing and Cultural Anxiety* (London and New York: Routledge, 1992), p. 11.

40 Communication with the author.

41 See McMullan and Williams, 'Contemporary Irish Women Playwrights', *The Field Day Anthology of Irish Writing*, eds Angela Bourke, et al. (Cork: Cork University Press, 2002), p. 1237.

42 Communication with the author.

Figure 1: Photo: No Talk, No Walk/Re-route the Flute graffiti, Ormeau Road, Belfast, July 1998.

Figure 2: Photo: *You Won't Reroute This Fruit!* sign, Pride Parade participant, Belfast, August 2004.

Figure 3: Photo: Belfast Sightseeing Bus with Kremlin gay bar
employees and pink, red and white Union Jack, Belfast Pride, 2006.

Figure 4: Photo: Giant rainbow flag, Belfast Pride, 2006.

Figure 5: Photo: Drag queen, Belfast Pride, 2006.

Figure 6: Poster for *In These Shoes?* Courtesy of Niall Sweeney at Pony Ltd., 2007.

Figure 7: Poster for *All Dolled Up*. Courtesy of Niall Sweeney at Pony Ltd., 2007.

Figure 8: Panti speaking to the audience during *All Dolled Up*.
Courtesy of Fiona Morgan, 2008.

Figure 9: Panti's *Make and Do Do Display Cabinet*. Courtesy of Rory
O'Neill, 2008.

Figure 10: Tony Flynn (seated) in the 1987 BCT production of *Sign on the Dotted Line*.

Figure 11: Early 1980s Hunger Striker mural from the gable wall of a terraced house on the Falls Road in West Belfast.

Figure 12: A socialist protest poster that was fly posted around Belfast in the 1970s.

10 | Queer Wanderers, Queer Spaces:
Dramatic Devices for Re-imagining Ireland

Todd Barry

Expanding the idea of queerness into realms other than its traditional locus in sex and gender is not new. Queerness is also a useful modern philosophy ultimately unanchored in the body, although it originates from queer bodies and is projected out into a new collective understanding of the world. In *Tendencies* (1993), Eve Kosofsky Sedgwick observes, 'a lot of the most exciting recent work around 'queer' spins the term outward along dimensions that can't be subsumed under gender and sexuality at all: the ways that race, ethnicity, postcolonial nationality criss-cross with these *and other* identity-constituting, identity-fracturing discourses, for example'.[1] Applying queerness to the dramatic use of space is just such an extension. Three Irish playwrights who employ this kind of strategy are Frank McGuinness, Brian Friel, and Brendan Behan. Using queer characters as catalysts, the playwrights under consideration are able to enact a national re-imagining of the spaces and boundaries of Ireland. This study will examine how this type of spatial awareness manifests itself in McGuinness's *Observe the Sons of Ulster Marching Towards the Somme* (1985) and *Carthaginians* (1988), Friel's *The Gentle Island* (1971), and Behan's *The Hostage* (1958).

In this chapter I will apply Una Chaudhuri's work on the role of place in modern drama and Jean-Ulrick Désert's theoretical work on queer space, in order to establish how these plays utilize a type of queer wanderer that activates the queering of Ireland's spaces, which in turn allows for a re-imagining of Ireland itself. This queerly precipitated national re-imagining leads to the potential for healing wounds caused by sectarian strife. However, once the queer wanderer catalyzes a restorative re-imagining of Ireland's boundaries and the identities dwelling within them, that queer character is expelled from these dramas, Behan's play being an important exception, in order to restore heteronormativity as the controlling centre of twentieth-century Irish community. In this respect, these dramatic strategies mirror the precarious position of gays and lesbians living in twentieth-century Ireland, and are closely connected with the political and social position of very real bodies.

Jean-Ulrick Désert provocatively writes in his theorizing about queer urban space, 'A queer space is an activated zone made proprietary by the occupant or *flâneur*, the wanderer. It is at once private and public. Our cities, our neighborhoods, our homes are loosely defined territories inscribed not merely by the laws of proprietary ownership but by implicit and shifting inflections of presence, conspicuous or otherwise.'[2] In his essay 'Queer Space', Désert formulates helpful definitions:

> 'Space' is commonly defined as a delineated or loosely bounded area occupied cognitively or physically ... This terrain of physical space, both natural and designed, increasingly includes literary, media, and electronic space. Queer space crosses, engages, and transgresses social, spiritual, and aesthetic locations.[3]

In the plays under consideration, there is always some kind of queer wanderer who catalyses a new understanding of the play's places and the literal dramatic space of the theatre, because he 'crosses, engages, and transgresses' a multiplicity of spaces. In addition, Una Chaudhuri's work on place in modern drama helps us to understand the significance of queer dramatic space. Chaudhuri characterizes the central concern of Western modern drama as that of 'geopathology', which she defines as 'a century-long struggle with the problem of place'.[4] She argues that 'this struggle ... unfolds as an incessant dialogue between belonging and exile, home and homelessness'.[5] Chaudhuri's theoretical model works quite well if we consider the central preoccupations of modern Irish drama. Christopher Murray argues that twentieth-century Irish drama is 'based on a need for a narrative of identity'.[6] This need was very pointed indeed at the start of the twentieth century, when there was only an independent country to be imagined because it had not yet come into existence; however, the eventual partition between the

Republic of Ireland and Northern Ireland served to further pronounce this need for identity narratives that addressed or attempted to resolve acute problems of place. These identities are inextricably bound up with the national boundaries and the sovereignty accorded them on the Irish island; the composition of any resulting identity is often a disjunction between one's current space and one's perceived home, or a conflict between one's dwelling place and the allegiances of one's identity. The use of queer space in modern Irish drama is a dramaturgical strategy used by certain Irish playwrights in response to Chaudhuri's problem of geopathology and the various geopathologies in the Republic of Ireland and Northern Ireland.

Growing up in Donegal, a geographical threshold in the Republic of Ireland because it borders Northern Ireland, had an impact on playwright Frank McGuinness, as he made clear in an interview: 'I come from a very unique position as I was born in Donegal, which is geographically North but politically is part of Southern Ireland. So we had a confusion there, we had conflict there that I grew up with, and I think that is in many ways the ideal setting, the ideal background for a playwright, to have that confusion, that sense of conflict in your sense of place.'[7] Writing for a tourist magazine called *Ireland of the Welcomes*, he noted the etymology of Donegal and its import for Irish self-conceptions: 'Dún na nGall – the fort of the foreigner; is it so called to remind us all that each of our most distant ancestors came to this island as a foreigner? We are all invaders. All seeking refuge, seeking home. To protect a home, each tribe, each family, will fight, until proximity, time, culture and sheer tiredness make us Irish, simply because we share this island.'[8] Donegal's etymology is so interesting because it highlights the paradox inherent in recognizing that one's home can also be a locus of self-alienation from certain perspectives.

Frank McGuinness often places his queer protagonists at the centre of theatrical exorcisms of trauma. Their queerness in these particular McGuinness plays is rooted in the characters' homosexuality, although we will see that the wanderers in Friel and Behan are queer more because of how they deconstruct the dramatic space they enter. McGuinness's queer wanderers re-evaluate, reclaim, and rewrite historical narratives that before had been silenced in war, sectarian strife, and their attendant traumas. *Observe the Sons* depicts a re-imagining of Ulster's contribution to World War I, and *Carthaginians* presents traumatized characters finally giving voice to the events of Bloody Sunday. Pyper and Dido dramatically articulate a unique perspective through which to imagine the past: this queer lens produces a vision that is de-centred because of the fragmentary nature of space and time in these plays. It is inclusive, moving away from hetero-normative and patriarchal societal models and additionally stresses the contingent and performative nature of gender and identity, including sectarian and nationalistic identities. It values artistic over historical fact, employs irony and parody as subversive strategies, and questions the role and make-up of the traditional Irish hero: instead of Yeats's arcane mythological band, most notably represented in *On Baile's Strand* (1904), we are presented with a drag queen as the Puckish orchestrator of events and a gay soldier who survives the bloodiest battle of World War I and is responsible for carrying forth its legacy in Northern Ireland. Pyper and Dido can be interpreted as filling the role of queer judges who preside over an interrogation of Ireland's mytho-historical past. They activate a re-imagining of Ireland's historic and present spaces. The various Irish audiences who first witnessed these performances (Republican and Loyalist, Catholic and Protestant, hetero- and homosexual, along with the varying shades of these binarisms) re-examined the past and the present of the Troubles through the imaginative lenses of Pyper and Dido. These queerly focal characters threaten the very nature of Ireland's self-conceptions by serving as catalysts for potential alterations in the collective Irish identity. If a queer lens is employed to heal and re-imagine a country's identity, there is the possibility that queerness ascends to a central interpretive lens of culture, rather than that of heteronormativity; this initial move towards a queer paradigmatic centrality is resisted in these plays through the expulsion of the queer characters after they have set restorative events into motion.

Observe the Sons takes place in a liminal space and time. The location of the setting that frames the entire play is unclear. The opening locates an ambiguous place where Pyper continuously embarks on his endless remembrance. The play opens with a stage direction suggesting a 'low drumbeat' — evocative of ceremonies ancient and modern, up to and including the drumbeat of the Orange parades — that awakens the Elder Pyper and his first line is 'Again'. Tom Herron remarks that the play is a 'devastating staging of insubstantiality'.⁹ It creates a set of empty spaces, overlapping but still immaterial. Pyper awakens in such a liminal space, and indeed,

Observe the Sons is fully concerned with what McGuinness calls 'that sense of conflict in your sense of place'. Pyper is ostensibly in Northern Ireland during the Troubles when the play opens: 'The house has grown cold. Ulster has grown lonely. We discourage visitors. Security. Men my age have been burned in their beds. Fenian cowards.'[10] He is in a 'house', which is also meant to symbolize Ulster itself. This house of Ulster is also a temple, a deserted temple of the Lord. It is all these things and places simultaneously.

McGuinness's theatrical space is often used to represent liminal spaces of the imagination, and images of places are projected simultaneously outward onto other geographies and inward on personal memory, simultaneously centrifugal and centripetal. Eamonn Jordan has noted this effect in *Carthaginians*: 'The theatrical space is represented in such a way that it both contracts and expands ... It is Dido alone, who transgresses the spatial boundaries.'[11] *Observe the Sons* demonstrates a similar treatment of theatrical space: the trajectory from Pyper's memory toward a manifestation in physical action on stage; the trajectory from an invisible to visible homoerotics, a trajectory which varies depending on the time in which the play is produced and the choices of the particular production; the split scenes that work with a splintered space and time coalescing at certain junctures; and the simultaneity of disparate spaces and times represented on the one stage (1980s Northern Ireland, France, the Battles of the Somme and Boyne).

In *Tendencies* (1993), Eve Sedgwick claims, 'That's one of the things that "queer" can refer to: the open mesh of possibilities, gaps, overlaps, dissonances and resonances, lapses and excesses of meaning when the constituent elements of anyone's gender, of anyone's sexuality aren't made (or can't be made) to signify monolithically.'[12] Sedgwick is mainly writing in spatial terms: these 'gaps, overlaps, dissonances and resonances' are at the core of McGuinness's queer vision in these plays (dissonances and resonances, while they obviously have an auditory meaning, also can be metaphorically applied to the structures that are imposed upon space). These theatrical strategies are employed in order to show how strong and dangerous a hold many of the Irish collective narratives maintain over the divided cultures and fractured identities on that island. They are also employed as a means of cleansing the audience members in a catharsis of realization that their national identities are as constructed and malleable as their sexual, gender, and religious identities.

A major critical debate over *Observe the Sons* involves whether it is a condemnation of Ulster Protestantism. In fact, the play questions *all* traditional markers of Irish national identity, both in the Republic and the North, whether moored in geography, religion, or sexuality. In altering the traditional mytho-historical framework, McGuinness suggests that the attempt to articulate and defend Irishness can sometimes be an insidious undertaking. In 'There's Something Queer Here': Modern Ireland and the Plays of Frank McGuinness*, David Cregan states this in a more positive way in terms of McGuinness's work expanding existing identity paradigms: 'By creating characters which represent subjective diversity, McGuinness artistically expands the boundaries of Irish identity, cracking the cohesive veneer of collective memories in order to create the possibility for the articulation of identities which have been suppressed in the project of nation building.'[13]

Displacement and projection of space and time in *Observe the Sons* is a theatrical strategy used by McGuinness, and a survival strategy used by his characters, in order to make historical myths justify otherwise horrific and meaningless realities. It is queer in nature because the strategy is deconstructive of historical and cultural mythologies; the result is also self-defeating in *Observe the Sons*. Throughout most of the play, the younger Pyper lays bare the artificiality of the men's constructs of country and identity, sexuality and Ulster Protestantism. However, Pyper's character undergoes a change when he falls in love with Craig, which marks the moment when he wants to survive the War and fully embrace the imperialist project of Ulster Protestantism. In the play's final scene, Pyper returns to the comfort of loyalist iconography and it consumes him in a repetition of communal bloodletting. In 'Reconstructing History in the Irish History Play', Claire Gleitman notes: 'The nature of that tragedy is best revealed in the conversion of Pyper, whose transformation from the gadfly sceptic of 1916 to the righteous scourge of unionism is a dramatic articulation of mytho-historiography. Pyper participates in uncovering the hollow centre of myth at the same time as he helps write another chapter of it.'[14] The iconography has such allure because their deaths at the Somme would have had no meaning without a certain mythologizing of the historical moment. In that respect, the characters take their strength from symbols, and the geographical place of the Somme is transformed into a symbol of the Boyne in order to give meaning to the men's sacrifice.

This transformation of space and place allows the Elder Pyper and his original audience in the 1980s world of the Troubles to look back for justification to the Somme and the Boyne. The best example of this spatial projection and displacement is at the end of the play when Pyper attempts to inspire the men before they go over the trench. They had just been comparing and boasting about their various local rivers in Ulster – the Bann, Foyle, Lagan, Erne – when Pyper projects their current location on the Somme back to these very local geographical locations:

> **PYPER**. It's bringing us home. We're not in France. We're home. We're on our own territory. We're fighting for home. This river is ours. This land's ours. We've come home. Where's Belfast, Anderson?
> **ANDERSON**. You know as well as I do where –
> **PYPER**. It's out there. It's waiting for you. Can you hear the shipyard, McIlwaine? ... You weren't dreaming about Lough Erne, David. You're on it. It surrounds you. Moore, the Bann is flowing outside. The Somme, it's not what we think it is. It's the Lagan, the Foyle, the Bann –
> **CRAIG**. You're trying too hard, Pyper (73-74).

Although the rhetoric is beautiful, it comes at a point when the other characters have already begun to experience a certain disillusion with their allotted place in the vulnerable trenches of the Somme, on the brink of almost certain annihilation, and Pyper's use of space may be a failed strategy in this instance. He is undercut by Craig, who does not want to die with any illusions about the meaning of his impending death: 'You won't save us, you won't save yourself, imagining things. There's nothing imaginary about this, Kenneth. This is the last battle. We're going out to die' (74). Oddly, Craig is at peace with this imminent death, and does not need the comfort of loyalist iconography and geographical symbols to comfort him, because, he says ambiguously, 'you can't teach us what we already know'. What do they already know? Is their loyalty to their particular mytho-historiography so strong that they do not even need to be reminded of it? Or do they 'already know' what Anderson says in despair during the 'Pairing' section, that 'Pyper the bastard was right. It's all lies ... We're going to die for nothing' (59). Perhaps they know that but also know they are dying for each other. It is this emphasis on the personal relationships between the men, the primacy of fraternal love that provides any kind of justification for their death. The historical narratives on their collective scale contain nothing but unrequited horror; rather, it is these personal relationships that provide the only positive historical meaning. Before the men go over the trench, they are putting on their own sashes when Craig suddenly gives his to Moore, and the other characters exchange sashes with others not in their normal pairings. A cynical interpretation of this is that they have become the mindless cannon fodder of the British Empire and that they have lost their individual identities to nationalism. However, something more complex and moving is occurring in that scene, something that dramatically contains McGuinness's impulse towards enacting performances of positive human value.

Carthaginians (1988) is also set in liminal spaces: a graveyard, the central play-within-a-play, and the memories of the characters. It takes place in Derry, a predominantly Catholic city in Northern Ireland. As a geographical location, it is simultaneously part of Northern Ireland and a site of civic resistance to British rule for Republicans. It is a border town and its inhabitants have varying conceptions and constructions of Irishness. The partition of Ireland along a physical border was hopelessly inexact: the problems of national boundaries and their conflict with sectarian identities is of course not unique to Ireland. Catholic Republicans were forced to navigate living in Northern Ireland with its attendant nationality while envisioning a different national identity for themselves. In her work with nationalism and sexuality, Eve Sedgwick draws on anthropologist Benedict Anderson's formulation of nationalism and its relationship with modern conceptions of gender:

> 'In the modern world,' Benedict Anderson writes, 'everyone can, should, will 'have' a nationality, as he or she 'has' a gender' ... The implication, I think, is that just as every culture has *some* mechanism ... to constitute what Gayle Rubin refers to as a 'sex/gender system,' a way of negotiating back and forth between chromosomal sex and social gender, so every *modern* culture and person must be seen as partaking of what we might (albeit clumsily) call a 'habitation/nation system.' The 'habitation/nation system' would be the set of discursive and institutional arrangements that mediate between the physical fact that each person inhabits, at a given time, a particular geographical space, and the far more abstract, sometimes even apparently unrelated organization of what has emerged since the late seventeenth century as her/his national identity ... [15]

According to this model, one's physical habitation does not necessarily correspond neatly with one's national identity. McGuinness's characters exhibit varying degrees of ambivalence about their national identity and allegiances. The playwright's use of theatrical space exploits the weaknesses inherent in a culture that ignores Anderson's paradigm. McGuinness writes for actors to inhabit the literal physical space of the theatre, playing characters who exist in another geographical space that, through his dramatic devices, is often projected onto a separate imagined space. This happens not only throughout *Observe the Sons*, but also in a significant way at the end of *Carthaginians* with the Northern Irish city of Derry.

At the end of *Carthaginians*, after the names of the dead in Bloody Sunday have been uttered, and after a quasi-resurrection scene has taken place, Dido awakens in the graveyard among the other sleeping characters:

> What do I believe? I believe it is time to leave Derry. Love it and leave it. Now or never. Why am I talking to myself in a graveyard? Because everybody in Derry talks to themselves. Everybody in the world talks to themselves. What's the world? Shipquay Street and Ferryquay Street and Rossville Street and William Street and the Strand and Great James Street. While I walk the earth, I walk through you, the streets of Derry. If I meet one who knows you and they ask, how's Dido? Surviving. How's Derry? Surviving. Carthage has not been destroyed. Watch yourself.

Dido drops flowers on the sleepers.[16]

Dido imagines Derry as a larger space than it is; the threshold-city is projected outward in space and onto the world. By equating the world with Shipquay and Ferryquay Street, streets in Derry, he in effect explodes their locality and contingent provincialism. Derry loses its borders by becoming international in scope, and the physical lines that cause its conflict are momentarily removed. Therefore, the city becomes all-encompassing and simultaneously obliterated by Dido's imagining. By moving from the local to the international, by being able to simultaneously tend to past wounds but also move forward to create new stories, McGuinness suggests that all of Ireland may be able to transcend past troubles. This threatens rigid conceptions of 'Ireland', which may lie at the centre of people's unwillingness to forget past stories. In *Carthaginians*,

Dido will read Derry in all cities he may encounter in his future wanderings: 'While I walk the earth, I walk through you, the streets of Derry' (379). *Observe the Sons* projects Ulster into a negative space in the past, with no hope of salvation because Pyper is obsessed with the past and does not overcome it, while *Carthaginians* tries to heal the past because Dido projects Ireland's spaces forward to a resurrected future.

While the use of space at the end of *Carthaginians* may imply a redemptive vision, Dido, while the vehicle for the centrifugal force, collapses as a character. Scholars commenting on Dido view him as a figure of redemption, and it may be useful to query their potential rationale for doing so. In *Feast of Famine* (1997), Eamonn Jordan asserts that 'Dido, as he is the youngest, remains somewhat protected from the event [Bloody Sunday] and it is through him that hope is possible.'[17] Following suit, Helen Lojek insists he offers a positive role, even while acknowledging that Dido goes into exile. She writes, 'As a gay, as an artist, as an individual, Dido finds Derry, his home, inadequate ... His final choice, though, is exile – a choice routinely made by McGuinness's artist figures, many of whom are gay. The choice is also, though, and most significantly, a choice of life, not death ... '[18] Lojek attempts to paint exile in a positive light. Dido's play *The Burning Balaclava* causes the rest of the characters to begin dealing with their trauma, through reliving repressed memories and attempting to purge their guilt and sins in the time since Bloody Sunday. As soon as the individual characters have begun to exorcize the trauma of Bloody Sunday, and as soon as they gather in the graveyard to collectively purge the souls of the victims of that day, Dido immediately leaves the community. The queer artist serves as a vehicle for cultural memory and healing in this McGuinness play, but not a participant in the actual framework of a functioning society.

Both queer characters in these plays serve as a mirror to the community, but never actually become a part of that community. Even Pyper, who may have joined the fraternal band of brothers before the Battle of the Somme, now 'lives' alone in a spectral whirlwind outside of time. If old and unsuccessful national stories are queered, de-centred, and subverted, what stories are put in their place, and what happens to the queer 'hero' who brought the old imaginative structure down? In these two plays, the queer hero is sacrificed for the community: Pyper is sacrificed in order to self-defeatingly preserve the cyclical violence of the Troubles, and Dido is exiled in order to restore a heteronormative foundation to the community. There does not seem to be a viable space for Pyper or Dido in these plays. No realistic space exists for Pyper and Craig in Northern Ireland after the conflict: as Craig says to Pyper only moments before the former's slaughter, 'What kind of life do you see for us when we're out of here? It might be many things, but it won't be together' (77). Dido is cruelly rejected by Hark, who, while he exhibits a potential queerness, goes back to Sarah. The queer energy that McGuinness utilizes in these plays serves to destabilize potentially harmful conceptions of an inflexible Irishness, but the queer characters are sacrificed in the name of freeing up space for a country's more heteronormative self-conceptions.

A similar dramatic phenomenon occurs in Brian Friel's play *The Gentle Island* (1971). The play premiered just two months before Bloody Sunday and had a great impact on McGuinness.[19] Friel holds a similar relationship as Frank McGuinness to the liminal spaces of Ireland. Several years before he wrote *The Gentle Island*, Friel moved from the city of Derry in Northern Ireland to County Donegal in the Republic of Ireland.[20] Michael Parker observes that *The Gentle Island* shows 'a gathering and profound disillusion with both states of Ireland, North and South, and a determination on the part of the forty-year-old author to re-view the ideological baggage he had inherited'.[21] *The Gentle Island* presents a space that is in the process of emptying out and deflating, as well as becoming sterile and non-reproductive. The island of Inishkeen, off the coast of Donegal, is in the process of being deserted by its inhabitants – which is evocative of Ireland's overall problem with emigration – and the few remaining characters who remain still struggle over their definition of the place in relation to their previous conceptions of family and home.

The struggle over ideas of home that the characters in *The Gentle Island* undergo is a metaphor for the larger contestation over the contours of the Irish state. In Michael Parker's article 'Telling Tales: Narratives of Politics and Sexuality' in Brian Friel's *The Gentle Island*, he persuasively draws the analogy between the contested space of a family and that of its encapsulating Irish national space:

> the island – like the Irish state? – no longer functions as a secure ground, stable centre or transcendental signified, exerting an unquestioned faith and loyalty ... Joe and Philly fluctuate between a scepticism about and deep attachment to 'home'.[22]

This intra-familial contestation over the contours and location of home is precipitated when the gay Peter Quinn and queer Shane Harrison come ashore on the island. I make the differentiation between Peter being gay and Shane being queer because it is clear from the text that Peter fits the more solid identity that 'gay' connotes, what with his love for Shane and desire to maintain a permanent relationship with him, while I will define Shane as 'queer' because his sexuality is harder to delineate. Shane is an object of desire for Peter, Sarah, and probably Philly, but the contours of Shane's own desires are ambiguous, if they are present at all. In response to Peter telling Shane that the others admire him, Shane replies, 'Which of me?'[23] Shane is a playful character, always performing for the others and it is hard to tell when he is being sincere, similar in many ways to the younger Pyper's antics and Dido's camp persona. He is also an orphan with unknown origins; a mystery clouds his lineage, and in that respect his identity is in a constant state of uncertainty.

Shane is a queer wanderer, much like Pyper and Dido, while his patron/father-figure/lover Peter wishes to put roots down and settle into a normative semblance of family and home. After Shane expresses a desire to leave the island, Peter criticizes him, 'Fine, fine, fine, we'll go. We'll keep moving, talking, laughing, providing vast entertainment for every damn lorry driver that picks us up. What a jolly young man he is!' (27) It is because Shane is a personality constantly in flux, and because his words and actions are performed with a heightened sense of self-reflexivity and performativity, that he becomes an object of queer desire; because the desires he generates are queer, they seem to precipitate volatile responses on Friel's island. When the desire that Shane elicits becomes incapable of a neat delineation and discernible genealogy rooted in the parameters of heterosexual marriage, it provokes a violent response, especially when that desire verges toward non-reproductive homosexuality: Sarah shoots Shane when he is suspected of homosexual relations with her husband Philly. This makes sense in the historical context: homosexual acts were illegal in Ireland until the 1993 Sexual Offences Act decriminalized homosexuality. It also makes sense within the theoretical context of a hetero-patriarchy: male supremacy depends upon the principle that heteronormativity is an essential component to male identity.

Shane is an object of queer desire because the desires he generates are legally and culturally transgressive, and thus the

spaces those desires inhabit and cross are queered: Peter wishes to
set up a same-sex domestic space on the island with Shane; Sarah
wishes to commit adultery with him (her desire is voyeuristically
kindled from afar with French binoculars); and Philly has an
ambiguous, homo-erotic and violent response to him. Both Sarah
and Philly project unfulfilled and imagined desires onto Shane: their
own and also their jealous imaginings of his sexual liaisons with the
other. While it is textually credible that Philly and Shane have a
homosexual encounter at the boathouse, Sarah may just be
retaliating for her own rejected sexual advance upon Shane. When
Manus tells his family about Peter's desire to return to the island for
Christmas (this story is contradicted by Peter, who says it is Manus's
desire, thus raising the possibility of a queer energy transferred
between Peter and Manus), Sarah exclaims, 'There's no room for
them in this house or in any other house here either' (49). Here we
again have an example of queer characters being expelled from the
community when they threaten that community's self-conceptions.
When the subject of Shane and Peter returning to the island is
broached, Sarah immediately thinks of the idea in terms of
containing them; despite all of the empty houses in the village, she
still insists there is no room to hold the two men. If the men were to
be given their own house, traditional male and female roles would
have to be re-defined; when gender is seen as fluid or constructed,
the voluntary choices inherent in the way families and societies are
constructed become apparent.

Michael Parker has argued that *The Gentle Island* is a play of
competing narratives about Ireland, as a mirror and presaging of the
cultural and sectarian conflicts that would erupt in the Troubles
soon after the play opened. I would suggest that the play is also a re-
imagining of Ireland's geographical spaces, in part because the
competing narratives about the ultimate location of 'home' break
down in terms of credibility, and boundaries are continuously
transgressed when characters reorient themselves toward a new
space to consider their own. The character that serves to show the
ease with which boundaries can be crossed is Shane, whether he
crosses them himself or, as is more the case in the play, others
imagine him as transgressing those boundaries. Ireland is queered
in *The Gentle Island* in that it becomes an unstable and contested
site, as a metaphorically geographic extension of the queer identities
and desires that are performed and imagined in the play. Queer
spaces are often described and evoked off-stage: Peter's and Shane's

tent, an imagined site of homosexuality; the mysterious caves that the islanders want to show to the strangers; the sea and what occurs on the sea and the mainland; and the boathouse where Shane and Philly may or may not have had a homosexual encounter. They are sites of imagination, which allows them a potentially positive value alongside the volatility of their fluctuating and uncertain energies.

These re-imaginings of Ireland occur because a queer character, Shane, forces different introspections within the characters regarding their relationships with the idea of home. Whether or not Sarah actually sees anything occur between Shane and Philly, she wants Manus to kill Shane because he has supposedly usurped her own role as the object of Philly's reproductive desire: 'That he's down there with that Dublin tramp, Shane. That they're stripped naked. That he's doing for the tramp what he couldn't do for me. That's what I'm trying to say. And that if you're the great king of Inishkeen, you'll kill them both—that's what I'm saying' (61). When Manus cannot, she shoots Shane herself with a chilling deter-mination: 'Give it to me! I'll kill the tramp' (68). Notice that Sarah continuously calls Shane a 'tramp', someone who wanders without roots or a home, as indeed is the case with Shane's unknown origins. Sarah also equates Shane with the city and its uncertain and threatening spaces when juxtaposed with those of rural Inishkeen. When Shane is shot and brought to the mainland, Joe reports that 'Even if he lives he'll never walk again. His spine's shattered' (70). The wandering queer character is immobilized and possibly destroyed, but Friel's ending shows that the community cannot restore itself to its past familial structures because they have been irrevocably changed.

The clearest realization about home's queer spatiality occurs within the heterosexual Joe, who realizes from Shane's ill treat-ment that his home is actually somewhere off the island, away from the people he has considered his family. The queer characters are expelled from the community, but in a sense the community ceases to function when this occurs, at least in terms of being a self-sustaining and reproductive entity, and a sustainable centre to home is removed. The hearth fire is out in the final scene and it appears that Philly will not have children with Sarah. Manus looks for a scapegoat and shouts, 'it's them—them queers! I should have killed the two of them when I had them! What we had wasn't much but what there was was decent and wholesome! And they blighted us! They cankered us! They blackened the bud that was beginning to grow again! My curse on them!' (72) But Manus's rage seems misplaced because all that Shane brought to the island was the queer consciousness of the uncertainties inherent in constructed identities and spatial boundaries. The audience should have been made aware of this by the play's end; unfortunately, Friel's prescience and cultural perceptiveness about the roots of violence was not enough to prevent the real bloodshed that would soon follow in the 1970s.

Brendan Behan's play *The Hostage* (1958) is queerly structured because it is constantly shifting among dramatic tones and genre. The space of the actual performance of the play becomes queered because of its direct engagement with the audience. There is bawdy humour, songs, characters who break the fourth wall and speak directly to the audience, tongue-in-cheek reference to the playwright himself, and even points of melodrama with tragic undertones. Michael Patrick Gillespie notes that the play 'appears as an amalgam of confusion and contradiction. Frenetic digressions disrupt the systematic progression of the plot, and radical shifts in temperament and attitudes frustrate efforts to delineate a linear character development ... Elements within Behan's play repeatedly underscore disorientation as an integral component of its dramatic development.'[24] Gillespie thinks that this dramatic 'disorientation' is a metaphor for the seemingly irreconcilable political and sectarian conflict between Northern Ireland and the Republic of Ireland.

The Hostage takes place in a brothel full of 'pimps, prostitutes, decayed gentlemen and their visiting "friends"', as well as several prominent queer characters: Rio Rita, 'a homosexual navvy,' Princess Grace, 'his coloured boyfriend', and eventually it is revealed that Mr. Mulleady, 'a decaying Civil Servant' is also queer (or he is 'made' to be queer by Rio and Grace). There is some critical debate as to whether these three queer characters are truly homosexual or will ultimately be revealed to be only members of the secret police. Brett Cardullo thinks they are revealed to be members of the secret police and so not ultimately as homosexuals. I agree more with Ann Marie Adams, who thinks that Rio and Princess Grace are actually homosexual, but that the text serves to reinscribe heterosexist assumptions about homosexuals. I do not see why they cannot be *both* homosexual and members of the secret police. These queer characters are at the centre of the play's main plot twist when they inform on the IRA activities in the brothel; however, when the police raid the house the British soldier being held hostage, Leslie

Williams, is accidentally killed, so in some respect they are responsible for the soldier's death, a point which Ann Marie Adams suggests is part of the play's hetero-sexism.

Queerness is figured as a kind of contagion in Behan's play. Although Mulleady conspires with Rio and Princess Grace, we are told in the stage directions that the two queer men 'have corrupted his morals',[25] which is an odd bit of stage direction considering that Mulleady is the one who includes Rio and Grace in his schemes to inform on the IRA activities in the house. Regardless, it appears that Rio and Princess Grace have 'queered' Mulleady when the three of them agreed to inform. We are told in the stage directions that 'the action takes a very sinister turn' at this moment in the play when the queer characters begin to conspire: 'They go into a huddle. The other inhabitants of the house are mystified. All that can be seen are three pairs of twitching hips, as they mutter and whisper to each other' (95). They sing a song, and the stage directions state, 'The song ends and the three queers gyrate across the stage, twisting their bodies sinuously and making suggestive approaches to LESLIE. LESLIE is about to join in when MISS GILCHRIST throws herself at him' (97).

Leslie is susceptible to the advances of the queers, just as Mulleady succumbed to their advances. Miss Gilchrist prevents him from entering the gyrating fray, but it is a telling stage direction. It also gives one pause to consider Leslie's relationship to Behan's use of queer space in the play; although the queer trio of Rio Rita, Princess Grace, and Mulleady seem to be the obvious locus for locating queer space in the play, it is actually Leslie who precipitates the queering of a space which is already fairly queer, a brothel inhabited partly by homosexuals. Act I is concerned with establishing the brothel as a space full of degenerate characters, prostitutes, and queers; it is already a subversive space, but the dramatic action does not truly get under way until the end of the act when Leslie is brought into the house. He is a British soldier brought into a Dublin house run by the IRA. Add to that the fact that the play was originally produced in London and there are plenty of spatial disjunctions with which to contend. Act I ends with a song, Leslie beginning, 'There's no place on earth like the world/There's no place wherever you be.' The song concludes:

MONSEWER. The South and the north poles are parted,
MEG. Perhaps it is all for the best.

> **PAT**. Till the H-bomb will bring them together,
> **ALL**. And there we will let matters rest (41-42).

The song ends with a pessimistic view of the spatial boundaries that plagued Ireland during 'The Troubles'. The only way to break down those barriers that cause sectarian strife, the song suggests, is through total annihilation in war, 'Till the H-bomb will bring them together'. There is no homoerotic energy that suffuses the end of Act I in *The Hostage*, and yet I would argue that Behan is queering the dramatic space: in the London theatre where it premiered, mostly British audience members looked in on a Dublin house where they witnessed the spatial disjunctions attendant upon a British soldier being held hostage by the IRA within that house. The end of Act I is a song about the impossibility of bringing disparate spaces together without violence, thus setting up the dramatic tension for the play.

The ostensibly heterosexual British soldier Leslie is the queer wanderer in *The Hostage*, who catalyzes an effect on the use of dramatic space in the play, which in turn highlights the spatial roots of the conflicts during 'The Troubles'. This device is used again at the end of Act Two, when Leslie has been informed he will likely be killed in exchange for the IRA soldier being executed in Belfast. Leslie is left alone in the room and sings a song that reorients the location of home to where he presently is:

> I love old England in the east, I love her in the west,
> From Jordan's streams to Derry's Walls,
> I love old England best.
> I love my dear old Notting Hill, wherever I may roam,
> But I wish the Irish and the niggers and the wogs,
> Were kicked out and sent back home (78).

Leslie is currently in Dublin, though, away from his own home, even though he takes control of the space and sings from a proprietary position. He is transgressing boundaries and changing the composition of their contents in his imaginings. Of course, his sentiments are violent and vulgar, which is to say that subverting the contours and ownership of space is often an act of aggression and not always a justified subversion. The justifications for this dramatic device, and its analogues in reality, vary depending upon one's place in a certain space at a given time, and one's confidence in the sustainability of whatever boundaries have been constructed.

Irish Catholic Teresa says of her lost love the British Protestant Leslie, 'He died in a strange land, and at home he had no one' (108).

That is the abyss that queer space evokes, because it threatens the stability of all we have known. It is also a warning of what happens when rigid spaces are maintained and policed with the fervour of certainty. These modern Irish dramas continue to be excellent vehicles for elucidating these thorny cultural concerns in a safe space. Queer space is an inspired doubt in the solidity of boundaries, locations, and identities: this doubt in boundaries need not have a destructively deconstructive effect, but rather can achieve a kind of cultural unification. Although Leslie is killed, Behan resurrects him in the final moments of *The Hostage*, and in this respect significantly breaks from the usual mould of exiling the queer character in order to re-establish a controlling hetero-normative lens. A 'ghostly green light' glows on Leslie's body as he rises from the ground to sing a song that serves to actually unify the space in the closing moments of the play. The entire cast approaches the audience and sings, 'The bells of hell,/Go ting-a-ling-a-ling,/For you but not for him,/Oh death, where is thy sting-a-ling-a-ling!/Or grave thy victory' (109). The characters direct their words toward the audience and suggest an end to previous ways of destructive seeing. The dramatic space is collapsed at the end of *The Hostage* because it is paradoxically unified between audience and actors: the divided dramatic space is queered in order to reveal itself to be the actual communal space it is or should be.

---

[1] Eve Kosofsky Sedgwick, *Tendencies* (Durham, NC: Duke University Press, 1993), p. 9.

[2] Jean-Ulrick Désert, 'Queer Space', *Queers in Space*, eds Gordon B. Ingram, Anne-Marie Bouthillette, and Yolanda Retter (Seattle: Bay Press, 1997), p. 21.

[3] Désert, p. 20.

[4] Una Chaudhuri, *Staging Place: The Geography of Modern Drama* (Ann Arbor: University of Michigan Press, 1995), pp. 14-15.

[5] Ibid, p. 15.

[6] Christopher Murray, *Twentieth Century Irish Drama: Mirror Up to Nation* (Manchester: Manchester University Press, 1997), p. 246.

[7] Maria Kurdi, 'An Interview with Frank McGuinness', *Nua: Studies in Contemporary Irish Writing* 4. 1-2 (2003), p. 113.

[8] Helen Lojek, *Contexts for Frank McGuinness's Drama* (Washington, D.C.: Catholic University of America Press, 2004), p. 222.

9 Tom Herron, 'Dead Men Talking: Frank McGuinness's *Observe the Sons of Ulster Marching towards the Somme*', *Éire-Ireland: a Journal of Irish Studies* 39.1-2 (2004), p. 137.

10 Frank McGuinness, *Observe the Sons of Ulster Marching toward the Somme* (London: Faber and Faber, 1986), p. 11. All subsequent quotations are from this edition.

11 Eamonn Jordan, *The Feast of Famine: the Plays of Frank McGuinness* (Bern: Peter Lang, 1997), p. 85.

12 Sedgwick, p. 8.

13 David Cregan, '"There's Something Queer Here": Modern Ireland and the Plays of Frank McGuinness', *Australasian Drama Studies* 43 (2003), p. 71.

14 Claire Gleitman, 'Reconstructing History in the Irish History Play', *The Cambridge Companion to Twentieth-Century Drama*, ed. Shaun Richards (Cambridge: Cambridge University Press, 2004), p. 223.

15 Sedgwick, pp. 147-48.

16 Frank McGuinness, 'Carthaginians', *Plays One* (London: Faber and Faber, 1996), p. 379. All subsequent quotations are from this edition.

17 Jordan, p. 71.

18 Lojek, *Contexts*, p. 182.

19 Helen Lojek, 'Brian Friel's *Gentle Island of Lamentation*', *Irish University Review* 29.1 (1999), pp. 48, 55.

20 Michael Parker, 'Telling Tales: Narratives of Politics and Sexuality in Brian Friel's *The Gentle Island*', *HJEAS: Hungarian Journal of English and American Studies* 2.2 (1996), p. 78.

21 Ibid.

22 Ibid, pp. 64-65.

23 Brian Friel, *The Gentle Island* (County Meath, Ireland: Gallery Press, 1973), p. 41. All subsequent quotations are from this edition.

24 Michael Patrick Gillespie, 'Violent Impotence and Impotent Violence: Brendan Behan's *The Hostage*', *Éire-Ireland: a Journal of Irish Studies* 29.1 (Spring 1994), p. 92.

25 Brendan Behan, *The Hostage* (London: Eyre Methuen, 1958), p. 104. All subsequent quotations are from this edition.

11 | 'Crying' on 'Pluto':

'Queering the "Irish Question" for Global Film Audiences'

Charlotte McIvor

This chapter explores the overlaps between Neil Jordan's *The Crying Game* (1992) and *Breakfast on Pluto* (2005)[1] and situates them in relationship to social change in the Republic and the North, the relationship between Irish and international politics, and evolving theoretical discourses of global(ized) queerness between their releases. *The Crying Game*'s surprise success in the early 1990s marked a new visibility for Jordan as a filmmaker and Irish cinema as a global art form, particularly in the United States. By 2000, Lance Pettitt was able to claim: 'I contend that film is now the pre-eminent medium through which Ireland examines itself and projects its image to the wider world.'[2] Notably, the queer focus of its plot was a major ingredient of *The Crying Game*'s success, although audiences were initially urged to keep it secret. The revelation of transgendered romance interest in Dil's male genitalia in a love scene featuring full-frontal nudity drove Miramax's US marketing campaign for the film and was thus marketed as the centre of the plot.

Jordan's love quadrangle of Black British Dil (Jaye Davidson),[3] Antiguan Black British soldier Jody (Forest Whittaker), and Irish IRA members Fergus (Stephen Rea) and Jude (Miranda Richardson) in *The Crying Game* plays out a litany of anxieties over Irish and British colonial/postcolonial history, racialization, sexuality and gender. Jody is held hostage by the IRA as a demand for the release of prisoners held by the British after being seduced by Jude, a volunteer. Fergus is charged with watching him, and the two develop a friendship bordering on the homoerotic. Fergus is charged with shooting Jody, but falters, and Jody escapes, only to be run over by a tank as the British army arrives to destroy the hideout. Fergus flees Ireland, reinventing himself as 'Jimmy' and finds Dil. He begins to fall for her, but is also preoccupied with guilt-ridden fantasy images of Jody in cricket whites, even while receiving oral sex from Dil. As they are about to make love, Fergus discovers she is biologically male. Meanwhile, Jude is back, and demands that Fergus aid her in assassinating a well-known official, implying that Dil's safety is at risk if he refuses. When Fergus reveals to Dil that he had a part in Jody's death, she confines him to his apartment. Jude tracks Fergus down after he misses the assassination, and a bloody showdown ensues between Dil and Jude. The film ends with Dil lovingly delivering Fergus's multivitamin tablets in prison after he takes the rap for Jude's murder.

The queer, racialized, gendered and postcolonial aspects of this film's plot inspired a storm of criticism that centralized Jordan's film within those fields of study up until the present. However, while *Breakfast on Pluto* covers remarkably similar ground, the film has not received the same international critical or popular attention as *The Crying Game*[4], despite featuring popular theatre and film star Cillian Murphy as Patricia (Patrick) Kitten Brady. How is the figure of the transgendered heroine recycled in what Lir MacCárthaigh of *Film Ireland* termed 'Neil Jordan's most Irish production in many years'?[5]

In *Pluto*, Kitten's queerness is anything but a secret in her fictional border town of Tyreelin. A queer aesthetic of camp and kitsch overwhelm the film as it features talking birds as narrators, among other spectacles, although this playfulness is often hidden just below the surface of an otherwise dreary and violent world. Kitten is the illegitimate son of the village priest, played by Liam Neeson, and his briefly employed Mitzi Gaynor look-a-like housekeeper. Left to the mercy of an unsympathetic foster family, Kitten discovers early on that there is a lot about her world that she wants to change, starting with free access to her foster mother's lipstick and dresses. She is not, however, interested in what she repeatedly terms 'serious'[6] matters, like the mounting violence of 'The Troubles'. She bands together with other misfits in her small town: Laurence (Seamus Reilly), a young man with Down's syndrome: Irwin (Laurence Kinlan), who eventually turns his aggression towards becoming a volunteer for the IRA, and Charlie

(Ruth Negga), who will bear Irwin's baby out of wedlock following his execution by the IRA.

Violence consistently forces its way into Kitten's life, despite her protestations. After Laurence's death from an IRA car bomb, Kitten makes her way to London in search of her mother and is nearly murdered in the course of doing sex work. She is also accused of being a terrorist after a bomb explodes in a nightclub where she is dancing at the time. She eventually returns to Ireland after Irwin's death to comfort a pregnant Charlie in the safety of the church rectory. She reconciles with her father, Father Liam, in the process. The rectory is firebombed by the local community in anger at the flagrant disobedience of this group of illegitimates and sinners in a sacred space. Charlie and Kitten leave for London again, and the film ends with a parting shot of this queer family that now includes a baby carriage. Ultimately, Kitten does not make peace with her mother, but she does make a family with Father Liam and Charlie that confounds her earlier expectations.

In *Breakfast on Pluto,* queerness becomes an actively deployed force against violent Irish nationalisms, rather than a titillating secret, but what does this repetition and refocus of queer energy and bodies permit Jordan to say anew in 2005? Additionally, it is not only the queer, as in homosexual or transgressive, that continues to be a focus for Jordan in these two particular films, but a fascination with *transgendered* queer bodies. Judith Halberstam's 2005 work *In a Queer Time and Place* examines the representation of transgenderism in popular culture, media, and art following a number of recently visible events and productions, such as the murder of Brandon Teena and companions and subsequent films and books about the case, as well as, of course, *The Crying Game.* She observes:

> Transgenderism, with its promise of gender liberation and its patina of transgression, its promise of flexibility and its reality of a committed rigidity, could be the successful outcome of years of gender activism; or, just as easily, it could be the sign of the reincorporation of a radical subculture back into the flexible economy. [7]

How does *Breakfast on Pluto* build upon the queer-/transgendered legacy of *The Crying Game* in popular mass film culture and its diagnosis of national(ist) Irish identity formations? How does the reframing of Irish terrorism for global audiences post-Troubles and post-9/11 transform the figure of the Irish terrorist and how does queerness mediate this transformation for Jordan? What is the relationship of social, economic, political and cultural shifts in the Republic and the North to the production of these two similar films, as well as global trends in queer cinema?

In the 12 years between the releases of these films, the Republic of Ireland and the North have undergone a multitude of changes. The year after *The Crying Game* was released, homosexuality was legalized in the Republic. In the Republic of Ireland, the Celtic Tiger's roar was beginning to make itself heard throughout the world, and the Belfast Peace Agreement was signed in 1998. The 1990s overall were an unprecedented moment of visibility for 'Irishness' as global product through *Riverdance, Angela's Ashes*, the music of the Cranberries, etc., and as a site of violence through continuing media coverage of 'The Troubles' and the lead-up to the passing of the Belfast Peace Agreement.

As a consequence of the economic boom, unprecedented im-migration from European Union member and non-member states, Africa, and Asia also began to shift the demographics of an island that had long appeared to be superficially white and Christian. Irishness as a political, nationalist and ethnic category was simultaneously being marketed as a global commodity as never before and stretched beyond its previously imagined limits through challenges from within. These rapid changes have been criticized for encouraging images of a post-modern, post-nationalist cos-mopolitan Ireland when in fact there is greater economic inequality than ever in the Republic. Reports of racism and racially motivated attacks have been unprecedented, and there is continuing controversy over issues concerning who counts as an Irish citizen, and what rights are to be applied to immigrants, refugees and asylum seekers. The mounting recession has only exacerbated these issues. In this period of transformation, Irish literary and cultural critics have vacillated between exhortations for Irish film, literature, and culture not to forget its traumatic past of Famine, poverty, and colonialism in the glow of the Celtic Tiger and challenges to deal more actively with the changing social, political, cultural, and economic dimensions of contemporary Ireland without employing historical 'trauma' as an excuse for creating new structures of racism and inequality that are complicit with global capitalisms and US led neo-imperial hegemonies.

This pull between traumatic Irish pasts and shifting con-temporary geometries of global power and influence for Ireland brought on by the Celtic Tiger is made manifestly clear in the resonances between *The Crying Game* and *Breakfast on Pluto*. When Jordan returned to the topic of the Troubles, queerness, transgenderism and Irish nationalism in 2005 with *Breakfast on Pluto*, he argued that he did so as a response to the post-9/11 global atmosphere, particularly following the London bombings in summer 2004. He says:

> I looked back on my memories of the 1960s and 1970s in Dublin and London and found an eerie resemblance to that time – think of the London bombings that have just happened – and it made me a little reluctant to do this film. I had the script for three or four years and I didn't push it, but then I finally decided that the experience that the film represents is really quite instructive for anybody living in these times. With all these nasty ideologies trying to tell you what you should be, in a world where you can go into a bar and the bar may explode, how do you make your way in the world? Patrick does a pretty good job.[8]

Rather than an explicit engagement with the history of the Troubles, Jordan positions this film as an instructive allegory for global audiences dealing with the aftermath of 9/11 and an aggressive focus on global terrorism from the US, Britain, and their allies. 'The Troubles' status as an allegory for Jordan rather than a current event telegraphs the new place of Ireland in the global world order as an affluent and peaceful country, no longer officially troubled by a divisive civil war with Britain.

Breakfast on Pluto does have the power to challenge narratives of dominant Irish nationalism through the queered perspective of Kitten Brady, but Jordan's use of Kitten to translate contemporary events for non-Irish audiences should not be overlooked. Jordan has frequently been criticized for the lack of political analysis in his films. These criticisms have cited bland condemnations of Irish republicanism without a consideration of the (post)colonial context or other complex relationships of class and/or religion between Catholic and Protestant communities and Irish and British security forces. This lack of political focus allows him to foreground the redemption of the individual, rather than collective social liberation. His focus on the generic and unsituated individual positioned against unnamed global forces of terror post-9/11 as the representative audience for his work reproduces this politically limited perspective. Queerness stands in as the force that can dissolve politics and allow individual liberation, but at what cost and for what (queer) subjects? *Breakfast on Pluto* is far from a film that is only in conversation with Irish (nationalist) histories and its blind spots reveal the manner in which queerness has been marshalled as a global commodity that frequently distracts from deeper inter-rogations of the imbrication of race, nation, sexuality, and power post 9/11. Kitten's tale therefore can be read as a comfort and inspiration to people who live with violence as a clear and present danger in everyday life, but it suggests no analysis of contemporary political situations, using queerness in the service of deflecting this potentiality. Kitten does not take politics seriously and neither by extension should the audience. Jordan thus potentially links a queer aesthetic to a lack of political awareness.

Jordan's queer characters, plots, and spectacles in *The Crying Game* and *Breakfast on Pluto* are simultaneously used to reveal the limits of 'Irishness' based on nationalism as a conceptual and political project and translate Ireland and the Troubles to global cinema audiences. This marshalling of queerness as globalized commodity by Jordan in his 1992 film was in fact the beginning of a trend for global queer cinema,[9] and *Breakfast on Pluto* ultimately feeds back into this genealogy. Jordan's critique of Irish nationalism is predicated upon a rejection of compulsory whiteness, Catholicism/Christianity, heterosexuality and Republicanism for Irish subjects, north and south, with queer characters as the catalyst for their dissolution. The concept of queer in these two films implicates not only a range of sexual practices and gender presentations that deviate from the heterosexual as linked to biological male and female 'sex' roles in socially sanctioned arrangements (i.e., marriage). Rather, queer sexuality itself takes on a particularly normative Irish articulation understood again by Jordan through the lens of Catholic heterosexual nationalisms. Thus, in these films, queer Irish sexuality includes not only male/male, female/female activity or transgenderism, but also clergy/laity intercourse and sex outside marriage. Charlie, Kitten's best friend and unmarried pregnant mother, and Father Liam, his priestly father, are therefore also 'queered' in *Breakfast on Pluto*.

Nevertheless, the homosexual or transgendered characters (Kitten, Dil, Jody) serve as the major catalyst for the trans-formations at the centre of each film's plot: Fergus leaves the IRA, Charlie leaves Ireland and starts a queer family with Kitten, Father Liam renews a relationship with his son and is freed of guilt over his indiscretions despite the anger of the community and church. Queer characters' sexual transgressions are understood as linked with their failed political and religious virtues, which Jordan frames positively as a necessary step in rejecting pathologically violent Irish nationalisms, but it is the *homosexual* and *transgendered* characters that are able to force change and the evolution of other characters away from limited scripts of Irish nationalist identity. This slippage between the queer (Fergus, Charlie, Father Liam) and practising homosexuals and transgendered characters (Dil, Jody, Kitten) allows Jordan to use the *idea* of queerness as a mode of unpacking Irishness through national and transnational contacts, but its practice is limited to the aesthetic and thematic. Dil, Jody, and Kitten never find love, and *The Crying Game* has been particularly criticized for using Jody and Dil as props for Fergus's own self-realization. By mixing the 'queer' and the Irish, the films address national and international audiences, with the queer/homosexual characters serving as the site of translation for both. Fintan Walsh observes in his examination of queer Irish theatre and performance: 'What social agency, after all, can we really apportion to the homosexual who only functions as a queering "device", or worse still, exists as pathology or symptom? Where is homosexuality not just a dissident strategy but also a force actively invested in the generation of meaning?'[10] Significantly, Jordan's Ireland gains entrance into global cinema markets precisely by using themes of queerness as a globally recognizable trope that distances both films from the violence of the Troubles, even as it evokes the events as background and initial draw.

Through Dil, Jody, and Kitten, Irishness can re-imagine itself as a post-national and queer identity that transcends the trauma of nationalism, the Troubles and Christianity (esp. the Catholic Church) in a national(ist) and international context. But, Jordan's version of Irish queerness can only articulate itself as a tale of ambivalent individuality and not social redemption or liberation. This is often viewed as a strength of *The Crying Game* in particular, and the reason for its place in the canon of Irish cinema. Irish film scholars Emer Rockett and Kevin Rockett argue: '*The Crying Game* marked a decisive shift from the political arena to the personal which had not been appropriated in such a bold manner prior to this.'[11] This move towards the 'personal' in Irish cinema with *The Crying Game* in 1992 suggests sexual exploration as an anecdote to violent (Irish) nationalism but it significantly coincides with an aggressive globalization of queer identities in the 1990s which I

detail below. Thus, by charting the continuities between these films'
pre- and post-Celtic Tiger/Belfast Peace Agreement representations
of Irishness, nationalism, and the Troubles, it can be identified how
queerness recurs as a key concept in locating Ireland on a global
map of power and prestige.

This is not to dismiss race, class, nation and religion as categories always already implicated in queer sexualities, but rather
actually to relate Jordan's work to a body of queer and queer of
colour theorizing that has linked increased mobility of queer bodies
through migration, media, and organizing to aggressive modes of
globalized capitalist consumption. This has resulted in queerness as
an object of globalized consumption, as well as creating increased
opportunities for transnational queer activism that has pushed at
categories of home and nation, margin and centre. This body of
work has sharply criticized the de-linking of queerness and queer
bodies from contexts of race, class, nation, and religion in search of
'a term or a grammar that would dispel the complexity of these
cross-cultural interactions, making them universally legible'.[12] In
their anthology, *Queer Globalizations: Citizenship and the Afterlife
of Colonialism*, Arnaldo Cruz-Malavé and Martin F. Manalansan
state: 'Queerness is now global'.

Whether in advertising, film, performance arts, the Internet, or
the political discourses of human rights in emerging democracies,
images of queer sexualities and cultures now circulate the globe.'[13]
They cite the circulation of *The Crying Game* and other mainstream
films such as *Philadelphia* as evidence, as well as 'gay and lesbian
lifestyle products'.[14] In the same volume, Joseba Gabilondo
identifies *The Crying Game* as the film which initiated a 'global
taste for "queer" films'[15] in the 1990s, and was followed by *Farewell
My Concubine* (1993), *The Adventures of Priscilla Queen of the
Desert* (1994), *Fresa Y Chocolate* (1995), and *Madame Butterfly*
(1995). He claims

> at the risk of metanarrativizing the specific negotiations taking
> place between different national situations and globalization, I
> believe that these films use the same discursive strategy of
> mobilizing a desiring queer male character in order to re-
> legitimize and articulate a new global hegemony around the
> different national masculinities and hegemonies set in crisis by
> globalization.[16]

In the case of *The Crying Game,* while Dil and Jody inspire a
change in Fergus's worldview through the challenge of their

difference (race, nationality, sexuality, and transgenderism), the affairs are never consummated knowingly, and Dil and Fergus's tentative romance is finally scored in the mode of a parodied heterosexual love story with 'Stand By Your Man' playing over the final credits. In perhaps the most telling moment of the film, during Dil and Fergus's reconciliation scene after the revealing of Dil's penis, she challenges him flirtatiously: 'And even when you were throwing up, I could tell you cared.'[17] Was this sentiment also initially shared by audiences at this moment of transition in global queer film culture from abject to bona fide trend? Jordan mobilizes disgust in order to theoretically undo it, but this moment of shock is the lynchpin of its successful US marketing campaign. Dil's humiliation, as well as physical and emotional pain in this scene when Dil is struck by Fergus in anger at the discovery, reinvents queer *and* Irish culture for global cinema audiences.

Therefore, the remainders of Jordan's project of queering Irishness seem to be precisely the queer subjects upon whom translation falls in the films. Jody is dead and Dil never consummates her relationship with Fergus. And while Kitten and Charlie escape to London to start a new life with Charlie's baby, as Judith Halberstam notes in regard to *The Crying Game*: 'The film characterizes Irish nationalism as a heartless and futile endeavour while ironically depicting England as a multicultural refuge, a place where formerly colonized peoples find a home.'[18] The relevance of her comment on both films is highly revealing. Jordan's de-privileging of material economic and social circumstances in favour of romantic queer utopias can certainly be read as empowering in the blush of the films' final frames and their accompanying swells of pop music. Yet, pleasure comes to queer characters only in the form of narrative twists or filmic conceits (such as Kitten's multiple fantasy sequences) rather than con-summation of physical desires onscreen or final confirmation of their safety. This suggests a mode of filmic discipline in Jordan's work where queerness is positioned as conceit rather than practice, device rather than situated mode of living.

Nevertheless, the switch in genre register from dark romantic thriller in *The Crying Game* to *Breakfast on Pluto's* violent camp fantasy suggests a transfer of agency to a queer(er) gaze, one which references a long history of queer camp performance as a mode of resistance. Through privileging the perspective of Patricia Saint Kitten Brady as narrator, *Breakfast on Pluto's* camp stylistic inversion of *The Crying Game* transforms the disgust experienced by Fergus at the centre of its plot into a prolonged engagement with visual queer pleasures in *Pluto*. *Pluto* also foregrounds a refusal to follow social or dramaturgical scripts, like that of the thriller or Irish Republican nationalism. Therefore, *Breakfast on Pluto* could be read as a comment on *The Crying Game,* a reworking of limited agency granted to Dil, Jody and Fergus. Conn Holohan argues: 'By repeatedly reinterpreting events within his own camp sensibility, Kitten both insists on his own integrity as an acting subject and queers the interpretive framework which has dominated the historical circumstances in which he finds himself.'[19] Holohan's reading of Kitten views her refusal to engage with the serious politics of Irish republican nationalism as a political gesture 'given the restrictive nature of nationalist political discourse, particularly in relation to issues of gender and sexuality'.[20] But Kitten's price for being given this voice by Jordan is to be subjected to multiple and prolonged acts of violence onscreen. She refuses to take the identity expected of her as a young man or by the Troubles as a whole seriously, transforming encounters with her foster mother and sister, violent British police interrogators, and IRA thugs into endless opportunities to flirt or question the logic of their tactics or beliefs. After one of her best friends, Laurence, a young man with Down's Syndrome, is killed by a car bomb planted by the IRA, she is inspired in her grief to dispose of guns that her rock band lover and IRA gun runner, Billy Hatchet, has hidden in their mobile home. When the IRA comes to collect the guns and discovers them missing, they first plan to shoot Kitten and then decide 'he's not worth the bullet, the mental nancy boy'.[21] Kitten challenges them, asking what's wrong with nancy boys 'that you can't be bothered killing them. You kill everybody else'.[22] Kitten's queerness therefore renders her beyond life or death to the IRA, and implicates the maintenance of sexual and gender norms as complicit in the reiteration of violent Irish nationalisms which manufacture victims and aggressors without resolving the source of political and social problems. Jordan grants queerness a dynamic power in dissolving commonly accepted Irish nationalist narratives and structures of feeling, but this power is still subject to regulation and death, even if it operates under the radar.

In the most powerful moment of parallel between the films, Kitten, like Dil, is subjected to a revelation of her secret. Unlike in *The Crying Game,* however, the audience already knows, and

Kitten's revelation is forced through police action, rather than as an act of erotic agency in the home. After a bomb explodes in a London nightclub as Kitten dances with a handsome soldier, she is accused of being a transvestite terrorist when her genitalia is discovered. Her Irishness and transvestism render her a terrorist by association, and she makes front page headlines. Nevertheless, the titillation of visual revelation is refused, operating essentially as a parody of the trope of discovering the *'true* identity' of transgendered characters in *The Crying Game* and other works.[23] But, in arguably the most violent scene of the film, Kitten is subsequently subjected to a brutal beating at the hands of British investigators, a scene which Holohan characterizes as 'deeply familiar to Irish audiences from cinematic and television representations of the Guilford Four and Birmingham Six'.[24] The reprise of this familiar scene, however, comes with a twist. Kitten enjoys her beating, flirting with the officers and smiling as she is thrown up against a window. She asks, 'If I wasn't a transvestite terrorist, would you marry me?'[25] She later has to be forcibly removed from the prison.

Kitten's methods of coping within that abusive situation that include even erotic pleasure during a police beating can be understood as what José Muñoz terms a practice of 'disindentification.' Muñoz defines disidentification partially as a mode of

> dealing with dominant ideology, one that neither opts to assimilate within such a structure nor strictly opposes it; rather, disidentification is a strategy that works on and against dominant ideology.[26]

Kitten's continued flirtations and expressions of pleasure throughout the entire beating incident, as well as her reluctance to leave the jail after she is cleared of charges, may seem twisted. But it is this twisted queer pleasure that undoes the terror the officers try to inflict upon her through her disidentification with its intended effects and eventually win them over to her side. The police officers are forced to view her in Holohan's words as an 'idiosyncratic individual'[27] rather than a Paddy terrorist. Muñoz argues, 'To disidentify is to read oneself and one's own life narrative in a moment, object, or subject that is not culturally coded to 'connect' with the disidentifying subject.'[28] Kitten reads pleasure into a moment of humiliation, and remakes a prototypical scene of Irish/British (post)colonial trauma into a romantic fantasy. Dil ends up on the floor from Fergus's blow, ultimately reading care into a moment of disgust, delivering vitamins to a distant love until the very end, but Kitten lives actively and pleasurably within the constraints of the moments, objects, and subjects not culturally coded to connect with her (Irish) queerness.

Since the release of *The Crying Game* in 1992, queer film and culture has become greatly mainstreamed leading to fears of the cultivation of what Lisa Duggan terms: 'the new homonormativity – it is a politics that does not contest dominant heteronormative assumptions and institutions, but upholds and sustains them, while promising the possibility of a semi-mobilized gay constituency and a privatized, depoliticized gay culture anchored in domesticity and consumption.'[29] *Breakfast on Pluto* offers a reprise of trans-genderism, queerness and Irish nationalism that certainly critiques 'heteronormative assumptions and institutions'[30] but nevertheless renders the queer body openly and repeatedly subject to violence in service of that critique. It also employs a longing for domesticity and consumption of US and British films and movie magazines as the primary strategy of Kitten's queer disidentification. This portrayal represents the material available for fantasy in a much-censored Ireland of the 1970s, but the film's release in 2005 draws attention back towards the rise of consumerism in Ireland post-Celtic Tiger, connecting *Breakfast on Pluto's* reinvention of 1970's Ireland to new geopolitical questions that have emerged during the upheaval of the last 20 years. Walsh also highlights the connection between these issues and queer communities in Ireland through interrogating the embrace of gay markets by the Irish economy: 'The contradiction is that while gay people remain unprotected by the law and excluded from civil society, they are embraced in so far as they fuel the revitalization of the Tiger economy.'[31] Duggan's framing of homo-normativity too warns against the absorption of queerness into (white) heteronormative structures of power through consumption and visibility in a manner that ignores subtler workings of race, class, and gender through celebrating an acceptance of queerness within limits as proof of social tolerance and flexibility.

What then does Jordan's celebratory focus on Irish queerness potentially conceal? Jasbir Puar offers this critique of post-9/11 global discourses of queerness:

> The politics of recognition and incorporation entail that certain – but certainly not most – homosexual, gay, and queer bodies may be the temporary recipients of the 'measures of benevolence' that are afforded by liberal discourses of multicultural tolerance and diversity ... The contemporary

emergence of homosexual, gay, and queer subjects – normatized through their deviance (as it becomes surveilled, managed, studied) rather than despite it – is integral to the interplay of perversion and normativity necessary to sustain in full gear the management of life.[32]

Puar argues further:

The emergence and sanctioning of queer subjecthood is a historical shift condoned only through a parallel process of demarcation from populations targeted for segregation, disposal, or death, a reintensification of racialization through queerness.[33]

Writing after 9/11, Puar identifies 'connectivities that generate queer, homosexual, and gay disciplinary subjects while concurrently constituting queerness as the optic through which perverse populations are called into normalization for control'.[34] These newly perverse populations are exemplified through the figure of the 'monster, terrorist, fag' or Middle Eastern terrorist post-9/11. Just as in *The Crying Game,* Jordan again misses an opportunity to deal with the imbrication of race, sexuality, (trans)nation, and power in his eagerness to posit queerness as the most powerful dissolver of Irish trauma and sexual repression. Queerness is enlisted as the flexible identity that covers over more complex politics of the Troubles as well as post-9/11, post-Celtic Tiger Ireland, north and south. Given Jordan's remarks in relation to *Breakfast on Pluto's* relevance to an environment of 'nasty ideologies' post-9/11, this myopia is somewhat troubling and begs for a more sophisticated analysis of the issues that are being addressed.

The film ends with Charlie and Kitten in London with her new baby. Ruth Negga, who plays Charlie, is Ethopian-Irish. She came to Ireland as a child and was trained through Trinity College's acting program. Jordan stated in an interview: 'I didn't know much about her when she came to the casting, but the moment I saw her act, I decided to change the script so that she could appear in the movie.'[35] Any changes to the script, however, included a sublimation of her ethnicity, rather than a confrontation with its implications in 1970s Ireland, or possible relationship to problems of racism, violence and discrimination in the North and Republic today. She is visually troped as a misfit in the film along with Kitten, Laurence and Irwin, but her racial difference is never referenced. The violence directed towards her and Kitten at the end of the film rather seems inspired by her illegitimate pregnancy and Kitten's cross-dressing and flaunting of money around town while staying at the rectory. I have already commented via Halberstam on the irony of London as a recurring final destination of safety and liberation for queers and queers of colour in the 1970s and 1990s, especially Irish ones. Negga's performance in particular links this film back to the present. Her racial difference renders recent changes to Irish society unavoidable for a contemporary (Irish) viewer of this historical film.

Only one year before the release of this film, the Republic of Ireland passed the 2004 Citizenship Referendum by an 80% majority. Negga's appearance as Charlie highlights the role of race, gender, nation, and sexuality in co-formations of Irishness today, and the broader maps of power that Jordan frequently evokes but never engages directly. Her presence suggests that debates about Irishness are not and perhaps never were simply about defeating heteronormative masculinity, Republicanism, and the traumatic effects of Christian repression in the context of Ireland and Britain alone. Kitten's radical queer terrorist camp wreaks havoc on these three themes, but their escape to London in the 1970s should not be finally celebrated as a romantic triumph. Rather, it also necessarily prompts reminders of continued anti-Irish racism in Britain, queerphobia, and a mounting panic about former subjects of the colonies (particularly India, Pakistan, and the West Indies) coming to settle in the seat of the former British Empire during this period. In their final pairing, there is potential for a deeper dialogue about the role of not just sexuality/sexual orientation as easily accessible and marketable solutions to serious politics, but the shifting technologies of management of racialized *and* queered populations who seek survival amidst proliferating 'nasty ideologies'. An individual queer, even one as fabulous as Kitten, cannot do this on her own, while bearing the bruises and the blood for audience sport. It will take a deeper engagement with the serious politics that constitute national *and* transnational flows of power. This critical engagement must deal with Jordan's alliances not only to Irish national(ist) cinema and narrative, but queer and global cinemas as well through the funding, distribution and thematic concerns of his work.

It is difficult to determine whether Negga's disruption is intentional or is another productive blind spot in Jordan's body of work. The black (transgendered) female is a trope not only in *The Crying Game,* but in *Mona Lisa* (1986) as well, yet Negga's role does not reprise the 'black femme fatale' of progressive 'white' cinema in

Jordan's work that Joy James criticizes,[36] instead operating in a quieter key. The nuances her presence communicates would most likely not register for non-Irish audiences, with the queerness of the film and predictable depictions of the excesses of Irish Republicanism and Catholic hypocrisy finally serving as its dominant point of entry. This, in the end, remains the issue with the film. *Breakfast on Pluto* does take transgenderism beyond a mere gimmick and embed queer transgendered critique in the gaze of the film. These aspects of the film undoubtedly rework *The Crying Game's* shortcomings while again linking the management of sexualities with management of nation and its attendant violences. But other stories of race, Irish/non-Irish immigration, and diasporic identity are hidden below the surface of this film, and should also be addressed in subsequent criticisms of this work. The final goal is to avoid the co-option of queer as an automatic dissolver of nationalism(s) without a consideration of how queer itself has been assimilated in the global marketplace.

---

[1] The film is adapted from Patrick McCabe's 1999 novel *Breakfast on Pluto*, and this project represents a continuing collaboration between Jordan and McCabe. They produced *The Butcher Boy* in 1997, following upon McCabe's 1994 novel of the same name.

[2] Lance Pettitt, *Screening Ireland: Film and Television Representation* (UK: Manchester University Press, 2000), p. xvi.

[3] I do not mean to imply that Dil is 'generically' black. While Jody's ethnicity is specifically mentioned in the film as context for the similar colonial background of Fergus and Jody, Dil's is never mentioned.

[4] *Breakfast on Pluto* actually marginally outranks *The Crying Game* in Ireland as the 18th highest grossing film of all time (€981,256). *The Crying Game* comes in at #19 with €965,958. Worldwide, however, *Pluto's* numbers are weak, grossing less than a million in the US, and showing similarly low numbers elsewhere. See Ted Sheehy, 'Reaching the Audience', *Film Ireland* 31 October 2008. <http://www.filmireland.net/124/reachingtheaudience.htm>; '*Breakfast on Pluto*: Foreign Box Office' 30 October 2008. <http://www.boxofficemojo.com/movies/?page=intl&id=breakfasto npluto.htm>

[5] Lir Mac Cárthaigh, '*Breakfast on Pluto* Review', *Film Ireland* 20 October 2008, http://www.filmireland.net/reviews/breakfast_on_pluto.html>. Unlike *The Crying Game*, *Pluto* was partially financed through the Irish Film Board. It was distributed, however, by Sony Picture Classics through the Japanese media conglomerate Sony which has

its headquarters in Culver City, California. The complicated transnational pedigree of the film's production challenges its status as an 'Irish' film and invites a more nuanced analysis that considers what other interests may be at stake here. Sony Pictures Classics, 1 November 2008, <http://www.sonyclassics.com/index.php>.

6 'Serious' is what Kitten terms anything she wants nothing to do with, especially IRA politics. I will continue to invoke 'serious' as a term to describe Jordan and Kitten's aspirations throughout this paper due to its extreme repetition in the film. I feel that it is significant because it is what Kitten wants to avoid, and what Jordan is able to foreground for film audiences through her avoidance. Thus, it is a term that is able to turn back on itself.

7 Judith Halberstam, *In A Queer Time and Place: Transgender Bodies, Subcultural Lives* (New York and London: New York University Press, 2005), p. 21.

8 'Director Neil Jordan', Sony Pictures Classics: *Breakfast on Pluto,* a film by Neil Jordan.
<http://www.sonyclassics.com/breakfastonpluto/main.htm>.

9 Jaceba Gabilondo makes this claim in his essay: 'Border and Global Consumption in Rodríguez, Tarantino, Arau, Esquivel, and Troyan. Notes on Baroque, Camp, Kitsch, and Hybridization', *Queer Globalizations: Citizenship and the Afterlife of Colonialism,* eds Arnaldo Cruz-Malavé and Martin F. Mansalan, IV (New York and London: New York University Press, 2002), p. 236.

10 Fintan Walsh, 'Shirley Temple Bar at the Abbey: Irish Theatre, Queer Performance, and the Politics of Disidentification', *Irish Theatre International,* 1.1 (2008), p. 56.

11 Emer Rockett and Kevin Rockett, *Neil Jordan: Exploring Boundaries,* (Dublin: The Liffey Press, 2003) p. 142.

12 Arnaldo Cruz-Malavé and Martin F. Manalansan, IV, Introduction, p. 4.

13 Ibid, p.1.

14 Ibid.

15 Gabilondo, p. 236.

16 Ibid, pp. 236-37.

17 Jordan, *The Crying Game, Neil Jordan: A Reader* (New York: Vintage Books, 1993), p. 234.

18 Halberstam, p. 81. Thus, it is a term that is able to turn back on itself.

19 Conn Holohan, 'Trauma, Narrative, and Subjectivity in *Breakfast on Pluto*', *Irish Films, Global Cinema,* eds Martin McCloone and Kevin Rockett (Dublin: Four Courts Press, 2007), p. 144.

20 Ibid, p. 145.

21 *Breakfast on Pluto*. Dir. Neil Jordan, Perfs. Cillian Murphy, Stephen Rea, Brendan Gleeson, Liam Neeson. Sony Pictures Classics, 2005. DVD.

22 Ibid.

23 The other most notorious example being *Boys Don't Cry,* dir. Kimberly Peirce, Perfs. Kimberly Swank, Chloe Sevigny, Peter Saarsgard. Twentieth Century Fox, 1999.

24 Holohan, p. 147.

25 *Breakfast on Pluto.*

26 José Muñoz, *Disindentifications*: *Queers of Color and the Performance of Politics* (Minneapolis and London: University of Minnesota Press, 1999), p. 11.

27 Holohan, p. 148.

28 Muñoz, p. 13.

29 Lisa Duggan, *The Twilight of Equality*: *Neo-Liberalism, Cultural Politics and the Attack on Democracy* (Boston: Beacon Press, 2003), p. 50.

30 Ibid, p. 50.

31 Walsh, p. 60.

32 Jasbir Puar, *Terrorist Assemblages*: *Homonationalism in Queer Times,* (Durham and London: Duke University Press, 2003), p. xii.

33 Ibid, p. xii.

34 Ibid, p. xiii.

35 Jorge Guttiérrez, 'Ruth Negga: A Star Without a Label', 21 April 2008.

<http://www.cafebabel.com/EN/article.asp?T=T&Id=8984>.

36 See Joy James, 'Black *Femmes Fatales* and Sexual Abuse in Progressive "White" Cinema: Neil Jordan's *Mona Lisa* and *The Crying Game*', *Camera Obscura* 36 (September 1995), pp. 33-47.

12 |Living by the Code: Authority in *The Gay Detective*

Kathleen A. Heininge

Irish drama has few representations of police officers as anything but a trope for authority, tending to avoid any substantive character development. Likewise, it has few representations of homosexual characters, and when such representations do exist they are often caricatures. Reductive portrayals of police often arise from the complex relationship the Irish have with authority and with the legal system. But one of the few exceptions to this trend, and the only play to tackle the representation of a police officer and a homosexual at once, is Gerard Stembridge's play *The Gay Detective* (1996). The play offers up the character of Pat, a 'gay detective', a fascinating dramatic portrayal of the collision of two identities which, on the surface, contest each other. Alternately comic and tragic, poignant and gruesome, with an ambiguous ending, Stembridge's work defies attempts at easy categorization. He explores the comic possibilities in the tension between the codified identifiers of Irish police officers and of gay men, two codes which don't often 'speak' to each other, but he also demonstrates the tragedy in the misunderstanding between these two cultures. The collision provides a fascinating study of codified behaviour and the way different codes of identity recognition can clash in one individual. This paper will explore the implications of Pat's seemingly incompatible persona, implications that force a consideration of his adoption of these codes in terms of Judith Butler's concept of 'masquerade' allowing for a kind of interpellation.

At the start of the play, Bear, Pat's superior, dangles the possibility of promotion in front of Pat, but also hints he knows Pat is gay, implying Pat's successful future in the department hinges on Bear's will and on Pat's sexual discretion. Thus, when a case seems to involve homosexuals, Bear takes advantage of Pat's status by sending him undercover to investigate; Pat ends up catapulted into the treacherous secret world of wealthy and influential men, violent sex, and murder. Pat's sense of his own conflicted identities, in the meantime, is tested when he meets and begins a relationship with Ginger, the victim of a gay bashing incident being investigated by Pat.

The play is set at the moment in Irish history when the decriminalization of homosexuality, because of a 1993 court case, was being debated in Ireland. This liminal moment of debate is what Georg Lukács calls a revolution in thought, the result of a new class consciousness, and any possible change in law 'is the self-objectification of human society at a particular stage in its development; its laws hold good only within the framework of the historical context which produced them and which is in turn determined by them'[1], the historical context here being that precise moment in time when the law was least definitive. Laws are, ultimately, human constructs that are made to be resisted or changed when they no longer suit the parameters of a given society. Lukács continues:

> Now class consciousness consists in fact of the appropriate and rational reactions 'imputed' ... to a particular typical position in the process of production. This consciousness is, therefore, neither the sum nor the average of what is thought or felt by the single individuals who make up the class. And yet the historically significant actions of the class as a whole are determined in the last resort by this consciousness and not by the thought of the individual – and these actions can be understood only by reference to this consciousness.[2]

Because of the uncertainty of whether homosexuality would continue to be illegal, Pat is both secretive about his sexuality at work and indiscreet about his sexuality outside of work. He cannot yet know how far a new consciousness might extend, and his tension remains that between work and personal identity. There are 'appropriate and rational reactions' expected of him because he has a very 'particular typical position' in the process of production of the law: as a police officer, in fact, he holds the most typical position, the most visible authority figure with which the general public comes into contact. A society works smoothly when those who are in charge of maintaining it function in predictable ways. The behaviour of such people is guided by the expectations put upon them, and not by individual choices or preferences. Revolution occurs when the expectations are violated by personal choice or preference, but only when that personal choice or preference becomes more than just an anomaly. Pat, in alternately 'masquerading' as police officer and gay man, violates the codes of both law enforcement and homosexuality, which would seem to be an anomaly at any other given time in history. At the moment of change, however, he becomes the symbol of the tension, the symbol of revolution, of what may become a new class consciousness.

These codes help to mark Pat's moment of identity, and he has so cleanly compartmentalized them that he has difficulty recognizing one in the context of the other. The concept of 'gaydar', 'that seemingly indefinable social skill ... that allegedly allows lesbians and gay men to identify each other in heterosexually dominated social contexts'[3] is well-known as a form of recognition, although the specifics of such recognition may change from culture to culture, and it is certainly not a perfectly reliable means of identification. What is less discussed in anthropological or social studies is the fact that other social groups also have indefinable cues, whether linguistic or nonverbal, often enabling members of that group to recognize each other. Motivated by a similar desire to 'pass' in a social setting that may not be accepting of their career, many police officers, especially off-duty, investigative or undercover officers, have internalized the same kinds of cues, and are frequently able to recognize each other through signals both verbal and physical. Joseph Hayes identifies the verbal markers as 'insider jokes, play on words, exaggeration in speech ... part adaptation to the need for secrecy, part defensiveness, yet at the same time a kind of assertiveness'.[4] While Hayes specifically defines 'gayspeak', the same markers apply as well to police officers, and for similar reasons. Whether the style is clothing, hairstyle, mannerisms, speech patterns, stance, or some other 'indefinable' quality, the code allows for recognition. Pat's character functions in both of these two codes, able to recognize the way each one works. Homi Bhabha calls this interstitial position 'the ambivalent man'[5], a mode of functioning between two conflicting forces of subjectivity that precludes fully aligning with either force. Pat's attempts to negotiate between the codes, here operating as the signifiers of the forces of subjectivity (i.e., gay man and police officer), are both amusing and painful, and his failures to recognize one code when he is operating in the other, stifling one side of himself as it were, suggest that the two identities are entirely incompatible, and one must win out over the other.

The dilemma for Pat is in trying to reconcile the secrets in his life and in trying to prioritize and identify the true elements of his identity. As a police officer he is meant to uphold the law, while as a gay man he is breaking the law. The scenario of a police officer breaking a law is nothing new, but this goes further; for Pat, his homosexual identity is breaking the law at the same time his law enforcement identity requires him to force the lawbreaker to desist. His status as police officer is contested by the hierarchy above him, which threatens him with ever-increasing levels of authority and punishment. That punishment, however, can arise from either his public or his private life, and any 'authority' that he may have as a gay man is contested within the structure of police work. From the first scene in the play, the configurations of authority are subverted and confused. Pat himself seems to have only the vaguest understanding of which of his identities truly defines or authorizes him, and he seems to be masquerading in both, adopting the codes of being a gay man or a police officer according to the situation.

In her important work on the performance of gender Judith Butler describes this masked behaviour: 'Masquerade may be understood as the performative production of a sexual ontology, an appearing that makes itself convincing as a 'being''[6]. The performative aspect of Pat's behaviour is central to Stembridge's point: Does the masquerade slip into something more than a pose? In behaving as a police officer, or in behaving as a gay man, does Pat actually create a new reality for himself, or is the slippage between the two itself a deconstruction of that reality? In her later book, *Bodies That Matter*, Butler uses Althusser's concept of interpellation to illustrate her idea of the performative: when a police officer calls to us through the door, we are compelled by the law to obey, and it is more than a request. Something ontological is stipulated by the assertion of language; a reality is created through the use of language alone, which goes beyond mere description. Butler asks, 'Are there other ways of being addressed and constituted by the law, ways of being occupied and occupying the law, that disarticulate the power of punishment from the power of recognition?'[7], a question tackled directly within *The Gay Detective* when we see the layers of masquerade required of Pat. Pat is being 'addressed' by the law when he is given an assignment that, as a subordinate and as a police officer, he cannot refuse; he is constituted by the law when he is reminded that his very being is illegal. He is occupied by the law when he is the subject of interrogation; he is occupying the law when he is performing his occupational duties. Whether, however, that dual position manages to disarticulate the power of punishment from the power of recognition, whether this is a moment of successful 'revolution', remains to be seen.

Bear's confrontation of Pat at the beginning of the play is the first instance of tension between codes. Bear speaks as a representative of the law and as the authority within a hierarchy in which Pat participates, telling Pat, 'I'd have said now, you were the sort of fellow who'd be after promotion. Would you fancy that, promotion? ... I wanted you to see that we're paying attention.'[8] The double meaning of 'we're paying attention' – noting both Pat's work and Pat's sexuality – is clear to the audience and to Bear, but not yet to Pat, who has not suspected Bear's authoritative subtext. Bear reads aloud from Pat's file, and the linguistic and lexical codes begin to clash: 'Logical – good concentration ... stylish approach, that's an unusual one – that's not a comment I often hear about young Gardai – stylish '(8). Bear is confused – or pretends to be – by the language of Pat's evaluator, as if a 'normal' police officer would never use the word 'stylish' in an official document, but he senses an underlying meaning; since he is privy to Pat's differently coded world, he seems to be mocking Pat, although Pat, still functioning in the code of police work, fails to recognize the distinction. Bear insinuates there is something different about Pat, regardless of the fact that Pat is not responsible for the language used by his evaluator. Stylishness is clearly cause for suspicion, according to Bear.

Bear continues to toy with Pat, making Pat guess what Bear's next questions will reveal; Pat becomes both interrogated and interrogator, though he has no idea of the purport of Bear's remarks and his confusion increases with his sense of threat. Bear finally reveals that Pat has been spotted at a gay bar by Cat, an undercover officer. In fact, Pat has made advances to the officer without recognizing him as a fellow officer; Pat was, however, recognized and reported. He is threatened when his identities clash, and he is forced to operate simultaneously in both of his worlds, a condition he finds confusing. He recognizes the codes of police work, the

nature of interrogation and the positioning of authority, but is now
the subject of it rather than the object, a position that bewilders him
until he understands that his private life has just crossed over to his
public life. Keeping him off kilter, just as Pat 'cops on' to what is
happening and is about to confess to his superior that he is gay, Bear
assures him, 'You don't have to answer what you're not asked. Just
be very, very careful Sergeant, won't you? ... You know the law don't
you?' Bear's refusal to allow Pat to confirm his suspicion leaves
himself free to later utilize Pat's status without 'abetting' Pat's crime
of homosexuality. Furthermore, it allows Bear to assert the threat
his superiority represents, while posing as benevolent mentor. Pat
must balance between these two codes, these two worlds, until he
can feel safe, but the safe position shifts continually throughout the
play.

While investigating a report of a man having been beaten, Pat
meets Ginger, the victim. As Pat conducts the interview, Ginger
clearly assumes Pat knows what provoked the beating, finally
announcing bluntly, 'We were queer-bashed Garda ... Are you afraid
to say it out loud?'

> **PAT.** No. No. I'm sorry. I didn't ... didn't ... know. I didn't know
> you were –
> **GINGER.** Really?
> **PAT.** No really – it never occurred to me.
> **GINGER.** Oh I know sure, it never happens.
> **PAT:** I don't mean that either. I just wasn't thinking – So ... so
> ... you were attacked just because they thought you were –
> **GINGER.** Thought? No they didn't just think it. I'd have to say
> that. – To be fair we were asking for it (16-17).

Pat is again surprised at the intersection of the codes: he hadn't
been thinking as a gay man, and so he failed to see the signs which
were already there, clues that would have helped in his investigation. Ginger, far more camp than Pat, assumes it is obvious,
saying, 'You know why we were attacked so stop going round' – (16).
Pat vows that he will find the attackers and Ginger doesn't believe
him, seeing him as just another cop who would never investigate
such a beating. Ginger's neighbour, Puppy (the only female in the
play who speaks), is the one who called the police during the
beating, and Pat takes her to the gay bar with him to see if she
recognizes any of the men as the attackers. She does indeed, and Pat
suddenly changes his clothes and behaviour, becoming very camp,
to Puppy's surprise; he lures Bull after him and when Bull jumps

him, he makes his arrest, beating the man viciously in the course of it. When Pat goes to tell Ginger about the arrest, Pat kisses him, to Ginger's surprise; they end up in bed together.

While Pat is clearing this case, Bear asks him to find a way to secretly warn the local closeted TD to be more discreet in his homosexual activities. Cat, the undercover officer who recognized Pat in the gay bar, has been following Rat, an informant on a drug case, and saw Rat and the TD together. Reputations are at stake. It seems as if Bear is sympathetic to the TD's situation (and perhaps to Pat's), since sending a cop to warn someone about his illegal activities is outside the purview of the police department. Pat 'poses' as a gay man, approaching the TD in the park as if he wants sex, and warns the TD that Rat is about to expose him. He earns his promotion.

When the same TD is found murdered outside a gay bar, Bear is pressured to solve the case and he turns to Pat, relying on Pat's familiarity with the codes of the gay world, knowing his own authority is inadequate in this other code. Once again, Pat's two identities intersect. Pat again agrees to 'pose' as a gay man to find the killer; his first stop is the bar outside of which the TD was killed. Stembridge's use of the gay bar as the site of Pat's 'acting' gay reveals yet another layer of the tension between Pat's personae: while as a gay man he is comfortable frequenting gay bars, as a police officer he is there seen as the enemy. As Nancy Achilles demonstrates in her study of gay community, the gay bar is a most important symbol of social cohesion. 'If,' she argues, 'there is one particular issue which calls forth a unified protest from the homosexual Community, it is that of police activity. Many homosexuals remain passive until a favourite bar or close friend is threatened by the police.'[9] The gay bar is the place where contacts are made, where information is exchanged, where assignations are scheduled, and it must be protected as a safe haven. It is the place where Pat's own identity is more obfuscated than ever: he is a gay man pretending to be a straight police officer pretending to be a gay man. The masquerade continues.

While posing as a gay man who is just curious about recent events, Pat pretends to the bartender that he is also disgusted by all the police running around. He learns that Rat has not been seen for some time, but he meets Snake at the bar, who seems to know something about the murder, and who invites Pat to join him and his friends at a secret hideaway; Pat can be their 'special guest'. The names of the friends – Snake, Pig, and Wolf – interpellate them for us. In fact, the names of most of the characters are a form of interpellation, as nearly everyone in the play has the name of an animal and that animal's characteristics. Bear, the Superintendent, brooks no question to his authority. Ginger, who becomes Pat's lover, is flamboyant and charming. Puppy, Ginger's neighbour, is loyal to a fault, standing by Ginger even when Pat seems to abandon him, refusing to judge anyone. Bull is Ginger's attacker, the man Pat arrests in the bar. Rat is the informant. The murder of the TD, a man without name – and no identity except his political position – leads Pat to Snake. Snake is a brilliant musician whose proclivities are hidden behind his public display of Lizard, his female companion who does not speak in his presence but who provides cover for Snake's real interests (his 'fag hag,' according to Philip Core).[10] Pig is a criminal lawyer, and Wolf, the owner of the hideaway, is prominent, married, wealthy, and gets carried away with violent sex. Mouse is Wolf's houseboy, mute because, it is implied, Wolf did something horrific to him; he is desperate to escape the hideaway and enlists Pat's help. For each of these personae, identity is 'created' through the use of names. They are effectively reduced to their animal types, and don't exceed those boundaries.

The only two characters who differ in this respect are Ginger and Pat. While the other 'animals' are named for their species, Ginger, in being named for a particular kind of cat, is allotted more character development than the others. Cat is the undercover officer who told Bear about his encounter with Pat, and he is also the man with Ginger during the gay-bashing, but he scampered away for fear of having his 'real' identity discovered. While Cat denies that he is gay to his superiors – Bear notes, 'As I'm sure you realize, he's not that way inclined himself ... In fact, he has three lovely children' (19) – Ginger comments that he and Cat were 'asking for it':

> **GINGER:** That night we were the fairies from hell. If I was straight, I'd have beaten us up. Look picture the scene if you can, George's St. Two in the morning, two fine lads arm in arm, cheek to cheek, completely arseholes, and we are not by any stretch of the imagination being discreet. Rampaging queens in fact (17).

While he and Cat are the same species, Cat behaves as expected from a cat, somewhat sly and elusive when trouble arises, and Ginger gets further character development that allows us to see him as a human being rather than a type, more complex than simply a species.

The other exception to this interpellation is Pat, who is not named for an animal: his traits don't fit any one type. In fact, his name suggests some ambiguity in his gender, as Pat could be short for either Patrick or Patricia. But as he self-identifies, 'Pat' is not central; rather, his rank as a police officer is, a rank that no one can seem to remember accurately. Bear refers to him as Sergeant, accurately identifying his rank, but suggests that he could become detective, that he is the one able to confer that status, that interpellation. Puppy calls him 'Inspector' until Pat corrects her with 'Sergeant' (12); Ginger calls him 'Garda' twice and Pat corrects him (16); when Ginger gets it right, finally calling him Sergeant, Pat has been promoted, and then Pat has to assert himself as Detective (32). Pat's opening line in the play, directed retrospectively at Ginger, is, 'I am the Gay Detective. Remember it was you called me that' (7). When Ginger gave him the name of the Gay Detective, however, Ginger meant it differently, before Pat reveals himself as gay: 'Can I call you the Gay Detective now? ... I just mean the detective that gays can trust' (33). The interpellation ends up being more accurate than Ginger knew, as Pat is not only a detective for gays, but is himself gay. The commentary on interpellation becomes part of the comedy of the play, then, as Pat seeks to reinterpellate himself while others refuse to comply. The one time that Pat is likened to an animal is at the hideaway, after he has sex while he 'masquerades' as the new boy toy for the weekend, and Pig comments, 'Where does it come from? ... In you. The animal. What makes you like it this way? Don't misunderstand me. I'm not suspicious – you weren't faking or pretending' (68). In agreeing that he was not faking or pretending, Pat forces the audience to wonder again about his true identity, an identity clouded by the fact that he is 'pretending' to be gay while working 'undercover' as a police officer, a job he does while 'undercover' as a gay man. The truth seems to be obliterated in the masquerade. Is he, in fact, just as much an animal as all the others?

Even the physical interpellates self. The stage directions set up the doubling of characters, reinforcing the sense that the characters are only caricatures or types. Bear is also Wolf. Puppy is also Lizard. Bull is also Pig. The only two who do not double are Pat and Ginger. Pat changes his clothes on stage, effectively adopting a new identity with every change of clothing, 'becoming' the police officer when he dons his uniform or his anorak, 'becoming' gay when he abruptly dons his 'camp' clothing so he and Puppy can go undercover at the gay bar to find the man who beat up Ginger (29); he wears 'ordinary clothes' when he goes to the park to warn the TD and for sex (22); he turns in his uniform in exchange for an anorak when he is promoted to Detective (32). But in all these costume changes those around him fail to recognize the significance of the codes. Puppy understands the connection with the 'camp' clothing when they are hunting for Bull, but she sees it as a costume, assuring him that he will 'pass' as gay and not realizing he actually is (29). She is so convinced by his 'cover' that she demands that Pat kiss her in order to create a distraction when she sees Ginger's attacker (29). Ginger doesn't recognize the anorak as the uniform of new status and must be told of Pat's promotion. 'Ordinary clothes' do not mark Pat as 'different' (either as gay or as a police officer) in the park. The audience is reminded throughout the costume changes of the idea of masquerade, but are not allowed to see what lies beneath, leaving them to wonder at the effectiveness of the performative: can both aspects of Pat's identity be interpellated at any given moment, or does one cancel out the other continually?

The fact of this interpellation places the tension of identities beyond merely the binary of public versus the private, deconstructing them. The core elements of Pat's identity are incompatible given this social structure. He does not cease to be a police officer when he leaves work anymore than he ceases to be gay when he is at work. His masquerade is one of defence as well as assertion, and always must be. The superficiality of seeing public versus private as dichotomous is evidenced when we try to cleanly separate Pat's identities.

Refusing to allow the audience to consider the possibility that Pat is gay in name only, that his homosexuality is all just part of his 'masquerade' or 'pose', the audience sees him regularly having sex with men. Each time, the sex is in complete contrast to his official duties, becoming a violent rendering of his identity, taking place as it generally does at moments of stress in his work. Having sex with Ferret immediately after Bear has threatened him, he is distracted, swearing about Bear ('Bastard. Fucking bastard.') rather than focusing on sexual pleasure (10-12). He is again distracted while he is having a sexual encounter with an anonymous Man in the park, this time because he is delighted with himself for having successfully warned the TD off Rat (24). After he captures Bull, one of

Ginger's attackers, he congratulates himself while he is being orally copulated by Badger:

> **PAT.** I like my job. Do you like your job? I was getting to hate it. I was feeling you know – like a square peg in a round hole. But mmm – suddenly, suddenly, it's exciting, it's alive with possibilities – Oooh yeah – I can't believe it. It's as if –
> **BADGER.** Do you want me to stop?
> **PAT.** Sorry?
> **BADGER.** Look, if you're not into it just say so.
> **PAT.** Oh no sorry – no it's great – it's all great.
> **BADGER.** Well, will you shut up so. Or if you have to talk, cries of ecstasy would be nice (30).

In each instance, the sex is impersonal, violent, physical, without emotion or even apparent engagement on Pat's part. It is as if the physical act itself helps to remind Pat of who he is when he feels lost in the job, and he can reassert himself somehow through sex. Audience discomfort is at least partly due to the recognition of the ineffectiveness of such a ploy: he is disconnected, so why should we take it seriously? Jeff Nunokawa claims that 'Sex invokes an urge to get away from others as much as an urge to join with them.'[11] Only when he and Ginger are together is there intimacy rather than brute sex, as the only 'sex' the audience sees between them is given in the stage direction: 'They get into bed together and disappear under the sheets' (36). It is clear that this is different, that Ginger is 'a real lover' (40), someone with whom Pat can have a relationship, and with whom perhaps he can now become whole.

Pat's deepest frustration is his inability to read the codes of the one when he is operating by the codes of the other. If he is at work, he seems unable to distinguish the codes of gay life; if he is not at work, he seems unaware of the codes of police work. When he meets Cat at the gay bar, he does not recognize him as a police man, and his failure to do so puts him in a vulnerable position with Bear; when he meets Ginger at work, despite Ginger's innuendoes, he is unable to put together the fact that Ginger is gay, a fact that could have helped him with the investigation had he known it right away. While Bear assumes that Pat's familiarity with both codes would be an asset in the murder investigation, he does not realize the lengths to which Pat must go to keep his two identities compartmentalized. Stembridge seems to imply that audiences would also expect a greater level of awareness of codification from Pat; some of this lack of awareness is a source of the more amusing moments in the play, such as the *double entendres* when Ginger is flirting with him to which he is oblivious. Stembridge also clearly marks the other characters as unaware: Puppy, for example, seems to be completely unaware of the most basic of codes. While trying to describe Ginger's attackers, she announces that she is 'hopeless on men's clothes ... I just never notice what fellahs wear ... ' (14). All she can remember is that the attackers were big. She later has a flash of memory and pictures the attackers in her head, claiming she could recognize them if she saw them, but she cannot describe 'colour of eyes, or hair, or, or, you know things ... I can't think like that' (25). And yet, she has learned to distrust the police, living by the code taught by Ginger that keeps homosexuals and police as far away as possible from each other. She insists that she is not responsible for identifying the men in the way that Pat demands, telling him she is not the police, and she will not be one who mixes her identities: 'I didn't interrogate him you know – Jesus – the poor guy is – beaten and and bleeding and ... and God knows what – and I'm just trying to make things easy – I mean I'm not the police' (13). Until he convinces her that he is willing to help, she assumes the police would be uninterested in investigating a 'queer-bashing', and is surprised to learn that he has no intention of arresting Ginger for his homosexuality (18). The code that Puppy has learned is, oddly enough, a code that doesn't really apply to her since she is not homosexual; the seemingly obvious dominant cultural code that might help her to identify her friend's assailants is beyond her.

Bear, on the other hand, recognizes the existence of the varying codes, but is unable to convincingly operate outside of his own authoritative code of police work. He attempts to manipulate the codes of the gay world, as he tries to manipulate Pat, but he misunderstands them, either deliberately or because he does not care enough to learn. Bear's obstinate misreading of the gay codes reveals that the apparent sympathy for Pat's plight which he feigned in the beginning, when he was actually threatening Pat, was part of his own masquerade, though one that was consciously adopted. When he gives Pat the order to find and warn the TD about Rat, effectively giving him permission to 'be' gay, he tells Pat, 'Discretion. Just because you're legal doesn't mean you can go round like a nancy. No arriving to work in mascara and funny perfume – right?' (32) Whether his conflation of homosexuals and transvestites is deliberate or simply a misunderstanding of the codes, the audience can sense his disingenuousness. Later, when Bear learns of the TD's murder, he tells Pat, in frustration and anger, that 'queers are either sad or bad. They fuck up their own lives first, and then everyone else's lives after that'. When he allows that Pat could be 'the exception to the rule' (39), he also notes that the TD probably thought that too; clearly what we earlier mistook for sympathy was part of Bear's own pose.

While Pat is at the hideaway, he discovers that it was Mouse who murdered the TD, having been ordered to do so by Wolf, Pig and Snake because the TD was going to turn Wolf in for the murder of Rat, the result of Wolf's violent sex fetish. Pat feels sorry for Mouse and allows him to escape, certain justice would still be served when Wolf, Pig and Snake are prosecuted for Rat's death. Bear's response to Pat's elation at having solved the crime situates Bear clearly as entirely within the law enforcement code, with no further attempt to negotiate the code of homosexuality or to placate Pat:

> Are you being deliberately stupid? Do you seriously think we're going to arrest three distinguished citizens for the murder of a little shit, a little pansy rent boy do you? For Christ's sake get sense – we have to get them on a real murder (76).

Bear's unwillingness to consider that the murder of a homosexual constitutes 'real murder' reveals what is no longer a surprise: he has no interest in reconciling the two codes, and any effort he made at sympathy for Pat was a calculated game of manipulation. Despite knowing Pat as a law enforcement colleague, Bear clearly disregards that status in light of Pat's homosexuality, which, for Bear, overshadows everything else. Everything for Bear is a matter of spin, and he only feels compelled to spin for those who, like Snake and Wolf and Pig, and certainly the TD, uphold the society in which he believes, even if those people are leading what he considers to be a despicable private life. His attitude here puts his earlier sympathy for the TD in a new light, and therefore he is able to take the details of the TD having been found murdered in the alley behind a gay bar and conclude that, 'He was obviously innocently walking around the streets of Dublin at four in the morning, when suddenly – ooh – the heart goes and without knowing it he staggers thirty yards up a lane and falls dead' (38). Bear's entire position of authority is engaged in behaving as though there is no 'revolution' of class consciousness, and he must first deny and then denigrate any other possibility. For him, the police code is a refuge that protects the status quo.

Engagement with and failure to understand various codes seem, in these other characters, to be expected. The failure of either of these codes to truly help Pat when he needs it the most implies the binary nature of the codes, a binary that does exist where the binary of public and private does not. The codes do not seem to overlap for Pat in the way that Bear expects them to. It is as if while he is functioning by one code, the other code is obliterated. Pat has stifled his instinct so that his two worlds will not intersect, and doing so interferes with his ability to do the job. He manages so well that Ginger tries to set Pat up with Puppy before Pat kisses him, despite Ginger's obvious flirtation with him at the same time (29). Pat's career and his love life seem to be on parallel tracks to success, but his disconnect interferes. While pursuing leads in the TD's murder, he talks to Ginger about the case, even relying on Ginger's more finely-honed senses to identify possible suspects from the TD's funeral: 'You're an old scene queen – sniff 'em out for me' (47). He doesn't trust his own ability to know who might be involved, and it is Ginger who leads him to Snake. But at the same time he becomes so wrapped up in the case that he fails to see the clues that Ginger is leaving about his health, as though the success of his police identity stifles his ability to read the codes in his personal life. The audience is not shocked to find that Ginger's symptoms, ailments that he has taken little care to hide or to explain away to Pat, are signs that he has AIDS, and yet Pat is deeply shocked when he realizes it. Puppy has known all along, and is infuriated that Pat, the detective, could have missed the signs; she accuses him of being selfish, but it seems that the problem is that he is of two selves, only one of which can operate at a time. His distraction is made clear by the juxtaposition of his lives: when Ginger is coughing, clearly in distress, and Pat is comforting him, Pat is thinking only about the case, failing to read the signs of his personal life (46). When he does realize the enormity of what he is facing, he leaves Ginger and retreats to his other reality, his police work, immersing himself instead in the case, nearly killing himself in the performance of his duties as he uncovers the truth about both murders while he also 'performs' his gayness.

Pat's back-and-forth efforts to interpellate self at the same time that he masquerades culminate in the moment when Bear tells him the truth of his job: no police investigation will ever seriously focus on a crime committed on a gay criminal, a 'little pansy rent boy' (76). The fate of a gay man will not take precedence over the fate of a distinguished citizen in this social structure. Pat realizes, 'So I've gone into the gutter for nothing – I raped myself of my own dignity for nothing' (77). The lost dignity is in both of his identities. He allows Bear to manipulate and subvert his identities in order to solve a case when the solution will never be acceptable within the current system. He allowed his private life, his love for Ginger, to suffer in his effort to try to reconcile his work with his sexuality. His own dignity, his ability to avoid being merely animal, is betrayed. He announces that he is done with the case, that there is no more to be learned, and that he is going home to be with his sick friend. Bear is bewildered, feeling his authority slipping, again threatening Pat with suspension and a denial of promotion. Pat states: 'I'm just going to be with my friend. If he'll have me. That's all I want to be now – his best friend if I can, that's more than good enough. I'm not the Gay Detective anymore' (78). In rejecting the paradigms of either Detective or Gay, but adopting one belonging to all of humanity – best friend – Pat becomes the rounded character so long absent in Irish drama. He is neither only authority figure nor homosexual, but is all of the above and none of the above. He exemplifies here what Mary McIntosh insists when she urges that 'the homosexual should be seen as playing a social role rather than as having a condition'[12]. He is beginning to let his roles become fully integrated.

This would be true if the play ended there. But in the last scene, Ginger and Pat reunite affectionately. Ginger tells Pat that he will always be the Gay Detective, with which Pat concurs. They speak of unravelling 'the big mystery', and Pat insists that at last he is on the right track, that they will have to keep looking for at least a few years for a solution to the mystery. And then Ginger returns to calling Pat 'Sergeant', inviting the question of what exactly has been interpellated.

Throughout the play Stembridge allows the characters to be interpellated at the same time as they are resistant to that interpellation, so the codes that make up identity, those of language, costume, relationships, and mannerisms, constantly shift and require reinterpretation. Context is not even enough. When Ginger thanks Pat for having found his attackers, he admires Puppy's courage, saying that he would never do the same. 'I mean sneaking out on a cold night, hanging around dark alleys chasing after big brawny men – although now that I think of it...And dressing up – Yes it's sounding better and better ... ' (34). The comic moment is the way the same language changes its code when the context changes. That which is frightening given the context of police work sounds enticing to a gay man. Is the ending, then, in its context, an interpellation of Pat's private life or his public life? Is the stipulation that he is always going to be perceived and derogated as gay? Or as a detective? Does one self necessarily always betray the other? Is 'detective' here only metaphorical? And in calling Pat 'Sergeant', has Ginger acknowledged Pat's demotion, and implied that he will never be successful in detecting the 'big mystery'? Or is it possible that Pig, the criminal lawyer, is the only one who is able to fully interpellate himself, an interpellation that could apply to many of the characters but most especially to Pat: 'I am an enigma, wrapped in a mystery, tucked neatly into a contradiction' (61)?

The roles, for Pat, of public and private, gay and straight, police officer and citizen, are ineffectively performed because for him they are not the dichotomies they seem to be for others. In refusing to allow for one public and one private persona, each separate, Stembridge forces the question about what real identity is. The fact that Pat is homosexual does not stop when he is performing his police duties; the fact that he is a police officer does not stop when he goes home at night. The two identities are uniquely pervasive in all situations, and Pat must make a decision about identity that disallows a performative masquerade, thus creating a new 'reality'. Stembridge refuses the clean solution to the questions. Can the two identities, police officer and gay man, effectively intersect, developing into (finally) a well-rounded, complex character? Can a gay man be the figure of authority in a culture that presumes homosexuality is illegal? Can a police officer ever be afforded the right to a private life that does not interfere with his public one? Or does Pat have to choose between one and the other, reinstating the same familiar tropes about homosexuality and about police officers? The ambiguity of the ending, the ambiguity of the very genre of the play (is the audience supposed to laugh or cry at the ending?), allows Stembridge to leave the audience at the liminal moment in history when these answers might become relevant to all, not just to those who operate within these particular codes.

---

[1] Georg Lukács, *History and Class Consciousness*: *Studies in Marxist Dialectics* (Cambridge, Massachusetts: The MIT Press, 1968), p. 49.

2 Ibid, p. 51.

3 William L. Leap, 'Studying Lesbian and Gay Languages: Vocabulary, Test-making, and Beyond', *Out in Theory: The Emergence of Lesbian and Gay Anthropology*, eds Ellen Lewin and William L. Leap (Urbana and Chicago: University of Illinois Press, 2002), p. 142.

4 Ibid, p. 136.

5 Homi K. Bhabha, *The Location of Culture* (London: Routledge, 1994).

6 Judith Butler, *Gender Trouble: Feminism and the Subversion of Identity* (London: Routledge, 1990), p. 47.

7 Judith Butler, *Bodies That Matter* (London: Routledge, 1993), p. 122.

8 Gerard Stembridge, *The Gay Detective* (London: Nick Hern Books, 1996), p. 8. All subsequent quotations are from this text.

9 Gayle Rubin, 'Studying Sexual Sub-Cultures: Excavating the Ethnography of Gay Communities in Urban North America', *Out in Theory: The Emergence of Lesbian and Gay Anthropology*, eds Ellen

Lewin and William L. Leap (Urbana and Chicago: University of Illinois Press, 2002), pp. 31-32.

10 Philip Core, 'From Camp: The Lie that Tells the Truth', *Camp: Queer Aesthetics and the Performing Subject*, ed. Fabio Cleto (Ann Arbor: The University of Michigan Press, 2002).

11 Jeff Nunokawa, 'Queer Theory: Post-Mortem,' *The South Atlantic Quarterly* 106. 3 (Summer 2007), p. 561.

12 Rubin, p. 37.

13 | There's Nothing Queer Here:
The Abbey Theatre and the Problem of Practice

David Cregan

The Irish theatre has historically been described as a literary theatre. As a result, until recent times the art of theatrical technique for performance has rarely been the main point of focus in either drama studies or in production. The consequence of this literary focus has produced a type of theatrical criticism and praxis which has focused more on authorship, narrative-based historical analysis, and naturalism within the Irish tradition, and less on the development of a distinctly Irish method of representation or theatrical aesthetic of practice. By describing itself as a literary theatre the mainstream Irish dramatic tradition has avoided any prolonged attempt to experiment with performance genres, but has alternatively settled largely for the devices of dramatic realism in both acting and production design, and has favoured a decidedly erudite engagement with drama as text.

Although many domestic theatre companies have emerged in recent years in response to the rather conservative theatrical practices of much of the twentieth century in Ireland, the National Theatre, or the Abbey, remains the most internationally visible example of Irish theatrical practice. However, the Abbey has entered a period of serious reconfiguration due to substantial fiscal failures. Although the crisis at the Abbey has been detailed in the media and amongst theatre critics as a financial downfall of mismanagement and poor audience support of Abbey productions, in this paper I suggest that it is, additionally, a crisis of practice; a creative decline rather than simply financial.

The Abbey theatre is an important cultural commodity in the representation of Irish identity both at home and abroad, and remains a foundational identifier in the marketing of the prominence of Irish writers. As a result of its iconic institutional stature and rich historical legacy the work done at the Abbey is, arguably, the highest profile theatrical work being done in modern Ireland. Theatrical experimentation and avant-garde performance practices have rarely been the defining aesthetic at the Abbey. Instead, authenticity and historical accuracy in the reproduction of dramatic artefacts or dramatic historical memories have dominated the artistic values of the Irish National Theatre.

With a principal emphasis on authorship, Irish theatre is quite naturally text-based and cognitively – as opposed to visually – or linguistically driven. The accessibility of theatrical naturalism and the certainty of dramatic realism were the perfect means of expression for a theatre whose original aim was to define and stabilize Irish identity through the nation's postcolonial period and into its modern future. It is the early political roots of the Abbey that have created its venerable reputation and simultaneously limited its aesthetic vision to the protection of a dramatic legacy over theatrical aesthetic innovation and artistic growth. Commitment to the play as text is partial to an approach to theatre which views theorization as secondary, favouring, instead, authorial intention. At the Abbey this is a precarious artistic choice at a period in its history when the public is weighing its place in the culture of contemporary Ireland.

Drama Studies in the Irish Academy is a rather recent intellectual phenomenon. Instead, the study of theatre has been largely under the auspices of English departments. As a result the essential component of theatre called 'performance' has been undertheorized in favour of materialist, historical, or political readings. It is this gap in the analysis of Irish theatre that I am interested in. If performance is the missing link in the progress of Irish theatrical practice at the Abbey, as I would suggest it often is, then it is essential to try and frame the meaning of the word. The concept of performance is interdisciplinary by nature as it addresses a spectrum of human activity ranging from the overtly theatrical to the everyday banality of social transactions. For the purpose of a theatrical discourse I will define performance as the execution of demonstrable and organized skills that include the interdisciplinary interaction of text or play, actor, design and audience: a democratic relationship of value rather than hierarchical. Performance, therefore, embraces the conflation of human artistic theatrical activity in a more complete fashion than happens with an understanding of theatre primarily as text.

How does the notion of performance put pressure on the literary emphasis of traditional Irish theatre? In dramatic writing characterization is a defining characteristic of the genre. Although character development is based on human characteristics they are two dimensional in text until they are animated through the body of the actor, the ultimate aspiration of a dramatic writer as opposed to an author of fiction. It is the phenomenology of all aspects of theatre that performance most clearly and accurately articulates.

Performance is what makes a play more than a publication and transforms it into a living piece of temporal art. Victor Shklovsky defines art as the following:

> Art exists that one may recover the sensation of life; it exists to feel things, to make the stone *stoney*. The purpose of art is to impart the sensation of things as they are perceived and not as they are known. The technique of art is to make objects 'unfamiliar,' to make forms difficult, to increase the difficulty and length of perception because the process of perception is an aesthetic end in itself and must be prolonged. *Art is a way of experiencing the artfulness of an object; the object is not important.*[1]

The emphasis of art as experience is the defining characteristic of theatre, and the quality of analysis that includes the object of art as created by practitioner and the reception of that work by audiences. For 'performance is always performance *for* someone, some audience that recognizes and validates it as performance'.[2]

The academic discourse on theatre as performance embraces the multifaceted, interdisciplinary character of theatre as text, design, and action, and codifies the semantics that unify these diverse practices; this is the work of theatre theorists. 'Some theorists speculate about the role of theatre in relation to audience, society and state. Others consider how the stage can best represent humankind's existence on earth, battle with demons, and afterlife in heaven or hell.'[3] Theory is indeed technique, and in theatre it is a discourse of practice. For example, while deconstruction is a literary theory, which complicates meaning in textual analysis, it is a design aesthetic which alters semiotics in theatre practice to stimulate visual associations otherwise unexplored. This theatrical theoretical discourse is phenomenological in its desire to find a language of action and experience, and does so by acknowledging the social sciences from psychology to political science in order to articulate beyond text and into the fullness of live encounter.

For the purpose of how the queer functions as performance at the Abbey Theatre, I will focus on a revival of Oscar Wilde's *The Importance of Being Earnest,* and will trace what I would describe as a denial of practice and theory in this production. Additionally, I will highlight a crisis of aesthetic and theory in the production, and estimate what that means for the performance of queer identity on the stage of the National Theatre of Ireland.

As the year 2005 drew to an end the *Irish Times* theatre critic Fintan O'Toole described the Abbey's year-long misfortunes as '*annus horribilis*'.4 Half way through 2005, on 20 July *The Irish Times* reported that the Abbey was expected to release the results of a commissioned examination of the theatre's financial records. The Abbey had engaged the accounting firm KPMG in May of 2005 after assessing its projected losses from 2004. KPMG examined the theatre's accounting records as well as its financial control systems on both the management and the internal governance levels. *The Irish Times* predicted that KPMG's report was 'likely to show that widespread systemic failure, lack of monitoring of expenditure and a reluctance to address the issues are at the root of the financial crisis'.5 In the days that followed these revelations the Abbey took centre stage in a national scandal revealing an irresponsibility of management at the highest levels of the country's National Theatre.

Attempting to contradict the financial accounting jargon of reviewers and critics alike, the then Artistic Director Ben Barnes asserted an artistic prognosis much more in line with the perhaps less obvious fundamentals which underlie the transparent economic crisis at the Abbey:

> The truth of the matter is that theatre has become a minority art form unless you devise the most popular programme and shamelessly play to the lowest common denominator. To do this brings down the odium of the media art police but not to do it risks the wrath of boards and finance committees with their focus on the bottom line.6

Barnes struggles throughout this article to assert what he calls a 'new paradigm'7 to deal with the crisis of vision between artistry and economics at the Abbey. As artistic director, he published his prospectus in a forty-page document titled *Act 2*. In *Act 2* he made the following suggestions in an effort to revitalize interest in the Abbey as its artistic director:

> I argued for the establishment of a research and development studio to interrogate ways of making theatre which do not rely exclusively on the text and the spoken word. I believe that the over-reliance of the Irish theatre on drama of the spoken word will seriously hamper its future development as it seeks to attract young audiences who are multi-media literate but not literate in the sense that people of my generation understand that term. This is not to say that I wanted to throw the baby out with the bath water, as the media hysteria of last September would have it dismantle the Abbey as a writer's theatre.[8]

Barnes describes how his artistic vision and general influence at the Abbey began to diminish more and more as financiers positioned themselves in leadership, ushering in the old tension of art for the sake of art versus commercial theatre based on profit and popularity.

With the dissident voice of Barnes's struggle added to the dialogue on the past and future of the National Theatre, the idea of art is foregrounded in an otherwise predominantly corporate rather than aesthetic debate. What may appear to be insightful and creative artistic vision does not always translate well into an economic stability based on popular support of audiences and critics alike. And yet, the space between this divide is not one which can be simply dismissed as either an artistic intellectual superiority over the more base understanding of popular entertainment. At the root of the Irish National Theatre is a commitment to producing art which speaks to its constituency, whether positively or negatively, about the condition of Irish life.

Ben Barnes was attempting to move the Abbey Theatre into the new millennium based on an internationalization of theatre practice. This internationalization would focus on the interpretation of text by the director, or production concept, diminishing the Irish esteem for dramatic language in favour of imagery and visuals. Critics of his administration interpreted this move as a threat to the literary focus of the theatre for most of the twentieth century. Consequently, the failure of the theatre in the past year may be overtly associated with financial misgivings, but there is a larger menace to the perceived identity of the National Theatre inherent in an artistic policy which threatens established aesthetics and traditional modes of dramatic representation.

In order to analyse this tension between finance and art, tradition and progress, at the root of the Abbey's bankruptcy problems, it is illuminating to examine one of the theatre's major production endeavours during this troubled fiscal year. In its cultural objectives, the Abbey explicitly articulates its imperative to re-imagine its own foundational texts: 'The guardianship of the Irish repertoire through the reanimation of the wide canon of Irish writing already in existence.' 'Reanimation' at the Abbey has more often been preoccupied with questions of authenticity in the resurrection of dramatic artefacts than it has been in the illumination of latent themes within well known plays which speak to contemporary realities and thus elicit interest from modern audiences.

Interestingly, the production of Oscar Wilde's *The Importance of Being Earnest* stretched the Abbey's traditional production values through non-traditional, if not entirely original, casting choices. *The Importance of Being Earnest* opened at the Abbey on 23 July 2005 and ran through September. It was directed by the renowned young Irish director and playwright Conall Morrison. In pre-production the play was widely publicized as an all-male version of what many regard as Oscar Wilde's most famous play. This production was chosen for the theatre with the hope that its extensive popularity would draw larger audiences and increase revenue for the theatre during this sensitive period in which the public were weighing the viability of such a large national debit.

Ben Barnes had proposed to Morrison the possibility of directing the play, but also encouraged him to take the play beyond its sophisticated comedy and into the issues below the surface of the text that might make it more thought provoking. Being both an author and a director Morrison chose to write a new prologue for the play, one which placed Oscar Wilde himself as a character into the action of the piece. Morrison describes his concept for the piece:

> The idea of viewing it through Oscar's glasses really came to me through years of watching Wilde's plays ... And just feeling that all the plays were, much more so than a lot of dramatic writing, completely perfumed with his personality. *Lady Windermere's Fan* and *An Ideal Husband* are sort of circumscribed by Wilde's biography, the fact that ultimately society got him, it beat him, and so the great play of his life ended tragically and was, in its own way, a morality tale. 9

In exploring the play, Morrison saw the action of *Earnest* as portentous in its representation of the future fate that Oscar Wilde would experience due to the public revelation of his homosexuality. He continued: 'It is shot through with ironic foretellings of his own downfall. A play of double lives, about untruths, about unsympathetic fathers. About revelations.'[10] Ultimately, Morrison was interested in exploring the sexual politics which he felt were a subtext for the entire play. In order to do so he decided to cast the show entirely with male actors, with the intention of exploring the homosexuality which he believes exists throughout the text and the dramatic relationships it portrays.

With its new prologue in place, the Abbey's production of *The Importance of Being Earnest* begins with the entrance of the character of Oscar Wilde into a fashionable Parisian café whose patrons are exclusively male. Morrison's prologue is written largely in French which gives way eventually to English. The setting is flamboyant and the flirtatious interaction of the male actors onstage was unmistakably the atmosphere of a gay bar. As the character of Wilde sits at a table to enjoy a glass of champagne the various patrons of this exclusive establishment take on the characters of Wilde's original play. The actor playing Wilde on stage, Alan Stanford, transforms himself into the character of Lady Bracknell by skirting himself with a tablecloth and creating a stylish hat out of a lampshade which initiates a standard of cross-dressing which enables the all male cast to become the female characters which populate the play.

For Morrison, the casting was a technique which would allow the culturally dangerous question of homosexuality written beneath the play to emerge. He asserted, 'It allows us to examine the performative nature of gender, of gender construction'.[11] The male actors who played the female parts in this production were fully corseted, wigged, and given heavy make-up in order to transform them respectively into Lady Bracknell, Cecily Cardew, Gwendolen Fairfax, and Miss Prism. Morrison's desired intention was that this type of untraditional casting would provide additional support for the sophisticated wit and humour which have traditionally defined this play, as well as spark a debate about gender, identity, and cultural issues of the position of the homosexual in society both at the time of Oscar Wilde's death and now. He describes his artistic interpretation:

I suppose that like Oscar, with this play, I'm hoping to have my cake and eat it. In that I want it to be accessible, funny, popular, and in its own way moving. And I also want, for those who want to decode it a bit further, to think about all the different layers and levels, to have some extra resonances. Because for the gay community, the battle is not won. It's over a hundred years on from when I'm setting this, and the battle is still not won. Think of the rise in homophobia and homophobic attacks lately, particularly in the North. And if you think of Oscar casting men in these roles, look at Hollywood and how many stars still cannot come out of the closet. It's far from won. Far from won.[12]

The broad aspirations of comedy and cultural challenge placed a heavy weight on a play so well established in the minds of Irish theatre goers.

Critical response to the play was confused at best, perhaps a reflection of its wide-ranging aspirations in interpretation. There appeared to be little difficulty in grasping and enjoying the comedy of the homocentric pairings of men in drag, and yet, little seemed to be gained in the attempt to draw out the serious nature of homophobia and its deadly consequences for men like Oscar Wilde. Belinda McKeon of *The Irish Times* wrote of Morrison's strategy, 'He tries to make a virtue out of blatancy, and while the lens he holds up to Wilde's layers often proves a thought-provoking one, its battle with the sheer comedy of *Earnest* is never quite won.'[13] This critical remark indicates the success of the comedy but the disappointment of the political message intended.

What was it about the production which made it more frivolous than contentious? After all, it was obvious to audiences that the men on stage were, in fact, men; a reality which had the potential at least to cause discomfort in the expression of romantic love and desire which dominate the narrative of the play. In fact, the very device which promised to make this play thought provoking, the all male cast, was undermined by the director and the designers by the misuse of drag. The culturally contentious effects of male/male relationships which Morrison asserted were latent in the play and crucial to its political stance were, in reality, neutralized by an uncritical use of the performance strategy of cross-dressing. The desired political effect was truncated by an audience base accustomed to drag as a performance practice used in pantomime rather than as a tool to assert injustice towards the gay community. The literal attempts to costume the men playing women, combined with the directorial choice for the men to alter the octave of their voices up to mimic that of a woman, made this potentially challenging concept in theatrical practice merely funny.

The Importance of Being Earnest is written in an extravagant style which foregrounds homocentric thinking in its liberal application of camp to its narrative and action. Characters fall in love instantly only to turn in the next moment into wronged lovers or jealous suitors. Style, social convention, and class are prodded at and blatantly mocked for comic effect. This is certainly at the root of Wilde's authorial strategy. The gender theoretician David Halperin defines camp and its intent within social or political systems of meaning:

> Camp, after all, is a form of cultural resistance that is entirely predicated on a shared consciousness of being inescapably situated within a powerful system of social and sexual meanings. Camp resists the power of that system from within by means of parody, exaggeration, amplification, theatricalization, and literalization of tacit codes of conduct – codes whose very authority derives from their privilege of never having to be explicitly articulated, and thus from their customary immunity to critique.[14]

Susan Sontag describes camp as 'sensibility – unmistakably modern, a variant of sophistication ... esoteric – something of a private code, a badge of identity' and as a 'taste [that] tends to develop very unevenly.'[15] The sophistication of Wilde's satiric comedy fits into this description of camp nicely, and Morrison's intention of marking this particular production in order to speak to the politics of homosexuality would, ideally, find a source of artistic inspiration in the performance potential of the politics of camp's coded sensibility.

Camp is perhaps what Morrison detected as essential to Wilde's play, for comedy is a favoured genre for camp. And yet, comedy in writing such as Wilde's is rarely simply implemented to be funny. Esther Newton describes the double meaning of laughter for the camp style of performance: 'Camp is for fun; the aim of camp is to make an audience laugh. In fact, it is a system of humour ... a system of laughing at one's incongruous position instead of crying.'[16] When understood in this fashion, Wilde's writing reveals fear, danger, and injustice. For modern audiences sodomy laws have changed since the time of Oscar Wilde, and so the fate of the honest revelations of sexual identity detected below the surface of this play may be expressed more overtly with only the fear of cultural disapproval, not civic retribution.

Perhaps doing an all male version of the play in which the masculinity of the characters is emphasized, rather than negated as it can be by panto-like drag, would have brought the danger and the anxiety of Wilde's dramatic vision to the foreground more effectively. And yet, this type of interpretation may have drained the comedy away, an effect which would damage the popular appeal of a piece which held the promise of renewing interest in a bankrupt theatre. Ultimately, it was the lack of ability to focus on a theorized intention for practice that neutralized the potential of such an innovative reanimation. A theoretical engagement with the simple ideas which help critically illuminate Wilde's writing would have proved a wonderful bridge between the desired political effects of the director and its opposite effects in performance or practice.

A type of dramatic language and practice, which instigates a new hermeneutic for contemporary theatre audiences, has not been produced by the National Theatre. Instead, a random experimentation with under-theorized devices of both practice and writing has caused confusion and limited critical analysis of the practice of the theatre.

The German theorist Wolfgang Iser describes the type of mutual connection between artist and spectator required for basic interpretation or analysis of performance. 'As we cannot perceive without preconception, each precept, in turn, makes sense to us only if it is processed. For pure perception is quite impossible.'[17] If theatre is art and performance, with its complex conflation of practices and receptions, then successful theatre cannot be merely perceivable for the artist, but must create the conditions for audience processing. This mutual obligation of artist and spectator suggests an ethic of practice for theatre that cannot simply ignore audience reception.

The missing link in the evolution of theatrical practice at the Abbey is the absence of a clearly articulated discourse surrounding theatre and theory. Although Ireland remains to this day a cultural environment where academics are public figures, academic influence in theatre practice virtually does not exist. Certainly, there are public figures who review theatre and academics who discuss it as literature, but performance analysis is extremely limited and theory is continually held in opposition to the practice of theatre. This was not a problem during an inward-looking era in which the text and authorship were the greatest values of the National Theatre.

However, in a period in which the Abbey is articulating its vision as 'reanimating' the canon of Irish drama, in conjunction with the aspiration to increase dialogue between Irish and international practitioners, the demand for a thoughtful language of renewed theatrical semiotics is a glaring hole in the centre of the vision of a theatre in trouble. Theory stimulates a theatrical conversation which impacts the pre-production design of a play as well as structuring the language by which the live performance can be analysed and understood by audiences.

In analysing what is self-described as being a literary theatre, Irish scholars have failed to adequately engage the dynamics of theatre as practice in favour of a literary criticism of drama as text. While this intellectual endeavour has created excellent and necessary volumes of historical and materialist analysis, it has done little to promote and encourage the practice of reinterpretation or deconstruction demanded by the engagement of theory with theatre. Theory is often misunderstood as overly complex and exclusively intellectual, but, in fact, theory provides a type of language for theatrical analysis which codifies and organizes new and innovative forms of practice. It would seem an error for the Abbey to have assumed its contemporary audiences and critics would have the interpretive language to enter into an understanding of such a radical reinterpretation of traditional material without a previous and sustained engagement with the principles of deconstruction and theory, as related to drama and performance.

Patrice Pavis elaborates on the significance of the intersection of theory and theatrical practice:

> I would not go so far as to claim that the desire to create comes from theory, since every desire is defined by its object, not by its origin; creative desire, like theoretical desire (yes, it does exist), emerges from the wish to situate oneself in the world by assuming a point of view, by taking part in the debate of ideas, but also and above all in the debate of forms. Even if theory does not change institutional structures or artistic forms – which develop slowly as a result of long-range ideological and political changes – it is one of the structuring and destructuring factors, especially in regard to the always suspended sense of what *makes sense* [sic] in theatre.[18]

Clearly, Morrison as a director wanted to participate in the theoretical and ideological debates within culture suggested by Pavis. Theory was already present in the seminal ideas of production and writing, but absent from the larger cultural dialogue which surrounds reception and interpretation of intention. As a result theorized performance is performed for unsuspecting audiences unskilled in 'making sense' of postmodern theatrical practice.

Plans for the Abbey theatre include a new location along the docks in Dublin. Cultural observers are speculating that what the theatre needs is less government and more philanthropy. What seems to be essential for the health and development of both the artistry and the finance of the Abbey is the creation of a dialogue which brings together these disparate concerns in such a way as to stimulate a form of theatrical practice which is provocative and interesting enough for theatre-goers who, more and more, have eclectic experiences of both domestic and international entertainment. This type of union would reflect the desire for cultural preservation so important to the Irish theatrical tradition's search for authenticity and the emerging global sensibilities of contemporary Ireland. The Abbey and theatre in general, offers a space to renegotiate the past and re-envision the future. A dialogue of history, international and interdisciplinary ideas of theatrical theory, indigenous practice, and innovative form could, at the very least, diminish the Abbey's problem of practice and give hope to a promise of future financial and artistic viability.

---

[1] Victor Shklovsky, 'Art as Technique', *Russian Formalist Criticism: Four Essays*, trans. Lee T. Lemon and Marion J. Reis (Lincoln: University of Nebraska Press, 1965), p. 12.

[2] Marvin Carlson, 'What is Performance? ' *The Twentieth Century Performance Reader Edition*, eds Michael Huxley and Noel Witts, 2nd ed. (London: Routledge, 2005), p. 150.

[3] Daniel Gerould, 'Introduction: The Politics of Theatre Theory', *Theatre/ Theory/ Theatre*, ed. Daniel Gerould (New York: Applause Theatre and Cinema Books, 1999), p. 11.

[4] Fintan O'Toole, 'Playing to a New World Order', *The Irish Times* 12 December 2005.

[5] Deirdre Falvey, 'Abbey Report Likely to Criticise Poor Financial Controls', *The Irish Times* 7 July 2005.

[6] Ibid.

[7] Ibid.

[8] Ibid.

[9] Belinda McKeon, 'A Peek Through Oscar's Glasses', *The Irish Times* 27 July 2005.

[10] Ibid.

[11] Ibid.

[12] Ibid.

[13] Belinda McKeon, 'Review', *The Irish Times* 29 July 2005.

[14] David M. Halperin, Saint Foucault: Towards a Gay Hagiography (Oxford: Oxford University Press, 1995), p.29.

[15] Susan Sontag, 'Notes on "Camp"', Camp: Queer Aesthetics and the Performing Subject, ed. Fabio Cleto (Ann Arbor: University of Michigan Press, 2002), pp. 53-54.

[16] Esther Newton, 'Role Models', *Camp: Queer Aesthetics and the Performing Subject*, ed. Fabio Cleto (Ann Arbor: University of Michigan Press, 2002) p.106.

[17] Wolfgang Iser, 'The Interactive Spectator', *Performance Analysis: An Introductory Coursebook*, eds Colin Counsell and Laurie Wolfe (London: Routledge, 2001), p. 180.

[18] Pavis, 1992, p.92.

Contributors

Eibhear Walshe is a senior lecturer in the Department of Modern English at University College Cork. Dr Walshe's biography *Kate O'Brien: A Writing Life* was published by Irish Academic Press in 2006. He was a section editor for *The Field Day Anthology of Irish Writing*: Volume 4 (Cork University Press, 2002); a contributor to the *New Dictionary of Biography* (Oxford University Press, 2004) and guest edited *The Irish Review* in 2000. His other publications include the edited collections, *Ordinary People Dancing*: *Essays on Kate O'Brien* (Cork University Press, 1993), *Sex, Nation and Dissent* (Cork University Press, 1997), *Elizabeth Bowen Remembered* (Four Courts Press, 1999) and *The Plays of Teresa Deevy* (Mellen Press, 2003.) He co-edited, with Brian Cliff, *Representing the Troubles* (Four Courts Press, 2004) and *Molly Keane: Centenary Essays* (Four Courts Press, 2006) with Gwenda Young. He has completed a study of Wilde and Modern Ireland.

Kathryn Conrad is Associate Professor of English at the University of Kansas. Her book, *Locked in the Family Cell: Gender, Sexuality, and Political Agency in Irish National Discourse* (University of Wisconsin Press, 2004), addresses the centrality of gender and sexuality to national identity and nationalist discourses in the Republic of Ireland and Northern Ireland. She has recently published articles on James Joyce, mural photography, discriminatory surveillance, and Northern Irish counter publics. Her current research deals with visual culture, space, and political discourse in Northern Ireland, and her current book-length project is focused on the surveillance of sexually dissident subjects.

Mária Kurdi is professor in the Department of English Literatures and Cultures at the University of Pécs, Hungary. Her main fields of research are aspects of Irish Studies, modern Irish drama and English-speaking drama in general.

Fintan Walsh completed his PhD at Trinity College Dublin where he currently teaches part-time. He is a regular contributor to *Irish Theatre Magazine*, co-editor of *Crossroads: Performance Studies and Irish Culture* (2009) and author of the forthcoming monograph *Male Trouble: Masculinity and the Performance of 'Crisis'*.

Michael Lapointe completed his Ph.D. in English at the University of British Columbia, Vancouver, in 2006, specializing in twentieth-century Irish literature, specifically James Joyce, Irish drama, nationalism, and queer and gender theory. Currently, he is a lecturer both in literature and engineering communications at the University of Toronto.

Brian Merriman is the Founder/Artistic Director of the International Dublin Gay Theatre Festival. He is an award-winning director of over 300 productions and is a singer, actor, playwright, filmmaker and producer. He holds a Masters Degree in Equality Studies from UCD, is a journalism graduate and has been a gay rights advocate and fundraiser for HIV/AIDS causes for many years.

Niall Rea is Belfast born. He is a professional theatre designer and director. He has worked with many theatre companies across the UK, Ireland, Europe, and the US – including Tinderbox and The Lyric Theatre, Belfast; The Crucible Theatre, Sheffield; Fru Emilia, Iceland; Remote Control Productions, Amsterdam, and Puerto Rico National Ballet amongst others. He is artistic director of TheatreofplucK – the first publicly funded queer theatre company in Ireland.

Samuele Grassi is completing his PhD at the University of Florence. He is the author of *L'Apocalisse e la peste dei gay. L'AIDS come metanarrativa nella letteratura anglo-americana*, Il dito e la luna, Milano, 2007, a volume on AIDS representations in Anglo-American literature, and has translated and edited Rebecca Brown's *The Gifts of the Body* (*I doni del corpo*), Il dito e la luna, Milano, 2006). His previous publications include an essay on Neil Jordan's fiction ('Fathers in a Coma: Father/son relationships in Neil Jordan's Fiction', *Estudios Irlandeses*, 3, 2008). He is a member of the editorial board of the journal *Studi irlandesi*.

Todd Barry is a PhD student in English at the University of Connecticut, where he previously earned an MA in English and a JD at the University of Connecticut School of Law. His interests include modern drama, law and literature, and queer and gender studies. He is also an attorney.

Charlotte McIvor is a PhD candidate in Performance Studies at the University of California, Berkeley. She is currently at work on a dissertation entitled: 'Staging the Global Irish: Race, Culture and Performance After the Celtic Tiger.'

Kathleen Heininge is assistant professor of Writing and Literature at George Fox University in Newberg, Oregon. She received her doctorate from University of California at Davis, with research focusing on Irish drama. Her forthcoming book, *Buffoonery in Irish Drama: Staging Twentieth-Century Post-Colonial Stereotypes,* is due out in March 2009, from Peter Lang Publishing.

David Cregan is an assistant professor of Theatre at Villanova University where he also teaches in the Irish Studies Program. David received his PhD in Drama Studies at the Samuel Beckett School of Drama at Trinity College Dublin. He is a theatre director at Villanova and a theatre critic for *Philadelphia Magazine.*

Index

Carysfort Press was formed in the summer of 1998. It receives annual funding from the Arts Council.

The directors believe that drama is playing an ever-increasing role in today's society and that enjoyment of the theatre, both professional and amateur, currently plays a central part in Irish culture.

The Press aims to produce high quality publications which, though written and/or edited by academics, will be made accessible to a general readership. The organisation would also like to provide a forum for critical thinking in the Arts in Ireland, again keeping the needs and interests of the general public in view.

The company publishes contemporary Irish writing for and about the theatre.

Editorial and publishing inquiries to:
Carysfort Press Ltd., 58 Woodfield,
Scholarstown Road, Rathfarnham,
Dublin 16, Republic of Ireland.

T (353 1) 493 7383
F (353 1) 406 9815
e: info@carysfortpress.com
www.carysfortpress.com

HOW TO ORDER

TRADE ORDERS DIRECTLY TO:
CMD
Columba Mercier Distribution,
55A Spruce Avenue,
Stillorgan Industrial Park,
Blackrock, Co. Dublin

T: (353 1) 294 2560
F: (353 1) 294 2564
E: cmd@columba.ie

INDIVIDUAL ORDERS DIRECTLY TO:
eprint Ltd.
35 Coolmine Industrial Estate,
Blanchardstown, Dublin 15.

T: (353 1) 827 8860
F: (353 1) 827 8804
Order online @ www.carysfortpress.com

FOR SALES IN NORTH AMERICA AND CANADA:
Dufour Editions Inc.,
124 Byers Road, PO Box 7,
Chester Springs, PA 19425,
USA

T: 1-610-458-5005
F: 1-610-458-7103

Seán Keating in Context: Responses to Culture and Politics in Post-Civil War Ireland

Compiled, edited, and introduced by Éimear O'Connor

Irish artist Seán Keating has been judged by his critics as the personification of old-fashioned traditionalist values. This book presents a different view. The story reveals Keating's early determination to attain government support for the visual arts. It also illustrates his socialist leanings, his disappointment with capitalism, and his attitude to cultural snobbery, to art critics, and to the Academy. Given the national and global circumstances nowadays, Keating's critical and wry observations are prophetic – and highly amusing.

ISBN   978-1-904505-41-9   €25

Dialogue of the Ancients of Ireland: A new translation of Acallam na Senorach

Translated with introduction and notes by Maurice Harmon

One of Ireland's greatest collections of stories and poems, The Dialogue of the Ancients of Ireland is a new translation by Maurice Harmon of the 12th century *Acallam na Senorach*. Retold in a refreshing modern idiom, the *Dialogue* is an extraordinary account of journeys to the four provinces by St. Patrick and the pagan Cailte, one of the surviving Fian. Within the frame story are over 200 other stories reflecting many genres – wonder tales, sea journeys, romances, stories of revenge, tales of monsters and magic. The poems are equally varied – lyrics, nature poems, eulogies, prophecies, laments, genealogical poems. After the *Tain Bo Cuailnge*, the *Acallam* is the largest surviving prose work in Old and Middle Irish.

ISBN: 978-1-904505-39-6 (2009)   €20

Literary and Cultural Relations between Ireland and Hungary and Central and Eastern Europe

Ed. Maria Kurdi

This lively, informative and incisive collection of essays sheds fascinating new light on the literary interrelations between Ireland, Hungary, Poland, Romania and the Czech Republic. It charts a hitherto under-explored history of the reception of modern Irish culture in Central and Eastern Europe and also investigates how key authors have been translated, performed and adapted. The revealing explorations undertaken in this volume of a wide array of Irish dramatic and literary texts, ranging from *Gulliver's Travels* to *Translations* and *The Pillowman*, tease out the subtly altered nuances that they acquire in a Central European context.

ISBN: 978-1-904505-40-2 (2009)   €20

Plays and Controversies: Abbey Theatre Diaries 2000-2005

by Ben Barnes

In diaries covering the period of his artistic directorship of the Abbey, Ben Barnes offers a frank, honest, and probing account of a much commented upon and controversial period in the history of the national theatre. These diaries also provide fascinating personal insights into the day to day pressures, joys, and frustrations of running one of Ireland's most iconic institutions.

ISBN: 978-1-904505-38-9 (2008)   €35

Interactions: Dublin Theatre Festival 1957-2007. Irish Theatrical Diaspora Series: 3

Eds. Nicholas Grene and Patrick Lonergan with Lilian Chambers

For over 50 years the Dublin Theatre Festival has been one of Ireland's most important cultural events, bringing countless new Irish plays to the world stage, while introducing Irish audiences to the most important international theatre companies and artists. Interactions explores and celebrates the achievements of the renowned Festival since 1957 and includes specially commissioned memoirs from past organizers, offering a unique perspective on the controversies and successes that have marked the event's history. An especially valuable feature of the volume, also, is a complete listing of the shows that have appeared at the Festival from 1957 to 2008.

ISBN: 978-1-904505-36-5 €25

The Informer: A play by Tom Murphy based on the novel by Liam O'Flaherty

The Informer, Tom Murphy's stage adapatation of Liam O'Flaherty's novel, was produced in the 1981 Dublin Theatre Festival, directed by the playwright himself, with Liam Neeson in the leading role. The central subject of the play is the quest of a character at the point of emotional and moral breakdown for some souce of meaning or identity. In the case of Gypo Nolan, the informer of the title, this involves a nightmarish progress through a Dublin underworld in which he changes from a Judas figure to a scapegoat surrogate for Jesus, taking upon himself the sins of the world. A cinematic style, with flash-back and intercut scenes, is used rather than a conventional theatrical structure to catch the fevered and phantasmagoric progression of Gypo's mind. The language, characteristically for Murphy, mixes graphically colloquial Dublin slang with the haunted intricacies of the central character groping for the meaning of his own actions. The dynamic rhythm of the action builds towards an inevitable but theatrically satisfying tragic catastrophe. ' [The Informer] is , in many ways closer to being an original Murphy play than it is to O'Flaherty...' Fintan O'Toole.

ISBN: 978-1-904505-37-2 (2008) €10

Shifting Scenes: Irish theatre-going 1955-1985

Eds. Nicholas Grene and Chris Morash

Transcript of conversations with John Devitt, academic and reviewer, about his lifelong passion for the theatre. A fascinating and entertaining insight into Dublin theatre over the course of thirty years provided by Devitt's vivid reminiscences and astute observations.

ISBN: 978-1-904505-33-4 (2008) €10

Irish Literature: Feminist Perspectives

Eds Patricia Coughlan and Tina O'Toole

The collection discusses texts from the early 18th century to the present. A central theme of the book is the need to renegotiate the relations of feminism with nationalism and to transact the potential contest of these two important narratives, each possessing powerful emancipatory force. Irish Literature: Feminist Perspectives contributes incisively to contemporary debates about Irish culture, gender and ideology.

ISBN: 978-1-904505-35-8 (2008) €25

Silenced Voices: Hungarian Plays from Transylvania

selected and translated by Csilla Bertha and Donald E. Morse

The five plays are wonderfully theatrical, moving fluidly from absurdism to tragedy, and from satire to the darkly comic. Donald Morse and Csilla Bertha's translations capture these qualities perfectly, giving voice to the 'forgotten playwrights of Central Europe'. They also deeply enrich our understanding of the relationship between art, ethics, and politics in Europe.

ISBN: 978-1-904505-34-1 (2008)   €25

A Hazardous Melody of Being: Seóirse Bodley's Song Cycles on the poems of Micheal O'Siadhail

Ed. Lorraine Byrne Bodley

This apograph is the first publication of Bodley's O'Siadhail song cycles and is the first book to explore the composer's lyrical modernity from a number of perspectives. Lorraine Byrne Bodley's insightful introduction describes in detail the development and essence of Bodley's musical thinking, the European influences he absorbed which linger in these cycles, and the importance of his work as a composer of the Irish art song.

ISBN: 978-1-904505-31-0 (2008)   €25

Irish Theatre in England: Irish Theatrical Diaspora Series: 2

Eds. Richard Cave and Ben Levitas

Irish theatre in England has frequently illustrated the complex relations between two distinct cultures. How English reviewers and audiences interpret Irish plays is often decidedly different from how the plays were read in performance in Ireland. How certain Irish performers have chosen to be understood in Dublin is not necessarily how audiences in London have perceived their constructed stage personae. Though a collection by diverse authors, the twelve essays in this volume investigate these issues from a variety of perspectives that together chart the trajectory of Irish performance in England from the mid-nineteenth century till today.

ISBN: 978-1-904505-26-6 (2007)   €20

Goethe and Anna Amalia: A Forbidden Love?

By Ettore Ghibellino, Trans. Dan Farrelly

In this study Ghibellino sets out to show that the platonic relationship between Goethe and Charlotte von Stein – lady-in-waiting to Anna Amalia, the Dowager Duchess of Weimar – was used as part of a cover-up for Goethe's intense and prolonged love relationship with the Duchess Anna Amalia herself. The book attempts to uncover a hitherto closely-kept state secret. Readers convinced by the evidence supporting Ghibellino's hypothesis will see in it one of the very great love stories in European history – to rank with that of Dante and Beatrice, and Petrarch and Laura.

ISBN: 978-1-904505-24-2 €20

Ireland on Stage: Beckett and After

Eds. Hiroko Mikami, Minako Okamuro, Naoko Yagi

The collection focuses primarily on Irish playwrights and their work, both in text and on the stage during the latter half of the twentieth century. The central figure is Samuel Beckett, but the contributors freely draw on Beckett and his work provides a springboard to discuss contemporary playwrights such as Brian Friel, Frank McGuinness, Marina Carr and Conor McPherson amongst others. Contributors include: Anthony Roche, Hiroko Mikami, Naoko Yagi, Cathy Leeney, Joseph Long, Noreem Doody, Minako Okamuro, Christopher Murray, Futoshi Sakauchi and Declan Kiberd

ISBN: 978-1-904505-23-5 (2007)   €20

'Echoes Down the Corridor': Irish Theatre - Past, Present and Future

Eds. Patrick Lonergan and Riana O'Dwyer

This collection of fourteen new essays explores Irish theatre from exciting new perspectives. How has Irish theatre been received internationally - and, as the country becomes more multicultural, how will international theatre influence the development of drama in Ireland? These and many other important questions.

ISBN: 978-1-904505-25-9 (2007)   €20

Musics of Belonging: The Poetry of Micheal O'Siadhail

Eds. Marc Caball & David F. Ford

An overall account is given of O'Siadhail's life, his work and the reception of his poetry so far. There are close readings of some poems, analyses of his artistry in matching diverse content with both classical and innovative forms, and studies of recurrent themes such as love, death, language, music, and the shifts of modern life.

ISBN: 978-1-904505-22-8 (2007) €25 (Paperback)
ISBN: 978-1-904505-21-1 (2007) €50 (Casebound)

Brian Friel's Dramatic Artistry: 'The Work has Value'

Eds Donald E. Morse, Csilla Bertha and Maria Kurdi

Brian Friel's Dramatic Artistry presents a refreshingly broad range of voices: new work from some of the leading English-speaking authorities on Friel, and fascinating essays from scholars in Germany, Italy, Portugal, and Hungary. This book will deepen our knowledge and enjoyment of Friel's work.

ISBN: 978-1-904505-17-4 (2006)   €30

The Theatre of Martin McDonagh: 'A World of Savage Stories'

Eds. Lilian Chambers and Eamonn Jordan

The book is a vital response to the many challenges set by McDonagh for those involved in the production and reception of his work. Critics and commentators from around the world offer a diverse range of often provocative approaches. What is not surprising is the focus and commitment of the engagement, given the controversial and stimulating nature of the work.

ISBN: 978-1-904505-19-8 (2006)   €35

Edna O'Brien: New Critical Perspectives

Eds. Kathryn Laing, Sinead Mooney and Maureen O'Connor

The essays collected here illustrate some of the range, complexity, and interest of Edna O'Brien as a fiction writer and dramatist... They will contribute to a broader appreciation of her work and to an evolution of new critical approaches, as well as igniting more interest in the many unexplored areas of her considerable oeuvre.

ISBN: 978-1-904505-20-4 (2006)   €20

Irish Theatre on Tour

Eds. Nicholas Grene and Chris Morash

'Touring has been at the strategic heart of Druid's artistic policy since the early eighties. Everyone has the right to see professional theatre in their own communities. Irish theatre on tour is a crucial part of Irish theatre as a whole'. Garry Hynes

ISBN 978-1-904505-13-6 (2005)   €20

Poems 2000-2005 by Hugh Maxton

Poems 2000-2005 is a transitional collection written while the author – also known to be W. J. Mc Cormack, literary historian – was in the process of moving back from London to settle in rural Ireland.

ISBN 978-1-904505-12-9 (2005)   €10

Synge: A Celebration

Ed. Colm Tóibín

A collection of essays by some of Ireland's most
creative writers on the work of John Millington Synge, featuring Sebastian Barry , Marina Carr, Anthony Cronin, Roddy Doyle, Anne Enright, Hugo Hamilton, Joseph O'Connor, Mary O'Malley, Fintan O'Toole, Colm Toibin, Vincent Woods.

ISBN 978-1-904505-14-3 (2005)   €15

East of Eden: New Romanian Plays

Ed. Andrei Marinescu

Four of the most promising Romanian playwrights, young and very young, are in this collection, each one with a specific way of seeing the Romanian reality, each one with a style of communicating an articulated artistic vision of the society we are living in. Ion Caramitru, General Director Romanian National Theatre Bucharest.

ISBN 978-1-904505-15-0 (2005)   €10

George Fitzmaurice: 'Wild in His Own Way', Biography of an Irish Playwright

by Fiona Brennan

Fiona Brennan's...introduction to his considerable output allows us a much greater appreciation and understanding of Fitzmaurice, the one remaining under-celebrated genius of twentieth-century Irish drama. Conall Morrison

ISBN 978-1-904505-16-7 (2005)   €20

Out of History: Essays on the Writings of Sebastian Barry

Ed. Christina Hunt Mahony

The essays address Barry's engagement with the contemporary cultural debate in Ireland and also with issues that inform postcolonial criticial theory. The range and selection of contributors has ensured a high level of critical expression and an insightful assessment of Barry and his works.

ISBN: 978-1-904505-18-1 (2005)   €20

Three Congregational Masses by Seoirse Bodley

'From the simpler congregational settings in the Mass of Peace and the Mass of Joy to the richer textures of the Mass of Glory, they are immediately attractive and accessible, and with a distinctively Irish melodic quality.' Barra Boydell

ISBN: 978-1-904505-11-2 (2005)   €15

Georg Büchner's Woyzeck, A new translation

by Dan Farrelly

The most up-to-date German scholarship of Thomas Michael Mayer and Burghard Dedner has finally made it possible to establish an authentic sequence of scenes. The wide-spread view that this play is a prime example of loose, open theatre is no longer sustainable. Directors and teachers are challenged to "read it again".

ISBN: 978-1-904505-02-0 (2004)   €10

Playboys of the Western World: Production Histories

Ed. Adrian Frazier

'The book is remarkably well-focused: half is a series of production histories of Playboy performances through the twentieth century in the UK, Northern Ireland, the USA, and Ireland. The remainder focuses on one contemporary performance, that of Druid Theatre, as directed by Garry Hynes. The various contemporary social issues that are addressed in relation to Synge's play and this performance of it give the volume an additional interest: it shows how the arts matter.' Kevin Barry

ISBN: 978-1-904505-06-8 (2004)   €20

The Power of Laughter: Comedy and Contemporary Irish Theatre

Ed. Eric Weitz

The collection draws on a wide range of perspectives and voices including critics, playwrights, directors and performers. The result is a series of fascinating and provocative debates about the myriad functions of comedy in contemporary Irish theatre. Anna McMullan

As Stan Laurel said, it takes only an onion to cry. Peel it and weep. Comedy is harder. These essays listen to the power of laughter. They hear the tough heart of Irish theatre – hard and wicked and funny. Frank McGuinness

ISBN: 978-1-904505-05-1 (2004)   €20

Sacred Play: Soul-Journeys in contemporary Irish Theatre

by Anne F. O'Reilly

'Theatre as a space or container for sacred play allows audiences to glimpse mystery and to experience transformation. This book charts how Irish playwrights negotiate the labyrinth of the Irish soul and shows how their plays contribute to a poetics of Irish culture that enables a new imagining. Playwrights discussed are: McGuinness, Murphy, Friel, Le Marquand Hartigan, Burke Brogan, Harding, Meehan, Carr, Parker, Devlin, and Barry.'

ISBN: 978-1-904505-07-5 (2004)   €25

The Irish Harp Book

by Sheila Larchet Cuthbert

This is a facsimile of the edition originally published by Mercier Press in 1993. There is a new preface by Sheila Larchet Cuthbert, and the biographical material has been updated. It is a collection of studies and exercises for the use of teachers and pupils of the Irish harp.

ISBN: 978-1-904505-08-2 (2004)   €35

The Drunkard by Tom Murphy

'The Drunkard is a wonderfully eloquent play. Murphy's ear is finely attuned to the glories and absurdities of melodramatic exclamation, and even while he is wringing out its ludicrous overstatement, he is also making it sing.' The Irish Times

ISBN: 978-1-904505-09-9 (2004) €10

Goethe: Musical Poet, Musical Catalyst

Ed. Lorraine Byrne

'Goethe was interested in, and acutely aware of, the place of music in human experience generally - and of its particular role in modern culture. Moreover, his own literary work - especially the poetry and Faust - inspired some of the major composers of the European tradition to produce some of their finest works.' Martin Swales

ISBN: 978-1-904505-10-5 (2004) €40

The Theatre of Marina Carr: "Before rules was made"

Eds. Anna McMullan & Cathy Leeney

As the first published collection of articles on the theatre of Marina Carr, this volume explores the world of Carr's theatrical imagination, the place of her plays in contemporary theatre in Ireland and abroad and the significance of her highly individual voice.

ISBN: 978-0-9534257-7-8 (2003) €20

Critical Moments: Fintan O'Toole on Modern Irish Theatre

Eds. Julia Furay & Redmond O'Hanlon

This new book on the work of Fintan O'Toole, the internationally acclaimed theatre critic and cultural commentator, offers percussive analyses and assessments of the major plays and playwrights in the canon of modern Irish theatre. Fearless and provocative in his judgements, O'Toole is essential reading for anyone interested in criticism or in the current state of Irish theatre.

ISBN: 978-1-904505-03-7 (2003) €20

Goethe and Schubert: Across the Divide

Eds. Lorraine Byrne & Dan Farrelly

Proceedings of the International Conference, 'Goethe and Schubert in Perspective and Performance', Trinity College Dublin, 2003. This volume includes essays by leading scholars – Barkhoff, Boyle, Byrne, Canisius, Dürr, Fischer, Hill, Kramer, Lamport, Lund, Meikle, Newbould, Norman McKay, White, Whitton, Wright, Youens – on Goethe's musicality and his relationship to Schubert; Schubert's contribution to sacred music and the Lied and his setting of Goethe's Singspiel, Claudine. A companion volume of this Singspiel (with piano reduction and English translation) is also available.

ISBN: 978-1-904505-04-4 (2003) €25

Goethe's Singspiel, 'Claudine von Villa Bella'

set by Franz Schubert

Goethe's Singspiel in three acts was set to music by Schubert in 1815. Only Act One of Schuberts's Claudine score is extant. The present volume makes Act One available for performance in English and German. It comprises both a piano reduction by Lorraine Byrne of the original Schubert orchestral score and a bilingual text translated for the modern stage by Dan Farrelly. This is a tale, wittily told, of lovers and vagabonds, romance, reconciliation, and resolution of family conflict.

ISBN: 978-0-9544290-0-3 (2002)   €20

Theatre of Sound, Radio and the Dramatic Imagination

by Dermot Rattigan

An innovative study of the challenges that radio drama poses to the creative imagination of the writer, the production team, and the listener.

"A remarkably fine study of radio drama – everywhere informed by the writer's professional experience of such drama in the making…A new theoretical and analytical approach – informative, illuminating and at all times readable." Richard Allen Cave

ISBN: 978- 0-9534-257-5-4 (2002)   €20

Talking about Tom Murphy

Ed. Nicholas Grene

Talking About Tom Murphy is shaped around the six plays in the landmark Abbey Theatre Murphy Season of 2001, assembling some of the best-known commentators on his work: Fintan O'Toole, Chris Morash, Lionel Pilkington, Alexandra Poulain, Shaun Richards, Nicholas Grene and Declan Kiberd.

ISBN: 978-0-9534-257-9-2 (2002)   €15

Hamlet: The Shakespearean Director

by Mike Wilcock

"This study of the Shakespearean director as viewed through various interpretations of HAMLET is a welcome addition to our understanding of how essential it is for a director to have a clear vision of a great play. It is an important study from which all of us who love Shakespeare and who understand the importance of continuing contemporary exploration may gain new insights."

From the Foreword, by Joe Dowling, Artistic Director, The Guthrie Theater, Minneapolis, MN

ISBN: 978-1-904505-00-6 (2002)   €20

The Theatre of Frank Mc Guinness: Stages of Mutability

Ed. Helen Lojek

The first edited collection of essays about internationally renowned Irish playwright Frank McGuinness focuses on both performance and text. Interpreters come to diverse conclusions, creating a vigorous dialogue that enriches understanding and reflects a strong consensus about the value of McGuinness's complex work.

ISBN: 978-1904505-01-3. (2002) €20

Theatre Talk: Voices of Irish Theatre Practitioners

Eds Lilian Chambers and Ger Fitzgibbon

"This book is the right approach - asking practitioners what they feel." Sebastian Barry, Playwright

"... an invaluable and informative collection of interviews with those who make and shape the landscape of Irish Theatre." Ben Barnes, Artistic Director of the Abbey Theatre

ISBN: 978-0-9534-257-6-1 (2001) €20

In Search of the South African Iphigenie

by Erika von Wietersheim and Dan Farrelly

Discussions of Goethe's "Iphigenie auf Tauris" (Under the Curse) as relevant to women's issues in modern South Africa: women in family and public life; the force of women's spirituality; experience of personal relationships; attitudes to parents and ancestors; involvement with religion.

ISBN: 978-0-9534257-8-5 (2001) €10

'The Starving' and 'October Song': Two contemporary Irish plays

by Andrew Hinds

The Starving, set during and after the siege of Derry in 1689, is a moving and engrossing drama of the emotional journey of two men.

October Song, a superbly written family drama set in real time in pre-ceasefire Derry.

ISBN: 978-0-9534-257-4-7 (2001) €10

Seen and Heard: Six new plays by Irish women

Ed. Cathy Leeney

A rich and funny, moving and theatrically exciting collection of plays by Mary Elizabeth Burke-Kennedy, Síofra Campbell, Emma Donoghue, Anne Le Marquand Hartigan, Michelle Read and Dolores Walshe.

ISBN: 978-0-9534-257-3-0 (2001) €20

Theatre Stuff: Critical essays on contemporary Irish theatre

Ed. Eamonn Jordan

Best selling essays on the successes and   debates of contemporary Irish theatre at home and abroad.

Contributors include: Thomas Kilroy, Declan Hughes, Anna McMullan, Declan Kiberd, Deirdre Mulrooney, Fintan O'Toole, Christopher Murray, Caoimhe McAvinchey and Terry Eagleton.

ISBN: 978-0-9534-2571-1-6 (2000)   €20

Under the Curse. Goethe's "Iphigenie Auf Tauris", A New Version

by Dan Farrelly

The Greek myth of Iphigenie grappling with the curse on the house of Atreus is brought vividly to life. This version is currently being used in Johannesburg to explore problems of ancestry, religion, and Black African women's spirituality.

ISBN: 978-09534-257-8-5 (2000)   €10

Urfaust, A New Version of Goethe's early "Faust" in Brechtian Mode

by Dan Farrelly

This version is based on Brecht's irreverent and daring re-interpretation of the German classic.

"Urfaust is a kind of well-spring for German theatre… The love-story is the most daring and the most profound in German dramatic literature." Brecht

ISBN: 978-0-9534-257-0-9 (1998)   €20
